D1478886

LISTEN TO MOVIE MUSICALS!

Recent Titles in
Exploring Musical Genres

Listen to New Wave Rock! Exploring a Musical Genre
James E. Perone

Listen to Pop! Exploring a Musical Genre
James E. Perone

Listen to the Blues! Exploring a Musical Genre
James E. Perone

Listen to Rap! Exploring a Musical Genre
Anthony J. Fonseca

Listen to Classic Rock! Exploring a Musical Genre
Melissa Ursula Dawn Goldsmith

LISTEN TO MOVIE MUSICALS!

Exploring a Musical Genre

JAMES E. PERONE

Exploring Musical Genres
James E. Perone, Series Editor

GREENWOOD

An Imprint of ABC-CLIO, LLC
Santa Barbara, California • Denver, Colorado

Library of Congress Cataloging-in-Publication Data

Names: Perone, James E., author.
Title: Listen to movie musicals! : exploring a musical genre / James E. Perone.
Other titles: Exploring musical genres.
Description: Santa Barbara, California : Greenwood, An Imprint of ABC-CLIO, LCC, [2020] | Series: Exploring musical genres | Includes bibliographical references and index.
Identifiers: LCCN 2019046775 (print) | LCCN 2019046776 (ebook) | ISBN 9781440869716 (print) | ISBN 9781440869723 (ebook)
Subjects: LCSH: Musical films—United States—History and criticism.
Classification: LCC PN1995.9.M86 P47 2020 (print) | LCC PN1995.9.M86 (ebook) | DDC 791.43/6—dc23
LC record available at https://lccn.loc.gov/2019046775
LC ebook record available at https://lccn.loc.gov/2019046776

ISBN: 978-1-4408-6971-6 (print)
       978-1-4408-6972-3 (ebook)

24 23 22 21 20   1 2 3 4 5

This book is also available as an eBook.

Greenwood
An Imprint of ABC-CLIO, LLC

ABC-CLIO, LLC
147 Castilian Drive
Santa Barbara, California 93117
www.abc-clio.com

This book is printed on acid-free paper ∞

Manufactured in the United States of America

Contents

Series Foreword

Ask some music fans, and they will tell you that genre labels are rub-
bish and that imposing them on artists and pieces of music dimin-
ishes the diversity of the work of performers, songwriters, instrumental
composers, and so on. Still, in the record stores of old, in descriptions
of radio-station formats (on-air and Internet), and at various streaming audio and download sites today, we have seen and continue to see
music categorized by genre. Indeed, some genre boundaries are at least
somewhat artificial, and it is true that some artists and some pieces of
music transcend boundaries. But categorizing music by genre is a conve-
nient way of keeping track of the thousands upon thousands of musical
works available for listeners' enjoyment; it's analogous to the difference
between having all your documents on your computer's home screen
versus organizing them into folders. So, Greenwood's Exploring Musical Genres series is a genre- and performance group–based collection
of books and e-books. The publications in this series will provide listeners with background information on the genre; critical analysis of
important examples of musical pieces, artists, and events from the genre;
discussion of must-hear music from the genre; analysis of the genre's
impact on the popular culture of its time and on later popular-culture
trends; and analysis of the enduring legacy of the genre today and its
impact on later musicians and their songs, instrumental works, and
recordings. Each volume will also contain a bibliography of references
for further reading.

We view the volumes in the Exploring Musical Genres series as a go-to
resource for serious music fans, the more casual listener, and everyone
in between. The authors in the series are scholars, who probe into the
details of the genre and its practitioners: the singers, instrumentalists,

composers, and lyricists of the pieces of music that we love. Although the authors' scholarship brings a high degree of insight and perceptive analysis to the reader's understanding of the various musical genres, the authors approach their subjects with the idea of appealing to the lay reader, the music nonspecialist. As a result, the authors may provide critical analysis using some high-level scholarly tools; however, they avoid any unnecessary and unexplained jargon or technical terms or concepts. These are scholarly volumes written for the enjoyment of virtually any music fan.

Every volume has its length parameters, and an author cannot include every piece of music from within a particular genre. Part of the challenge, but also part of the fun, is that readers might agree with some of the choices of "must-hear music" and disagree with others. So while your favorite example of, say, grunge music might not be included, the author's choices might help you to open up your ears to new, exciting, and ultimately intriguing possibilities.

By and large, these studies focus on music from the sound-recording era: roughly the 20th century through the present. American guitarist, composer, and singer-songwriter Frank Zappa once wrote:

> On a record, the overall timbre of the piece (determined by equalization of individual parts and their proportions in the mix) tells you, in a subtle way, *WHAT* the song is about. The orchestration provides *important information* about what the composition *IS* and, in some instances, assumes a greater importance than *the composition itself*. (Zappa with Occhiogrosso 1989, 188; italics and capitalization from the original)

The gist of Zappa's argument is that *everything* that the listener experiences (to use Zappa's system of emphasizing words)—including the arrangement, recording mix and balance, lyrics, melodies, harmonies, instrumentation, and so on—makes up a musical composition. To put it another way, during the sound-recording era, and especially after the middle of the 20th century, we have tended to understand the idea of a piece of music—particularly in the realm of popular music—as being the same as the most definitive recording of that piece of music. And this is where Zappa's emphasis on the arrangement and recording's production comes into play. As a result, a writer delving into, say, new wave rock will examine and analyze the B-52's' version of "Rock Lobster" and not just the words, melodies, and chords that any band could sing and play and still label the result "Rock Lobster." To use Zappa's graphic way of highlighting particular words, the B-52's' recording *IS* the piece. Although they have expressed it in other ways, other writers such as Theodore Gracyk (1996, 18) and Albin J. Zak III (2001) concur with Zappa's equating of the piece with the studio recording of the piece.

In the case of musical genres not as susceptible to being tied to a particular recording—generally because of the fact that they are genres often experienced live, such as classical music or Broadway musicals—the authors will still make recommendations of particular recordings (we don't all have ready access to a live performance of Wolfgang Amadeus Mozart's *Symphony No. 40* any time we'd like to experience the piece), but they will focus their analyses on the more general, the notes-on-the-page, the expected general aural experience that one is likely to find in any good performance or recorded version.

Maybe you think that all you really want to do is just listen to the music. Won't reading about a genre decrease your enjoyment of it? My hope is that you'll find that reading this book opens up new possibilities for understanding your favorite musical genre and that by knowing a little more about it, you'll be able to listen with proverbial new ears and gain even more pleasure from your listening experience. Yes, the authors in the series will bring you biographical detail, the history of the genres, and critical analysis on various musical works that they consider to be the best, the most representative, and the most influential pieces in the genre. However, ultimately, the goal is to enhance the listening experience. That, by the way, is why these volumes have an exclamation mark in their titles. So please enjoy both reading and listening!

—James E. Perone, Series Editor

REFERENCES

Gracyk, Theodore. 1996. *Rhythm and Noise: An Aesthetics of Rock*. Durham, NC: Duke University Press.

Zak, Albin J., III. 2001. *The Poetics of Rock: Cutting Tracks, Making Records*. Berkeley: University of California Press.

Zappa, Frank, with Peter Occhiogrosso. 1989. *The Real Frank Zappa Book*. New York: Poseidon Press.

Preface

To late 20th-century and early 21st-century audiences, it might seem as though movie musicals have been around forever; such is the vast number of iconic works that can still be enjoyed in theaters, on DVDs and other physical forms for in-home viewing, and on the numerous streaming video services.

This volume traces the history of movie musicals back to 1927 and the premiere of the film *The Jazz Singer*. As important as that was, the year 1927 also saw the premiere of *Show Boat*, the Jerome Kern and Oscar Hammerstein II show, that was arguably the first important, mature, well-rounded Broadway musical. That crucial year was not, however, the beginning of the story of popular musical theater—a genre of which the movie musical is a part—, so the chapter "Background" discusses the pre-*Show Boat* era in order to fill out the story.

Unlike other volumes in this series that focus on bands, albums, iconic concert events, and songs, the chapter "Must-Hear Music" focuses entirely on 50 important and/or particularly interesting films. Many of these are among the most iconic movie musicals up to the present; however, I have included a few that might not have necessarily been the greatest films of their time. These somewhat-left-field examples, though, tell us something important about either the development of the genre or what was going on in the world of the popular culture of the movies' times. "Must-Hear Music" is arranged alphabetically, in the manner of encyclopedic entries.

Because I treat the 50 major entries in the chapter like standalone entries in an encyclopedic work, the reader will find some duplication of information. For example, I include discussion of the importance of *Show Boat* in "Background," a detailed discussion of the film versions of the musical in "Must-Hear Music," and references to *Show Boat* in the "Impact on Popular Culture" and "Legacy" chapters.

In the major entries in "Must-Hear Music," I discuss the overall importance of the movie, its reception by the public, some of the major songs that were featured, and the wider role of music in the film. In the case of adaptations of stage musicals, I also discuss distinctions between the stage and film versions. For example, the film version of *On the Town* uses the sights and sounds of New York City in a way that would have been impossible at the time on stage. Similarly, the film version of the show includes several songs that were not part of the Leonard Bernstein score for the stage version of *On the Town*—these were especially written to highlight the talents of the movie's stars, most notably Frank Sinatra.

As its name suggests, "Impact on Popular Culture" focuses on the immediate and longer-lasting impact of the musical—and particularly the best-remembered film version of the musical—on general popular culture. As one might imagine, gauging the impact on popular culture of a movie musical that was only or primarily known as a film (e.g., no stage version existed at the time of the movie's premiere or ever existed at all) is far easier than distinguishing between the possible impact of a stage version and a movie version, particularly when the two were prominent at the same time. In these cases, I discuss what seems to have impacted the popular culture of both the live and film versions of the show. In some cases, the popularity of the film itself continued to define the general public understanding of the musical for years and years after the film's premiere, sometimes eclipsing even the cultural impact of highly success-ful and star-studded runs of the stage version. Ask people, even in the 21st century, who they think of when they think of Maria in *The Sound of Music*, and Mary Martin, who played the show's heroine in the first Broadway production and won a Tony Award in the process, is often for-gotten because of Julie Andrews's portrayal of the character in the movie.

"Legacy" focuses on the continuing relevance, popularity, and/or notoriety of the film, or, in cases in which there have been several film versions of a musical produced over the years, the various movie ver-sions. Although for some of the longtime popular and iconic movie musicals there is some degree of overlap between the basic themes of the "Impact on Popular Culture" and "Legacy" chapters, I have attempted to minimize redundancy.

The book concludes with a bibliography. This chapter includes works cited in the narrative, sources that I used to research movie musicals and their impact, additional sources that might be of interest to readers who seek more information on various musicals (in their stage and film versions), and some of the movie musicals that I have not detailed. For many bibliographical entries, I have provided annotations, particularly for works that are somewhat on the periphery of providing a primary focus on movie musicals.

Acknowledgments

I wish to thank the entire staff at ABC-CLIO, as well as the copyeditors and others with whom they subcontract, for all their help in getting this volume from the concept to the published book. I also wish to thank my wife and best friend, Karen Perone, for all the support that she continues to give me on my writing projects. I especially want to thank Karen for her patience in watching numerous movie musicals—on both the big screen and on video—over the course of the writing of this book. I would like to think that Karen's biggest hope is that, upon the publication of this book, she never has to hear me sing the melody of the "Fugue for Tinhorns" from *Guys and Dolls* ever again. Apparently, I'm no Stubby Kaye, so I won't rock the boat . . .

CHAPTER 1

Background

The popular belief is that the mid-20th century represented the high-point of the Broadway musical, as well as the movie musical. However, the history of the movie musical is much broader than that. As we shall see, although those classic midcentury movies are still well known today and the nature of movie musicals has diversified, particularly since the 1960s, the musical is alive and well into the 21st century.

As one might reasonably imagine, the history of movie musicals is intimately tied with the history of the stage musical. Therefore, let us examine the history of both genres and their intersections to gain a more thorough appreciation of how the movie musical developed and continues to be an important part of popular culture.

The history of the popular stage musical can be traced back to the early 18th-century Britain and John Gay's work *The Beggar's Opera*. This piece included tunes that were already part of the British popular culture of the day and was framed around a story that resonated among common people. In its use of popular melodies and characters that were not gods, goddesses, prominent historical figures, or literary characters from the upper class, *The Beggar's Opera* represented an important landmark in the development of popular musical theater.

Minstrelsy developed in the 19th century in the United States. Although blackface minstrel shows were based on stereotypes of African Americans and racist humor and were basically plotless, they introduced styles and forms at least tangentially connected to African American music. This helped broaden the scope of what audiences might reasonably expect in musical theater, particularly in the United States. Although operettas from the British duo of W. S. Gilbert and Sir Arthur Sullivan and various other European composers were popular in the United States in the late 19th century and early 20th century, minstrel show classics such as Stephen Foster's "Camptown Races," "Oh, Susannah!," and others have proven to have had a longer shelf life than many of the one-time popular arias from these operettas, particularly among members of the general public. Foster also helped establish what would later be known as popular song form. Foster's song "I Dream of Jeanie with the Light Brown Hair," although an independent parlor ballad and not part of a minstrel show, provides a well-remembered example of the AABA form that would be a standard part of the structural vocabulary of numerous songwriters associated with stage musicals and their film kin.

Still, a loosely affiliated collection of popular songs and dance melodies does not make for mature musical theater. Arguably, at least in the United States, the dominant musical comedies of George M. Cohan in the early 20th century marked the next step in the development of what would become the Broadway musical, the form intimately tied with the movie musical. Cohan's upbringing in a traveling theatrical family unquestionably gave him an understanding of the entertainment industry that few others could match.

Beginning with *Little Johnnie Jones* in 1904, Cohan wrote, composed, and starred in numerous musical comedies that helped establish the theme of the easily defined American hero who overcomes all obstacles to triumph in the end. Cohan's work reflected the optimism of the United States during the years between the nation's victory in the relatively brief Spanish-American War and U.S. entry into World War I. Although Cohan's shows for the most part have long since been forgotten, songs such as "Yankee Doodle Boy," "Give My Regards to Broadway," "You're a Grand Old Flag," "Mary's a Grand Old Name," and others remain well known over a century after their premieres. In addition to the hits he wrote for his shows, Cohan was also responsible for "Over There," a rallying song for U.S. troops during both World War I and World War II. Although Cohan's musicals and his still-remembered songs date from before the era of movie musicals, his work and a semi-fictionalized story of his life were the subject of the must-watch musical *Yankee Doodle Dandy*. Ironically, this film, starring James Cagney as Cohan, was released shortly before Cohan's death.

Vaudeville shows and revues also played prominent roles in the story of early 20th-century musical theater in the United States. The Follies of 19-Whenever and a plethora of other such shows might never have been reproduced in later years, but many of these early 20th-century shows featured songs that became sing-along classics and are still heard from time to time today. The Tin Pan Alley songwriting and music publishing scene—which played a significant role in American popular music from approximately the 1880s to the mid-20th century—was intimately tied to the multitude of revues, post–George M. Cohan musical comedies and other Broadway offerings. The song, it seemed, was the thing.

So, was it entirely all about the song throughout the 1920s? Not really, as the year 1927 marked the next major milestone in both the development of popular musical theater and of the very possibility of the movie musical. The premiere of *Show Boat* in 1927 was one of the two crucial events in the development and establishment of the movie musical as an important genre in popular culture. In addition to classic songs, such as "Ol' Man River," "Can't Help Lovin' Dat Man," and "Make Believe," *Show Boat* mixed lighthearted comedy and series social issues (e.g., racism) into a composite that showed that popular and mature Broadway musicals could go well beyond the predictable plots of earlier musical comedies and the largely plotless follies, vaudeville, and other types of musical theater preceding this groundbreaking musical.

The other major event that defined the history of the film musical in particular was the premiere of *The Jazz Singer*. Starring singer-actor Al Jolson, *The Jazz Singer* might not have necessarily been the first film to include a soundtrack, but it was the first full-length movie with a soundtrack and synchronized singing and speaking. The early "talkies" did not necessarily feature the kind of film-soundtrack technology that would become the norm (e.g., the soundtracks of many of the earliest movies were recorded on a disc—a record—that was played along with the film), but they did prove that sound could be incorporated into commercial films and fairly quickly proved to be a nail in the coffin of silent films. Much more than just a film that included audio material, *The Jazz Singer* included six songs that were sung by its star, Jolson. Despite what very soon thereafter would seem to be a primitive, disconnected approach to connecting the visual and audio elements of the film, *The Jazz Singer* was the first movie musical and is detailed in the chapter "Must-Hear Music."

The movie musical came into full bloom within a couple of years of the premiere of *The Jazz Singer*. *The Hollywood Revue of 1929*, which included appearances by such film legends as Stan Laurel and Oliver Hardy, Buster Keaton, Joan Crawford, Jack Benny, and numerous others, took the concept of the revue, a large-scale production with numerous unrelated acts meant for the Broadway stage, and successfully brought it to the screen. Notably, Cliff Edwards, known professionally as Ukulele Ike, sang "Singin' in the Rain" in the production. As shown in the 1974 film *That's Entertainment*, this song became something of a recurring theme in Metro-Goldwyn-Mayer (MGM) musicals, as it was included in several of the studio's movies in the 1950s.

Credit for including music in the actual soundtrack of a film has to go to the 1932 movie *Love Me Tonight*. This film featured songs such as "Isn't It Romantic," "Mimi," and "Lover," written by composer Richard Rodgers and lyricist Lorenz Hart and sung by the movie's stars Maurice Chevalier and Jeanette MacDonald. Rouben Mamoulian also deserves credit for helping to advance the movie musical as the director and producer of *Love Me Tonight*.

Love Me Tonight, however, was just one of the many movie musicals that were in circulation in the late 1920s and early 1930s. Movie musical historian Thomas S. Hischak points out that the number of such films was so great that "by 1931 there were too many musicals on the market, the novelty of the new genre wore off, and audiences started to avoid movie musicals" (Hischak 2013, 617). Hischak points to the 1933 releases *42nd Street* and *Flying Down to Rio* as films that revived interest in movie musicals. In a way, this parallels what continues to occur even today: the movie musical would appear to be dying—or dead—only to have its popularity revived by a significant film that opens the floodgates to new movie musicals.

One of the more spectacular—but sometimes dismissed and often parodied—aspects of the movie musicals of the 1930s and 1940s is the work of director and choreographer Busby Berkeley. Berkeley ramped up the degree of spectacle in musicals through the use of elaborate sets, architecturally and geometrically conceived patterns, and provocatively clad female dancers. Writer Marcia Siegel points out that the influence of Berkeley's work during this period can be found in early MTV videos and in Cirque du Soleil productions (Siegel 2009). Berkeley's over-the-top work was also the impetus for the big production number "Your Mother Should Know" in the Beatles' doomed made-for-television film *Magical Mystery Tour* and arguably any other musical film sequence in which spectacular seems to be the primary aesthetic concern.

One could not possibly consider the history of movie musicals without giving a significant amount of attention to three letters: MGM. Formed by the merger of competing movie studios, Metro-Goldwyn-Mayer, more commonly referred to as MGM, was slow to the conversion from silent films to "talkies," but once it made the leap, the company produced some of the most iconic musicals of the 1930s, 1940s, and 1950s. *Singin' in the Rain, On the Town, Gigi, West Side Story, Meet Me in Saint Louis, Chitty Chitty Bang Bang, Brigadoon, Easter Parade, The Wizard of Oz*, and *Jailhouse Rock* are but a few of the movie musicals produced by MGM. These films were adaptations of stage musicals, musicals that were specifically designed for the film medium, works that were primarily comedies, and works that reflected some of the harsh realities of life. While other studios produced movie musicals in the mid-20th century, some popular classics, MGM remains the studio most closely associated with the mid-20th century, the period that is still regarded by many movie fans as the heyday of the movie musical.

Generally, MGM's musicals, although many are well remembered and during their day were among the most popular film musicals, were not as highly recognized by critics or the Hollywood establishment. It was perhaps just reward, then, when what was arguably the last great MGM musical, the 1958 movie *Gigi*, won the Academy Award for Best Picture.

Interestingly, writers such as Matthew Tinkcom and Steven Cohan studied the classic MGM musicals as examples of expressions of homosexual sensibilities in movies that occurred long before the gay pride movement of the late 1960s and 1970s brought homosexuality out into the open (see Tinkcom 2002; Cohan 2005). One of the films discussed in the chapter "Must-Hear Music" that critics and historians have spotlighted as an example of a pre–gay pride movie that contains covert references to homosexuality is *The Band Wagon*.

One thing that is important to consider about many—if not most—film adaptations of stage musicals is that they tended to be shorter in duration and punchier in impact than their stage counterparts. For example, scene changes could be instantaneous in a film, and they might take some time to accomplish on stage and require scene-change music to fill time. Depending on the movie and whether it was originally conceived for the screen or an adaptation from the stage, this can be a double-edged sword: although adaptations might seem to be fast-paced than their stage predecessors, sometimes truncated dialogue or the cutting of musical numbers can leave the viewer familiar with the original feeling that the adaptation was incomplete.

Another aspect of the film versions of musicals originally written for the stage is that they tended to take advantage of the resources available to filmmakers. For example, *On the Town* includes scenes—and soundstage sets—that fairly realistically depict a multitude of sites around New York City. Although some of the scenes were clearly shot on a soundstage—for example, the scene that takes place at the top of the Empire State Building—the entire feel of the film surpasses anything that could have been possible in a stage production. Later movie musicals would continue to expand upon this use of technical resources. In the film version of *Cabaret*, for example, sudden cut-to scene changes and briefly flashing images of scenes of Nazi brutality connect the songs and the ongoing subplot of the rise of the Nazis and the public acceptance of their agenda. Although the subplot ran through the stage version, one can easily argue that the film techniques heighten the immediacy and intensity of the message beyond what could be produced on the stage.

Some of the classic mid–20th-century movie musicals were specifically written for the film medium—for example, the MGM film *Meet Me in Saint Louis*. Although I have not included *Meet Me in Saint Louis* among the 50 "Must-Hear" movie musicals, it is an excellent example of a musical that was entirely conceived as a movie. It also remains well remembered for Judy Garland's performance of "Have Yourself a Merry Little Christmas," "The Boy Next Door," and "The Trolley Song."

Similarly, film musicals such as *Chitty Chitty Bang Bang*, a musical adapted from a novel for film, used scenery, mechanical devices (e.g., the car that "stars" in the film), and the like that never could have been depicted convincingly on the stage. Thus, the film musical genre took on a life of its own. Some of the musicals originally released as films were later converted into stage versions; however, some became so iconic that the film became so firmly etched into popular culture that it is difficult to imagine a stage version ever rising to the film's iconic status.

Since the late 1930s, the world of musicals originally known through their film versions has been dominated by the Disney franchise. The 1937 film *Snow White and the Seven Dwarfs* was followed by *Pinocchio, Fantasia, Song of the South, Peter Pan, The Jungle Book*, and numerous others that became quickly etched into popular culture. In fact, one could convincingly argue that some of the songs from Disney animated movie musicals of the 1930s–1960s were as well known, if not better, than the songs of stage musicals and non-animated film musicals from the same period. Disney, particularly after the company acquired the computer animation firm Pixar, continues to produce commercially successful animated movie musicals even today.

Many of the early Disney hits remain in the repertoire in the 21st century, appearing on cable television and on streaming services. The 1946 film *Song of the South*, which mixed live-action and animated sequences, is the most controversial of these. Based on the traditional Uncle Remus stories, *Song of the South* has long been considered offensive to African Americans; however, the film contained one legitimate hit song that continues to be well known: "Zip-a-Dee-Doo-Dah."

Beginning in the mid-1990s, Disney increasingly took their commercially successful film musicals to the stage, representing a flipping of the paradigm that had been established in the early days of the movie music.

Starting with the 1992 film *Aladdin*, which featured a nearly manic Robin Williams voicing the Genie, *Beauty and the Beast*, *The Little Mermaid*, *The Lion King*, and others brought the Disney franchise back to prominence and, in fact, leadership in the world of movie musicals. Adding to the popularity of some of these Disney musicals was the fact that some were released in "Jr." versions, abbreviated and designed for young performers.

Because Disney has produced so many animated movie musicals over the course of over eight decades now, it is interesting to study the studio's output to see how filmmaking technology has changed, how the audio quality of films has changed, and how cultural sensitivity and appropriateness have evolved over the years. Perhaps one of the better examples of this is the fact that films such as *Song of the South* gave way to *Pocahontas* and *Mulan*, both of which were considerably more culturally sensitive than Disney's output from the 1930s and 1940s. In fact, the principal critique of *Pocahontas* by *Rolling Stone*'s Peter Travers was that it was too much of a "civics lesson" (Travers 1995).

The treatment of race and ethnicity and the changes in that treatment over time were not limited to Disney cartoons. As detailed by Chang-Hee Kim (2013) in an article in *Cultural Critique*, Richard Rodgers and Oscar Hammerstein's 1958 film musical *The Flower Drum Song* was a popular and critical hit. The movie was unusual among the iconic Broadway songwriting duo's Asia-focused shows of the mid-20th century, as it featured Asian actors (as opposed to, say, Yul Brynner portraying King Mongkut in *The King and I* earlier in the decade). However, *The Flower Drum Song* relied on stereotypes of Asian characters. Playwright David Henry Hwang revised the book of *The Flower Drum Song* for a 2002 production, a version that eliminated the stereotypes. Although Hwang's rewrite was not adapted into the film medium, the fact that his stage version was written and produced illustrates the changes in racial and ethnics that had occurred over the intervening nearly 50 years.

Similarly, film and stage version of late 20th-century and early 21st-century musicals such as *Miss Saigon* demonstrated greater cultural sensitivity than had been the case in earlier times. Ironically, *Miss Saigon* did generate a considerable amount of controversy over the use of non-Asian actor-singers. Arguably, the musical that eventually broke down all ethnic and racial barriers was Lin-Manuel Miranda's 2015 Broadway smash *Hamilton*. At the time of this writing, *Hamilton* has not been made into a film.

Many of the classic Broadway musicals of the 1940s, 1950s, and 1960s found their way into cinema, including *Guys and Dolls*, *The Sound of*

Music, South Pacific, Oklahoma, The Music Man, and others. Although not as well recognized by the general public, several other notable movie musicals appeared in the mid-20th century. One of the more interesting movie musicals was Otto Preminger's production of *Carmen Jones*, a film that expanded on the stage musical of the same name and employed new lyrics for the music of Georges Bizet's 19th-century opera *Carmen*. With an all-black cast led by Harry Belafonte and Dorothy Dandridge, the film was recognized by the Library of Congress for preservation in the National Film Registry.

Writers Todd Berliner and Philip Furia detail a blurring of lines between film genres beginning in the 1960s (Berliner and Furia 2002). According to them, movies such as Mike Nichols's 1967 film *The Graduate*, which heavily incorporated contemporary popular music styles in the soundtrack, while not musicals in the traditional sense—the characters in *The Graduate* do not sing—were so infused with music in a different approach to non-diegetic music than what had been the norm before that they essentially became a new subgenre. The Simon and Garfunkel songs that appear throughout the film tie in with the overt and inner feelings of the characters and thus add depth to the characterizations. In addition to *The Graduate*, the 1969 Dennis Hopper film *Easy Rider* represented the best-known examples of this approach to song in film from this period.

The approach of building a soundtrack around popular songs in a non-diegetic and diegetic manner continued in a host of movies in the decades that followed, including *Ferris Bueller's Day Off*, *Pretty in Pink*, *Bachelor Party*, and numerous others. Although these are not movie musicals in the traditional sense, these films can be understood as providing a link to a new form of musical that appeared in the late 20th century: the so-called jukebox musical. These stage and film musicals were constructed around pre-existing songs, often originally performed by the same artist or group and placed into a context by a storyline. In some cases, the songs were used in such a way as to stretch the realm of reality. For example, in Julie Taymor's *Across the Universe*, Beatles songs were used to represent the general period of the second half of the 1960s and the dawn of the 1970s; however, some of the songs were used in conjunction with events that supposedly took place before the Beatles ever released the particular song. Although this might work sufficiently well for viewers unfamiliar with the exact sequence of the recording and release of the songs, it can be a head-scratcher for hardcore fans. However, it should be noted that regardless of how improbable the storyline of *Across the Universe* might seem to Beatles fans, the storyline of the

Beatles' cartoon musical, *Yellow Submarine*, released at the end of the psychedelic era, was itself a work of fantasy that stretched the meaning of the songs.

Some jukebox musicals in which fanciful plots were constructed around songs that were never meant to go together in a single narrative achieved critical and commercial success. Particularly successful was *Mamma Mia!*, the 2006 film based on the 1999 musical. In *Mamma Mia!*, the songs of the disco-era Swedish pop sensation ABBA were outfitted with a storyline that involved a Greek island, a wedding, and plenty of dancing. Although dancing certainly was at the core of the ABBA hit "Dancing Queen," other parts of the plot have little to do with ABBA's songs. The songs also did not necessarily provide the audience with a great deal of substance about the inner psyche of the characters. The fact is that they were unconnected songs written for various single and album releases by ABBA a couple of decades before the stage version of the show ever premiered. The point of a movie musical of this type seemed largely to revolve around the premise that the audience knew and loved the songs and might, just might, accept a somewhat contrived storyline that provided the pretense for the songs. It should be noted that perhaps the most critically lambasted example of the jukebox musical had been the 1978 Robert Stigwood film *Sgt. Pepper's Lonely Hearts Club Band*, a vehicle for the band the Bee Gees that used songs from the iconic Beatles album of the same name, as well as other well-known Beatles songs. Although films such as *Mamma Mia!* were not the unified whole of, say, a classic live Broadway musical such as *West Side Story*, *Porgy and Bess*, or *Show Boat*, they played a role in perpetuating the legacy of pop music of the second half of the 20th century, helping popularize them for new generations while bringing back nostalgic memories for older viewers who remembered the music from the first time around.

Even during the blurring of genres and the development of the jukebox musicals, there were new movie musicals of a more traditional structure that were being successfully produced. In particular, the rock opera—as a stage and film subgenre—came into prominence in the 1970s. There were slightly earlier stage rock operas, most notably *Hair* (which did not appear as a film until the late 1970s); however, one of the most prominent film rock operas was the 1973 Norman Jewison movie *Jesus Christ Superstar*. With music by Andrew Lloyd Webber and lyrics by Tim Rice, *Jesus Christ Superstar* was based on a 1970 concept album. The move from concept album/rock opera to the stage and/or film became a paradigm that marked a number of successful rock operas over the course of the next several decades.

One of the better-known examples is the 1975 rock opera *Tommy*, a work based on the Who's 1969 multidisc concept album of the same title. *Tommy* featured an all-star cast, including Roger Daltrey (lead singer of the Who), Elton John, Ann-Margret, Tina Turner, Oliver Reed, Jack Nicholson, among others. Although this Ken Russell film generated considerable interest upon its release, some fans of the Who preferred the original album, which left more of the story's details to the listener's imagination. The fact that some of the actors were not among the strongest of singers was another challenge that *Tommy* faced.

One of the most notable rock-based musicals, thought of by some viewers as a near rock opera, was the 1975 Jim Sharman production *The Rocky Horror Picture Show*, a movie based on a stage show of a couple of years before. Transvestitism, cannibalism, marital infidelity, and weird science fiction meshed in this quirky show written by Richard O'Brien, who played Riff Raff the handyman in the film. The character of the campy sexually ambiguous mad scientist, Dr. Frank N. Furter, was a perfect fit for the glam rock period. Although the movie was not a major hit when it first released, it eventually became part of the midnight movie circuit in cities across the United States. Audience members acted out scenes in front of theaters, sang along with the songs, did the dances (notably the "Time Warp") in the aisles, and brought and used props that aligned with the storyline, song lyrics, and dialogue—in short, *The Rocky Horror Picture Show* became part of a scene. The film is still shown in countless movie theaters each Halloween.

Although the Disney franchise continued to produce animated musical films, in the late 20th century and the dawn of the 21st century, large-scale movie musicals starring real people were becoming increasingly rare. There were some notable exceptions, such as the 1996 film *Evita*, based on the brief but eventful and politically important life of Eva Perón. *Evita* started out life as a 1976 concept album by composer Andrew Lloyd Webber and lyricist Tim Rice, the same sort of genesis that led to their *Jesus Christ Superstar* several years before. A stage version followed in 1978, with various film-rights and other business issues keeping a film version on hold for over a decade and a half. Starring pop singer-actress Madonna as Eva Perón, *Evita* represented a paradigm shift from the star-vehicle movie musicals of the 1940s. Although Leonard Bernstein's original score for *On the Town* had material extracted and substituted with material that was both deemed more commercial sounding and provided a greater focus on the singing of stars such as Frank Sinatra, *Evita* found Madonna actively working to convince Evita's producers and director to cast her in the title role and then undergoing extensive vocal training so that she could convincingly sing Lloyd Webber's music. The integrity of the film and the musical, at least in this case, took precedence over the commercial whims of stars, producers, and directors. In part, this may have been because of the large commercial and critical success the original concept album and the various long-running stage productions had enjoyed.

Some time elapsed between the premiere of *Evita* as a film and the proliferation of movie musicals that began several years later, and *Evita* received mixed reviews during its run; therefore, it makes sense to point to the 2002 film adaptation of the 1975 musical *Chicago* as the kick-off of a renewed vibrancy to the genre of the movie musical. *Chicago* was highly commercially successful and was followed in fairly short order by a film adaptation of *Phantom of the Opera*, *Dreamgirls*, *Hairspray*, and a fair number of others.

Although this volume concerns movie musicals and not those made for television, it must be noted that over the years, some musicals have been filmed specifically for the small screen. Arguably, remakes of classic movie musicals for television generally have not been as successful as the original film versions. For example, the 2003 Jeff Bleckner's television version of *The Music Man*, which starred Matthew Broderick as Professor Harold Hill, received a negative preview from the *San Francisco Chronicle*'s Edward Guthmann, due in large part to Broderick's less-than-energetic portrayal of the story's con man (Guthmann 2003). The television version of the film also suffered from the fact that it could not take advantage of the razzle-dazzle available on the big screen. This was particularly noticeable in the dance numbers; however, comparison of the film and the television adaptation reveals more close-up and fewer visually impressive wide-screen shots in the television version.

After such hits as *Hairspray*, *Cadillac Records* (which, although not a traditional movie musical, was filled with music originally released on Chess and Checker Records and reinterpreted by artists such as Beyoncé [who portrayed Etta James in the film]), and other movie musicals of the first decade and a half of the 21st century, the next significant uptick of interest in musicals occurred with the 2016 release of *La La Land*.

La La Land, written and directed by Damien Chazelle, starred Ryan Gosling, Emma Stone, John Legend, and Rosemarie DeWitt. The plot primarily concerns the relation between Gosling's character, a pianist, and Stone's character, an actress, and struggles with prevailing musical attitudes and the struggles between ambition and love. With its defense of the jazz idiom and old-fashioned storyline, *La La Land* suggests the musicals of the mid-20th century. Although some viewers might detect a sense of patronizing in a white character, Gosling's Sebastian Wilder, defending jazz (originally an African American genre) and trying to save the genre in a society in which it is no longer valued greatly, that aspect of *La La Land* only seemed to faze some movie critics. The title of Ruby Lott-Lavigna's *Wired* review, "*La La Land* Review: An Ambitious Musical Soured by Racist Overtones," reflects the reaction of some critics to the perceived nature of Gosling's character (Lott-Lavigna 2017). In stark contrast, *Rolling Stone*'s Peter Travers gave the film a thoroughly glowing review that ignored any supposed overtones of white patronization (Travers 2016). *La La Land* received 14 Academy Award nominations and won the Oscars for Best Actress, Best Director, Best Cinematography, Best Production Design, Best Original Score, and Best Original Song.

Interestingly, *La La Land* seemed to suggest that late in the second decade of the 21st century, the time might be right for a return to some of the techniques and styles of the classic musicals of the past, as well as for remakes of some of the classic film musicals. Benj Pasek, one of *La La Land*'s lyricists, was quoted as suggesting that the deliberately retro nature of the film appealed to a young generation of musical fans because of the popularity of late 20th-century and early 21st-century Disney animated musicals (Burlingame 2017). For example, director Bradley Cooper's 2018 remake of *A Star Is Born* starred Lady Gaga as a nightclub singer who is discovered by a has-been alcoholic and drug-abusing male country singer (played by Cooper). The premise of Cooper's version of the story held true to that of the popular 1976 remake of *A Star Is Born* that starred Barbra Streisand as an up-and-coming singer who was discovered by an established singer (played by Kris Kristofferson) whose career was on the downward track while Streisand's character is on her ascent. The even earlier 1954 version had starred Judy Garland as the up-and-coming singer discovered by an on-his-way-down actor, played by James Mason. In the original 1937 version of *A Star Is Born*, Janet Gaynor portrayed the star of the film's title, this time an aspiring actress who is discovered by an aging actor played by Fredric March.

Therefore, while in the 21st century, many moviegoers associate *A Star Is Born* with the movie musical genre, the film only worked its way into the genre gradually through the 1954 and 1976 remakes. Bradley Cooper's remake updates the musical styles and genres so that the story makes sense within the context of the movie's time. This latest remake of *A Star Is Born* generated significant buzz on the film festival circuit before its general release (see, for example, Coyle 2018).

Clearly, the writing team of Andrew Lloyd Webber and Tim Rice, and later Elton John and Tim Rice, had helped internationalize late 20th and early 21st-century musicals. The early 21st century has also seen the emergence of successful and significant film musicals from other countries. One example is the Chinese movie *Perhaps Love*, the work of filmmaker Peter Ho-sun Chan. A study of *Perhaps Love* by G. Andrew Stuckey compared the structure and techniques of the movie with those of the Australian director Baz Luhrmann in Luhrmann's international hit *Moulin Rouge!* (Stuckey 2014). The linkage of *Moulin Rouge!*, the successful work of an Australian director with the work of a respected Chinese filmmaker, illustrates how much more globalized the movie musical has become.

Interestingly, the question of the globalization of the movie musical has been studied in the 21st century from other angles, such as the reception of American movie musicals in other countries. For example, Olaf Jubin's article, "From *That's Entertainment* to *That's Entertainment?*—Globalization and the Consumption of the Hollywood Musical in Germany and Austria," examines the ways in which American musicals were modified and translated to be sold and to appeal to German-speaking audiences (Jubin 2009).

The wide range of the globalization, ethnic and racial expansions, and connections to the past represented in 21st-century movie musicals can be seen in recent academic study of Chinese movie musicals, the adaptation of English-language music musicals to the German language and culture, the commercial success of the deliberately retro musical *La La Land*, and musicals such as *Black Nativity* (which used techniques to make it appear as a film from an earlier era). At the time of this writing, there is talk of upcoming musicals based on *The Color Purple*, an adaptation of the book *Everything's Coming Up Profits: The Golden Age of Industrial Musicals*, a musical based on the early life of hip-hop legend Pharrell Williams, and continuing speculation that Andrew Lloyd Webber's stage musical *Sunset Boulevard* might be adapted for film. One of the brighter spots in the continuing story of the movie musical from late in the second decade of the 21st century was the 2019 release of *Rocketman*, a musical fantasy biopic about Elton John's childhood, ascent into stardom, and excesses of sex, alcohol, and drugs that led to his commitment to sobriety. *Rocketman*, a hybrid between the rock biopic and a fantasy musical, received generally favorable reviews (see, for example, Scott 2019). In some senses, *Rocketman* connects the 21st-century movie musical back to form of the iconic *Yankee Doodle Dandy*. With this film's commercial and critical success, and the other projects that are apparently in the works, the future of the movie musical looks bright and wide ranging indeed.

CHAPTER 2

Must-Hear Music

ALADDIN

The 1992 film *Aladdin* was part of a renaissance for Walt Disney Studios in the late 20th century. The renaissance included *Pocahontas, The Little Mermaid, Mulan, Beauty and the Beast,* and several other highly popular animated films. The original 1992 *Aladdin* remains popular nearly 30 years after its release, is widely available on home video, was adapted in 2011 into a significantly longer stage musical, was adapted as one of Disney's "Jr." musicals for youth theater performances, and was released in 2019 as a film using live (as opposed to animated) characters.

Aladdin featured voice actors such as Linda Larkin, who voiced Princess Jasmine; Scott Weinger, who voiced Aladdin; Robin Williams, who voiced the Genie; and Jonathan Freeman, who voiced Jafar, the movie's villain. Although Williams's work as the Genie generated the most interest among moviegoers, Freeman's voicing of Jafar gave the character a conniving, sinister feel, and Frank Walker's voicing of Abu, Aladdin's pet monkey, and Gilbert Gottfried's voicing of Iago, Jafar's parrot, helped lend a comic feel to the principal animal characters.

The credits for *Aladdin* include a lengthy list of technicians and illustrators. Ron Clements and John Musker produced the film, and Clements directed it. After *Aladdin*'s release, the film was criticized by some Arab groups for relying on stereotypes. The film also caused some controversy, as some of the improvised dialogue were apparently misunderstood; some audience members claimed to hear sexual references that were not necessarily present (Bradley 2015).

The principal people behind the movie's songs were composer Alan Menken, who, over the years, has been involved in other hit Disney and non-Disney projects, and lyricists Howard Ashman and Tim Rice. As a songwriting team, Menken and Ashman had previously collaborated on *Little Shop of Horrors*, *The Little Mermaid*, and *Beauty and the Beast*. For *Aladdin*, Ashman penned the lyrics for "Arabian Nights," "Friend Like Me," and "Prince Ali." After Ashman's death during the production of the film, Rice was brought in and wrote the lyrics for "A Whole New World," "One Jump Ahead," and "Prince Ali Reprise."

The settings of Menken's songs and the film's underscoring embrace several styles, including Middle Eastern–sounding music, big-band jazz, and a more general pop style. The Middle Eastern–sounding music, such as in the movie's opening song, "Arabian Nights," might be taken by some audiences as relying on instrumentation, scale-type, and melodic stereotypes from the Arab world; however, despite concerns that some audiences might have with cultural insensitivity, the music does not seem to mock Middle Eastern music; rather, it uses cues that Western audiences might recognize to help set the scene. That being said, this was a song for which one line of lyrics was changed from those of the original theatrical release after Arab groups complained about stereotypical references.

Similarly, the big-band jazz swing music of Aladdin's first song might be deemed stereotypical. At the very least, "One Jump Ahead" is not entirely removed from the style, tempo, and rhythmic feel of minor-key swing-era hits such as the Benny Goodman band's version of the Louis Prima's composition "Sing, Sing, Sing."

Musically, the more general pop-sounding songs, such as the movie's biggest hit, "A Whole New World," are more in keeping with the pop songs that Menken composed for his earlier musicals, and similar in accessibility to the songs that he would continue to compose for later stage and movie musicals.

In typical Disney manner, *Aladdin* uses human/animal interactions to set a mood and show the audience something about the character of the people involved (e.g., the interaction of the birds and Princess Jasmine), as well as the humorous animal characters (e.g., Jafar's parrot, Iago, voiced by Gilbert Gottfried). This ties *Aladdin* to Disney's animated films such as *Snow White and the Seven Dwarfs* and *The Jungle Book*. Also, in true Disney fashion, the characters are clearly defined. For example, the villain, Jafar, exhibits no redeeming qualities.

Although *Aladdin* is an approximately 90-minute musical that only included five songs, the movie includes a significant amount of under-scoring, including the action scenes in which the instrumental music is emphasized and even the more subtle scenes. However, *Aladdin* would seem to be one that would not be a natural to translate to the stage, in part because the film only featured five songs, more than most of the Disney-revival animated movie musicals. There is so much action to make the film almost a mixture of romance, Disney comedy, and adventure. Particularly visually interesting are the magic carpet sequences and those in which Robin Williams's Genie is at his most manic. The stage version was expanded considerably, but for some *Aladdin* fans, the original movie musical is definitive, particularly compared with the 2019 live-character version, which was not nearly as commercially or critically successful.

Like Aladdin's "One Jump Ahead," the Genie's first song also channels swing jazz, somewhat on the order of Cab Calloway's work. This sequence is at once reflective of the large production numbers of older, live-character musicals of the 1930s and 1940s while parodying those production numbers at the same time. In the songs and in his non-song sequences, Robin Williams references numerous pop culture icons, including Ed Sullivan, Jack Nicholson, and Arnold Schwarzenegger, as well as other stereotypes of popular culture of the late 20th century, including a campy tailor, a game show host, and so on. In this respect, *Aladdin* reflects the continuum of some of the great animated films and television programs of the past in providing not only material that children find entertaining but also references that perhaps only their parents and grandparents—the people who take young people to movies—will fully appreciate.

Variety's Susan King and other movie critics and movie historians consider *Aladdin* to be the start of the resurgence of the Disney franchise in the field of animated movie musicals (King 2017). In considering the popularity and significance of *Aladdin*, it must be noted that the performance by Robin Williams was so noteworthy and attention-grabbing for audiences that numerous reviews and retrospectives about the film, including King's 25th-anniversary report, either open by discussing or focus on Williams's work as the Genie.

Visually, the magic carpet sequences are spectacular. For example, the vivid colors and various effects during Jasmine and Aladdin's magic carpet ride during the movie's best-known hit song, "A Whole New World," are stunning. It is these sequences that make *Aladdin*, the film, a must-see for anyone who knows the stage version but not the film. The musical has proven to be so popular that Disney published a "Jr." stage version designed to be performed by children. It seems reasonable to presume that the popularity of the film will continue into the future as the truncated and simplified *Aladdin, Jr.* version of the musical continues to be marketed and made available by Disney. Unlike most musicals for which pit orchestra scores and parts are available for rental, Disney's "Jr." shows must be performed to a prerecorded accompaniment. From the standpoint of the original film, this stipulation guarantees that, irrespective of how talented the singer-actors are, the instrumental backing will be just as accurate as that of the movie's soundtrack. *Aladdin* also spawned a television series and two movie sequels that were released directly onto home video.

The legacy of *Aladdin* has more recently been perpetuated by the 2019 live-character version of the musical. Unfortunately for Disney, the live-character version did not receive the same highly favorable reaction as the original animated musical did. For example, NBC News commentator Ani Bundel wrote that, although some of the additional material was "often funny and well done . . . the rest of the movie feels like, at best, a pale imitation of the original cartoon, and at worst, embarrassingly bad" (Bundel 2019). To look at this negative reaction in a different manner, Bundel's review confirms the definitive nature of the original.

ALL THAT JAZZ

In the world of the musicals of the second half of the 20th century, dancer-choreographer-producer Bob Fosse was one of the giants. The 1979 film *All That Jazz*, which included Fosse's contribution as a writer and producer, included clear autobiographical references, particularly to his work in the 1970s just before he made *All That Jazz*. *All That Jazz* starred Roy Scheider, of *Jaws* and *Jaws 2*, in a role that was about as different as that of the shark-embattled Chief Martin Brody as an audience could possibly imagine.

The real-life Bob Fosse had been burning his proverbial candle at both ends in the mid-1970s, directing the film *Lenny* and producing the Broadway musical *Chicago*. One of the central songs in the latter show, "All That Jazz," provided the title for this movie, and a variety of situations and characters in *All That Jazz* are highly suggestive of both *Lenny* and *Chicago*. For example, one of the characters is a stand-up comic, suggestive of Lenny Bruce, on whose life *Lenny* was based. As Scheider's character, Joe Gideon, uses sex and drugs to fuel his workaholic lifestyle as a theatrical producer and director, his family tries unsuccessfully to save him from himself. The film, however, does not fictionalize the outward mid-1970s lifestyle and working situation of Fosse; there is also an element of fantasy to the story. Specifically, Jessica Lange's character, Angelica, represents an angel of death, as a kind of siren, calling Joe Gideon to destruction. Although the film is open to multiple interpretations, some viewers will undoubtedly sense that Gideon understands that his lifestyle might ultimately lead to his demise. He seems to be a character who is almost addicted to living life on the edge, though apparently believing that he can overcome the siren and death no matter how much he drives himself.

Ultimately, Gideon is hospitalized with angina, continues partying in his hospital room, dances with the angel of death, and suffers a severe heart attack, which leaves the backers of the show that Gideon was producing in a quandary: can they replace Gideon, can they recoup their losses, how can insurance money be leveraged, are the questions that run through the backers' discussions. One of the eerie ironies of *All That Jazz* is that Joe Gideon ultimately dies from the heart attack, and Bob Fosse himself, who suffered from heart ailments, died of a heart attack at age 60 in 1987.

Many of the dance and song-and-dance scenes that reflect Gideon's early life, as well as the sequences from the show that Gideon is choreographing, are short. These grow in length and complexity—as one might expect—as the show begins to take shape, and culminate in the "Airotica" production number, which is given as a demonstration to the show's backers. The backers are taken aback by the eroticism of Gideon's choreography, which includes simulation of heterosexual, homosexual, interracial, and group sex. Although Gideon's ex-wife, Audrey Paris, tells Gideon that this is the best work he has ever done, the show's backers are concerned with the marketability of the production (e.g., "It looks like we lost the family audience"). These opposing reactions show the conflict between musical theater as an art and as a business, a conflict that emerges at various times throughout the film and that seems to be the root of a deep insecurity in Joe Gideon.

Interestingly, as the dance and song-and-dance numbers expand and eventually climax in "Airotica" and the film's "Bye Bye Love" production number, Gideon's focus on the *Lenny*-like movie on which he is making final edits increasingly narrow on one part of the comedian's monologue: the part about Dr. Elisabeth Kübler-Ross's five stages of grief. Kübler-Ross's five stages are referred to by the comedian as the stages of dying (focusing on the one who dies, rather than on those who grieve). Curiously, although the vulgar comedian seems to be based on Dustin Hoffmann's portrayal of Lenny Bruce in Bob Fosse's production of the film *Lenny*, the real-life Bruce could have never built a routine around Kübler-Ross's work. Bruce died in 1966 and Kübler-Ross's *On Death and Dying* was first published in 1969.

Nonetheless, the film's structure is driven by the increasing size of the musical numbers against the increasing focus—or fixation—on the comedian's routine about the stages of dying. Also central to the exploration that Fosse gives to the exploration of Gideon's inner battles is a recurring fantasy in which the comedian tells Gideon that Gideon's biggest fear is that he is "ordinary."

All That Jazz included a mixed bag of music. Soundtrack music included George Benson's recording of "On Broadway," Ethel Merman's recording of "There's No Business Like Show Business," as well as performances of old standards such as "After You've Gone," "There'll Be Some Changes Made," and "Who's Sorry Now," and a dance sequence set to Peter Allen and Carole Bayer Sager's "Everything Old Is New Again" recorded by Allen.

The soundtrack songs lend *All That Jazz* a strong sense of dark irony, both in the context of the fate of Roy Scheider's character, but especially in the context of what was to happen to Bob Fosse less than a decade later. In this sense, it is interesting to consider this film as part of the continuum of movie musicals about show business, in general, and about musicals, in particular. This subgenre includes the innocence of Judy Garland–Mickey Rooney, Andy Hardy movies (e.g., "Let's Put on a Show"), *Top Hat*, and numerous others. By the time the 1954 version of *A Star Is Born* was released, elements of darkness (e.g., alcoholism and hints of child exploitation) had crept into the musicals on musicals and show business. This would intensify in the later iterations of *A Star Is Born. All That Jazz* ramps up the level of that darkness. Add to that the fantasy aspects, which seem to represent the inner thoughts, fears, and demons of Joe Gideon's character. *All That Jazz*, although containing humor and light moments, is also an exposé of the dark side of the entertainment industry. The fact that the producers of the show that Gideon is working on at the time of his initial hospitalization with angina learn that they could actually make money if Gideon dies might reflect the reality of Bob Fosse's work on various shows that he choreographed and/or directed over the years, but it also calls to mind the premise of Mel Brooks's *The Producers*.

One of the more notable uses of non-diegetic music in the film is near the opening scene during which a large group of dancers audition for Gideon. Although the audience sees that a rehearsal pianist provides the music to which the auditioners try out, the audience (but not the dancers) hears George Benson's 1978 recording of "On Broadway." Clearly, all of the would-be Broadway performers that crowd the stage in this sequence share the desire to be "a star" that runs through the song, originally a hit for the Drifters in the early 1960s. Perhaps because of the tempo difference between "On Broadway" and the dancers' movements, the sheer improbability of stardom given the number of dancers that are competing for a limited number of spots in Gideon's musical, or the lengths that the audience learns the dancers will go to, to be cast (e.g., sleeping with the choreographer), the "On Broadway" sequence is disconcerting. As such, it sets the stage for the darkness that is always lurking—but often overt—in the film.

The climax of the film features a major production number, a reworked version of Felice and Boudleaux Bryant's "Bye Bye Love," a late-1950s hit for the Everly Brothers. At the conclusion of the reworked "Bye Bye Love," as Gideon takes his bows and goes out into the audience for congratulations from the audience members, including his daughter, he is seen moving down a hallway—apparently in a wheelchair—toward Angelica, the siren of death. He kisses her and dies. As demonstrated in his production of the film version of *Cabaret* and some of his other works, Bob Fosse both celebrated life and show business and exposed their dark sides through darkly ironic humor. This is perhaps most striking as the body bag that encloses Joe Gideon is zipped closed and the end credits roll over Ethel Merman's recording of Irving Berlin's iconic song "There's No Business Like Show Business," for it was the excesses of the show business life that led to Gideon's early demise.

Like the later 2002 film *Chicago*, *All That Jazz* was one of the great film musicals that featured an unlikely cast. Notably, also like *Chicago*, *All That Jazz* was recognized by the American Film Institute as one of the 25 greatest movie musicals of all time; the American Film Institute ranked *All That Jazz* at No. 14 (American Film Institute 2006). The U.S. Library of Congress Film Preservation Board added *All That Jazz* to the National Film Registry in 2001.

AN AMERICAN IN PARIS

The title of the 1951 Vincente Minnelli film *An American in Paris* was based on the several-decades-old orchestral composition of the same name by George Gershwin. Alan Jay Lerner, best known as the book and lyrics writer of the Lerner and Loewe team, provided the film's story and screenplay. *An American in Paris* incorporates both the orchestral composition of the movie's title and numerous songs by brothers George (music) and Ira (lyrics) Gershwin. Gene Kelly, who starred as Jerry Mulligan—a play on the name of the well-known cool jazz baritone saxophone player Gerry Mulligan, who had just emerged a few years before the movie's premiere—provided the film's choreography.

The film's storyline revolves around Mulligan, an artist; his friend Adam Cook, a concert pianist, played by Oscar Levant; Henri "Hank"

Baurel, a cabaret singer, played by Georges Guétary; Baurel's girlfriend/fiancé Lise Bouvier, played by Leslie Caron; and Milo Roberts, a wealthy art collector, played by Nina Foch. The plot is not particularly novel, with Roberts becoming interested in Mulligan's work and in Mulligan himself on several levels, Mulligan and Bouvier accidentally discovering each other and falling in love, and Baurel recognizing that Bouvier and Mulligan belong together after overhearing their conversation just before Baurel was ready to whisk Bouvier off.

Several of the Gershwin brothers' songs appear in truncated form; however, the longer arrangements by music director Saul Chaplin really form the musical meat of the movie. For example, a set of instrumental variations of "Embraceable You" introduces the audience and Adam Cook to the various personality traits of Baurel's girlfriend. The variations also introduce the audience to snippets of the dance styles that Caron would exhibit more fully in her subsequent films, dancing *en pointe*, dancing seductively, and imitating a jazz-dancing showgirl. Another lengthy number, "By Strauss," might not be among George and Ira Gershwin's better-remembered songs, but it provides some comedy early in the film. Some songs, such as "Someone to Watch over Me," are interwoven into the soundtrack by being played in the background by a jazz band in a club.

Perhaps one of the most unusual uses of Gershwin songs in the movie is Mulligan's performance of "I Got Rhythm," which is in the context of a lesson in English that the artist gives to young French children. The song features the first of several Gene Kelly tap dance routines in the film. The section in which Mulligan mixes French and English is entertaining and adds to the unexpectedness of the song in the film's context. It is worth noting that the American Film Institute ranked Gene Kelly's performance of "I Got Rhythm" at No. 32 on its list of the 100 greatest movie songs of all time (American Film Institute 2004). Later in the film, the song "Tra-La-La" turns into another major Kelly tap dance routine.

One of the better-known songs included in the film, "Love Is Here to Stay," plays a role in defining the quickly developing relationship between Mulligan and Bouvier. The song comes into play at several key points as the relationship unfolds. Interestingly, its first appearance is the day after Mulligan and Bouvier first meet. Taken literally—the two characters have barely met each other, let alone fallen in love—the song's lyrics seem somewhat improbable. The song makes more sense when it occurs later in the film; however, because it occurs at several key points in the story, "Love Is Here to Stay" becomes a sort of leitmotif for the relationship.

Henri "Hank" Baurel's performance of "I'll Build a Stairway to Paradise" as part of his cabaret act suggests the influence of director/producer/choreographer Busby Berkeley with an elaborate set, numerous fancily and somewhat provocatively clad female dancers, and an overall grand production that uses a long winding staircase. Although Georges Guétary's performance in the film received critical praise (see, for example, The Staff of *Variety* 1951), his histrionic singing style in this song, as well as later in "'S Wonderful," has not aged particularly well.

Two major George Gershwin instrumental works, *Concerto in F* and *An American in Paris*, are used in dream sequences. The former is a part of concert pianist Adam Cook's fantasy of his performance of the work, which the film suggests was his own composition. This sequence is notable for the camera work and film editing, which makes it appear that Cook is not only the piano soloist but also part of a multi-Cook violin section, percussion section, and so on. In his book *Can't Help Singin': The American Musical on Stage and Screen*, Gerald Mast highlights, among many other movies, "five classic filmusicals of the 1950s" that demonstrate better than any others that the movie musical was about—particularly at that time—entertainment with an artistic sense that spoke to the audience (Mast 1987, 253). As Mast writes, "It is not now fashionable to admire the film that inspired the others: Alan Jay Lerner's script for *An American in Paris*, which seems loose and meandering, isn't funny; the ballet, which makes little sense in whatever plot the film has, seems pretentious" (Mast 1987, 253–254). I would argue that the use of *Concerto in F*, as part of the film's earlier fantasy sequence, actually sets up the fantasy ballet danced to Gershwin's *An American in Paris* well. In fact, to this viewer, it is the *Concerto in F* fantasy sequence—and not the ballet—that seems most to come out of nowhere in the film.

Although the ballet sequence set to the entire orchestral work of the film's title does not necessarily advance the plot, it functions as a fantasy/dream sequence-type piece for Gene Kelly's character, who finds himself at a proverbial critical juncture in his life after Lise Bouvier leaves him to marry Henri Baurel. Kelly's choreography breaks down barriers between modern dance, ballet, and vernacular styles such as tap in the work.

As Mast explains its historical significance, *An American in Paris* inspired *Singin' in the Rain*, *The Band Wagon*, *A Star Is Born*, and *Funny Face*, and that "number for number, no filmusical can rival *An American in Paris* for musical integrity" (Mast 1987, 254). Perhaps it was this excellent music that helped propel *An American in Paris* to No. 9 in the American Film Institute's ranking of 25 greatest movie musicals of all time (American Film Institute 2006). Although Mast's assessment suggests that the critical reaction to *An American in Paris* vastly improved between 1951 and the late 1980s, at the time of the film's release it was recognized by at least some reviewers as an important film. For example, the staff review from *Variety* referred to *An American in Paris* as "one of the most imaginative musical confections turned out by Hollywood in years." The *Variety* review also praises Gene Kelly as the film's star and identifies Leslie Caron and Georges Guétary as possible film stars of the future (The Staff of *Variety* 1951).

The musical integrity mentioned by Mast and other writers is important to consider on several levels. The songs and instrumental compositions are all by the Gershwin brothers. They come, however, from vastly different original contexts, and the songs originally represented a variety of different Gershwin shows spread out over many years. One of the strengths of *An American in Paris* is that this mixed bag of George and Ira Gershwin songs, including "Embraceable You," "Nice Work If You Can Get It," "I Got Rhythm," "By Strauss," "Love Is Here to Stay," "'S Wonderful," "I'll Build a Stairway to Paradise," and others rarely feels forced. In part, this is because the storyline does not move about artificially to accommodate the specifics of Ira Gershwin's lyrics. This is achieved in several ways, including by only using brief phrases from the lyrics of some of the songs and by including other tunes as underscoring in the soundtrack.

By taking this mixed bag of Gershwin songs and orchestral pieces and building a movie around them, *An American in Paris* might reasonably be considered one of the earliest and possibly one of the most influential jukebox musicals. Some musicals before *An American in Paris* had incorporated earlier material. For example, "Singin' in the Rain" was used in so many MGM musicals that it became something of a signature song for the company. Some other earlier movies—most notably the 1942 musical *Yankee Doodle Dandy*—had solely used earlier songs by a single songwriter. A movie such as *Yankee Doodle Dandy*, however, is akin to the biopic genre, being a stylized look at the life of Broadway legend George M. Cohan. *An American in Paris* is fundamentally different in that a fictional story was constructed by Alan Jay Lerner around the Gershwin pieces. In this respect, *An American in Paris* is the ancestor of *Mamma Mia!*, *Across the Universe*, *All Shook Up*, and other rock-era jukebox musicals.

The title of an article about the film "The Musical That Changed Movies" (McGovern 2017) suggests the cinematic importance of *An American in Paris*. The success of the film at the 1952 Academy Awards ushered in a new era of respect for movie musicals, as well as the era that included *Singin' in the Rain, Guys and Dolls*, the 1954 version of *A Star Is Born*, and *The Music Man*. Arguably, part of the respect for musicals associated with *An American in Paris* is connected to the integration of some of the most artistic examples of Tin Pan Alley songs—those of George and Ira Gershwin; however, the dance sequences are innovative and entertaining, and the cinematography creatively mixes what appear to be actual location shots with what are obvious studio backdrops. This is creatively done in the sense that the backdrops used in, say, the lengthy ballet sequence are supposed to look unreal as the entire sequence is a fantasy/dream piece based on Jerry Mulligan's sketch of a Paris scene.

Because so many movie musicals were actually film adaptations of earlier stage musicals, it is interesting to note that well over 60 years after the premiere of the film version of *An American in Paris*, a stage version with the same name opened on Broadway. This suggests a strong legacy for the film.

THE BAND WAGON

Starring Fred Astaire, Cyd Charisse, Oscar Levant, Nanette Fabray, Jack Buchanan, James Mitchell, and Robert Gist, the 1953 film *The Band Wagon* joined a list of early 1950s movie musicals about musicals. The film was preceded by a 1931 Broadway show of the same name with music by Arthur Schwartz and lyrics by Howard Dietz. In addition to songs from the 1931 stage show, *The Band Wagon* included songs from other Schwartz and Dietz shows of the 1930s, as well as material composed especially for the film. The movie included "That's Entertainment" and "Dancing in the Dark," two iconic songs of the golden age of the Broadway and film musical.

In her *Music & the Moving Image* article "Rethinking the Diegetic/Nondiegetic Distinction in the Film Musical," Nina Penner credits *The Band Wagon* with breaking down the distinctions between diegetic and non-diegetic music in films (Penner 2017). *The Band Wagon* set the stage for future musicals that straddled the barriers. It should be noted, however, that the work of other film scholars suggests that *The Band Wagon* perhaps was more part of a continuum of changes that had been underway in the movie industry from the 1940s. For example, David Neumeyer's article, "Merging Genres in the 1940s: The Music and Dramatic Feature Film," details how the lines between diegetic and non-diegetic music were beginning to blur both in dramatic non-musicals (e.g., *Casablanca*) and musicals (e.g., *Meet Me in St. Louis*) (Neumeyer 2004), both released approximately a decade before *The Band Wagon*. Although other films anticipated this aspect of *The Band Wagon*, it is true that one of the more noticeable scenes in the movie is the finale, a reprise of the song "That's Entertainment," that concludes by the movie's principals singing directly into the camera—to the audience in the movie theater. Throughout the movie some songs are part of the show-within-a-show, some are used as part of the dialogue between characters, and some seem to be directed at the film's audience.

The story and screenplay by Betty Comden and Adolph Green is predictable: writers create a show; writers team up with a producer who completely misinterprets the intent of the show; the show is a failure in early performances; aging Broadway star (Tony Hunter, played by Fred Astaire) takes over leadership and restores the entertainment focus of the original script; the show is a success. In addition, the relationship between Hunter and ballet star Gabrielle Gerard (played by Cyd Charisse) is also predictable: at first, the two cannot seem to get along but end up in a strong professional and personal relationship. Despite this, the storyline is interesting for semiautobiographical nods to writers Comden and Green, as well as to Astaire. Astaire had left the Broadway stage for the world of film, and by the early 1950s was in his early 50s and had already been semiretired from show business. Although Astaire would enjoy a resurgence in his career, in 1953, viewers could easily have detected a bit of Astaire in Tony Hunter.

Writer Robert Alford mentions that *The Band Wagon* had not received the sort of "queer" analysis that many other classic MGM musicals received from scholars such as Matthew Tinkcom and Steven Cohan (Alford 2014, 49). Alford writes, "*The Band Wagon* . . . appears positively sedate when compared to other films that [Vincente] Minnelli made there [MGM], such as *The Pirate* (1948) and *Yolanda and the Thief* (1945), which tend towards camp sensibility their flamboyant stylistic excess" (49). Throughout his article, however, Alford contends that *The Band Wagon* included abundant gay and queer references. For example, as Fred Astaire breaks into the song "A Shine on My Shoes," a neon sign behind the shoeshine stand reads "The Gayest Music Box." There are also references to Jack Buchanan's flamboyant character tied to "gay [musical] numbers." Near the beginning of the shoeshine scene mentioned above, Astaire's character mentions that the location used to be the site of the Eltinge Theatre (which was named after the female impersonator Julian Eltinge) as he is handed a hotdog by a vendor. Incidentally, the apparent change in the location of the Eltinge included in *The Band Wagon* anticipated the theater's 1998 physical move (when it was known as the Empire Theatre) approximately 170 feet away from its original location.

Regardless of to what extent Vincente Minnelli intended for these implications to exist, particularly in the first part of the film, audiences perhaps more commonly think of *The Band Wagon* as a movie musical about the entertainment industry and not as a film to be watched for alleged references to sexuality. One of the movie's songs that centered on the entertainment industry and the work of those in the industry was "That's Entertainment." In its list of the 100 greatest movie songs in the first 100 years of the film industry, the American Film Institute ranked "That's Entertainment" at No. 45. This was one of the songs that Schwartz and Dietz wrote especially for the film over 20 years after they had written some of the others for the original stage version of the musical. The song itself appears several times in the film and became a metaphor for the great MGM musicals of the 1930s through 1950s. In fact, the 1974 retrospective of the studio's contributions to the movie musical genre, *That's Entertainment*, took its title from this new Schwartz and Dietz song.

The prominence of the song—and the movie's basic theme that audiences go to a musical to be entertained—suggests that entertainment was the main aim of the musicals of the first half of the 20th century. Works such as *Show Boat*, *Porgy and Bess* and some others dealt with some of the social issues of their day and of the past; however, by and large, "That's Entertainment" sums up the overall goal of most stage and movie musicals at least until the 1960s.

The film includes several highlight scenes, including the memorable "Dancing in the Dark" sequence, as well as other dance sequences that feature Astaire and Charisse. One of the other highlights is the first encounter of their characters, Tony Hunter and Gabrielle Gerard, in which Astaire and Charisse trade barbs. Also notable is the scene that follows, in which the two appear briefly in front of the potential backers of the musical in which the two are to star. Here, in stereo entertainment industry style, Hunter and Gerard put on a false front to try to convince the potential backers to invest.

The movie contains a number of perhaps unexpected references to the early 1950s. One is when Astaire's character, after quitting the show, trashes his hotel room. He throws a bunch of records on the floor. Most of them shatter, except for one. When Astaire picks it up, the label reads "Unbreakable." The unbreakable single record had first appeared just before *The Band Wagon* was made.

As mentioned earlier, some of the songs came from post-1931/pre-1950 Schwartz and Dietz shows, including "Louisiana Hayride." Interestingly, this early-1930s song years later became associated with a popular country music radio and television program. Insofar as *Louisiana Hayride* was around at the time of the premiere of the movie version of *The Band Wagon*, the song ties the movie to the popular culture of its time.

"The Girl Hunt" sequence in the show-within-a-show clearly oozes the spirit of the popular detective novelist Mickey Spillane, who had published the first of his numerous Mike Hammer novels by the time *The Band Wagon* was shot. The entire sequence is suggestive of the ballet sequences in Gene Kelly's films from the 1940s to the early 1950s. Although this lengthy sequence uses a fair number of special effects, the dance sequence between Astaire and Charisse firmly moves Astaire from the world of the top hat and cane into the 1950s.

The film's "Dancing in the Dark" sequence is one of Astaire's classic film performances. Charisse and Astaire's characters ride through New York's Central Park trying to determine if they will be able to dance together. Ultimately, they dance together in one of the more famous dance duets in 20th-century movie musicals.

Rehearsals of the show-within-a-show parody the elaborate staging techniques of Busby Berkeley. As might be imagined, with all the complexity of Berkeley-like staging, set, and choreography, everything that can go wrong does go wrong. Adding to the comedic disasters is the subsequent scene in which pyrotechnics go awry, providing one of the funnier sequences in the entire movie.

Ultimately, the show opens in New Haven, Connecticut. As might be expected, given the premise of a musical adaptation of *Faust*, the technical problems that plagued rehearsals, etc., the premiere of the show is a flop. In stereotypical Broadway and Hollywood style, however, the show must go on, and with Tony Hunter asserting leadership and Buchanan's adaptation of *Faust* out of the way, the show-within-a-show becomes a hit. In the end, Tony Hunter and Gabrielle Gerard not only can tolerate each other they work well together, and there are hints that the two might share a deeper romantic tie, making *The Band Wagon* a classic opposites-attract story.

The American Film Institute recognized the importance of *The Band Wagon* by ranking the film at No. 17 on its list of the 25 greatest movie musicals of all time (American Film Institute 2006).

BEAUTY AND THE BEAST

The story at the core of the 1991 Disney animated film *Beauty and the Beast* has a long history, originating in a fairy tale from France. The famed French writer, poet, and filmmaker, Jean Cocteau had produced a film version in the 1940s, but the Disney organization turned the story into a musical. *Beauty and the Beast* proved to be popular and took its place among animated films such as *The Little Mermaid* and *Aladdin* as part of the Disney Renaissance from approximately the late 1980s through the 1990s.

Beauty and the Beast featured voice actors who were well experienced in film and on stage, including Paige O'Hara (Belle), Robby Benson (the Beast), Jerry Orbach (Lumière), and Richard White (Gaston). White deserves special mention for his exaggerated deliberately over-the-top interpretation of the conceited Gaston. Gaston's singing features an operatic vibrato that calls to mind the *Mighty Mouse* theme to which actor-comedian Andy Kaufman famously mimed early in his career. Although not necessarily among the principal characters, Angela Lansbury voiced the teapot and Jo Anne Worley voiced the wardrobe.

Throughout the film, in the musical numbers and the fairly lengthy periods between songs, there is an inherent cuteness to the animated inhabitants of the Beast's castle, particularly "Chip," the chipped teacup, who ultimately becomes one of the story's heroes. This balances the harshness that the Beast exhibits when and just after he takes Belle as a prisoner of the castle. It is interesting to note, though, that generally the characters are not really terrified of the Beast, perhaps suggesting that the candlestick, the wardrobe, and so on sense that the Beast might actually be able to change and that the curse might be broken.

One of the film's musical highlights is the production number "Be Our Guest." Here, Lumière sings and speaks with a humorous Maurice Chevalier-inspired French accent, suggesting the inspiration of Chevalier's work in *Gigi*. The production includes other cues from older musicals, such as the use of Busby Berkeley-inspired geometric formations of the "dancers" (dinner plates, cups, cutlery, and so on) and a reference to the Esther Williams synchronized swimming scenes that were popular in the late 1940s and early 1950s. These references brought the stuff of movie musicals that the grandparents of the young audience of 1991 might have been familiar with from the first time around, and the parents of youngsters would have been at least partially familiar with because of the extent to which Chevalier's performance of "Thank Heaven for Little Girls," the over-the-top Berkeley-style staging, and the synchronized swimming scenes of Williams had become a general part of popular culture that transcended the decades.

Some reviews of the 1991 film mentioned the Broadway-like nature of the production. Viewers can sense this in the staging of "Belle," early in the movie. The townspeople sing and dance as they go about their business early in the song. Near the end of the piece, however, the townspeople sing directly to the audience, as one would typically experience in a live-character movie musical or on stage in a song that informs the audience about the nature of a character or a situation. Apparently, the Disney organization also recognized the stage-friendly nature of *Beauty and the Beast*: a commercially successful live version was produced just a few years after the premiere of the animated movie.

As the original animated *Beauty and the Beast* was nearing completion, Disney took the unusual step of showing unfinished versions at prestigious film festivals. The fact that an animated musical would receive such treatment speaks to the quality of the movie, which goes beyond that of the average movie musical. In 2006, the American Film Institute ranked *Beauty and the Beast* No. 22 on its list of the 25 greatest movie musicals of all time, which is further evidence of the recognition of the film's high quality (American Film Institute 2006). The American Film Institute also ranked the movie's title song at No. 62 on its list of the 100 greatest movie songs of all time (American Film Institute 2004). Composer Alan Menken won the Academy Award for Best Original Score, and Menken and lyricist Howard Ashman won the Academy Award for Best Original Song for "Beauty and the Beast." Perhaps just as noteworthy as the wins, however, is the fact that Menken and Ashman's songs "Be Our Guest" and "Belle" were also nominated for the Best Original Song. Rare for an animated movie, let alone an animated movie musical, *Beauty and the Beast* was nominated for the Academy Award for Best Picture, losing to *Silence of the Lambs*.

The second half of the 2010s was a fertile time for sequels and remakes of classic movie musicals. *Beauty and the Beast* was among those remade during this period despite the fact that, arguably, the 1991 original was still relevant when the remake was made in 2017. As I discuss in the chapter "Legacy," remakes such as the 2017 live-actor version of *Beauty and the Beast* were lengthier and more complex than the animated originals. In fact, the production of *Beauty and the Beast* might appear to some movie fans to take some cues from the classic movie musicals of the mid-20th century, particularly in terms of production numbers. Given that audiences who were perhaps around 10 years old at the time of the release of the original animated version would be in their midthirties at the time when Emma Watson portrayed Belle in 2017, it would appear that the remake was designed to bring the story more into the realm of the original audience now as adults, while perhaps giving their children—perhaps young teenagers—a new version of *Beauty and the Beast* to call their own. Critical reaction to the 2017 live-character remake, however, was not particularly favorable.

In addition to many of the sequences being expanded in the 2017 live-character remake (e.g., the entire opening "Once upon a time . . ." sequence leading up to the Prince transforming into the Beast), some of the one-liners that would seem to be more fully aimed at adult audiences are handled noticeably differently. One example is near the beginning of the film in the song "Belle," when a male character is trying it on with one of the female street vendors. In the 1991 film, the comeback line, "How's your wife?" is tossed out and becomes part of several lines that seem to represent casual on-the-street conversation. In the 2017 film, the come on and response take longer and are given more of a wink-wink-nudge-nudge feeling that betrays the man's naughtiness and desire for sexual adventure. This kind of treatment provides additional evidence that the 2017 *Beauty and the Beast* might have been intended for people who had first experienced the musical as children but would now get some of the more mature references.

One area in which the 2017 remake holds its own against the original is in the orchestrations. After experiencing the live-character version, the instrumental accompaniments of the songs and the instrumental under-scoring of the non-song scenes seems thin in retrospect. In the animated musical, the accompaniment of the song "Beauty and the Beast" sounds synthetic, albeit not as synthesizer-oriented as the Céline Dion and Peabo Bryson recording that plays through the final credits and became a hit single.

CABARET

Cabaret was one of the more notable and edgy musicals of the 1960s and 1970s. The film version was set at the end of the 1920s in Berlin and starred Liza Minnelli as Sally Bowles, a cabaret performer at the Kit Kat Klub; Michael York as Brian Roberts, an English teacher and doctoral student from Cambridge University; Helmut Griem as Maximilian von Heune, a rich German playboy; and Joel Grey as the Kit Kat Klub's androgynous master of ceremonies, a role that Grey had played earlier in the stage version of *Cabaret*.

The original stage version of *Cabaret* was produced in 1966 and featured music by John Kander and lyrics by Fred Ebb. Bob Fosse directed and provided the choreography for the 1972 film version. The movie's screenplay included some material from the stage musical, some material from the book on which the stage version was based but was never used in the stage version, and some plot twists that were unique to the film. Because the relationship between the play and the film was so loose, the movie *Cabaret* must be considered as its own work and not as a slightly truncated and modified version of a stage musical. In fact, because the movie is relatively song-free for a movie musical, and because nearly all the musical numbers take place in the cabaret itself while much of the action takes place outside the cabaret, it is perhaps one of the least "musical" movie musicals included in this volume. Despite this, *Cabaret* was one of the most critically acclaimed and commercially successful movie musicals of its time. Ultimately, it places the rise of the Nazis into the context of the excesses of Berlin during the late 1920s and early 1930s. It also raises questions about values, particularly in the way in which the relationships of the characters develop and resolve.

The complexity of the relationships of the characters might best be seen in the fact that the well-educated doctoral student teaching English in Germany (Brian Roberts) is in a relationship with the bohemian cabaret performer (Sally Bowles). However, Maximilian invites Brian and Sally to his country estate, where he manages to have sex with both of them, initially unbeknown to the other. Adding to the issue of sexuality in *Cabaret* is the difficult-to-decipher nature of the sexuality of the master of ceremonies.

Mitchell Morris's 2004 essay "*Cabaret*, America's Weimar, and Mythologies of the Gay Subject" (Morris 2004) explores the differences in the sexual dynamics and the dramatic use of homosexuality and bisexuality—implicit and explicit—of the film version of the musical versus the earlier stage version, as well as the differences and similarities that the musical versions have with Christopher Isherwood's original novellas that were the original material from which the storyline and setting of the musicals was born. Morris makes the case that director Bob Fosse played a prominent role in both connecting the film version of the musical to late-1920s and early-1930s Berlin and to the "'new' social problems" of the late 1960s, such as the emerging gay rights movement, through changes that he had writers make to the original show and through the performance demands he put on the film's stars, including Minnelli and Grey.

Cabaret is a movie musical that has more sizable gaps between musical numbers than many other musicals. In fact, the number of musical numbers is considerably fewer in the film than in the stage version. Some of the songs were cut and some appear only as instrumentals, either produced in low fidelity on the phonograph or in high fidelity as part of more standard placement as soundtrack underscoring. Part of the challenge of this approach, as well as the fact that virtually all the songs that are actually sung in the movie are part of performances in the Kit Kat Klub, is that it is quite a different approach than that used in the traditional Broadway musical or movie musical. Because all the music in the film is diegetic—or source—music, the audience gets virtually no "insider" information from the soundtrack that the characters themselves do not experience—this distinguishes *Cabaret* from the norm in films. Although nearly all the songs are part of the Kit Kat Klub shows, they do tend to foretell the basic theme that is expanded in the action that follows. However, unlike the typical musical, the characters do not sing to each other to express their emotions. To put it another way, the action in *Cabaret* does not suddenly stop for a song as is the case in many earlier live and film musicals.

The one notable song that is not performed by the master of ceremonies or Sally Bowles in the Kit Kat Klub is also one of the most chilling musical numbers, "Tomorrow Belongs to Me," which is a song in a biergarten by a young man in a Hitler Youth uniform. The song foretells the full rise of the Nazis. As the song continues, a multitude of people—young and old—join in a massive chorus behind the young man, with very few not joining in. As Maximilian and Brian leave the biergarten, the young man raises his arm in a Nazi salute and Brian expresses his doubt that the Nazis can ever be controlled.

Although this scene is a pivotal point in the film, the growing ascent of the Nazis both in numbers and in power and influence is also shown in the makeup of the Kit Kat Klub audience and in the progression of the songs and repartee of Joel Grey's master of ceremonies. What started out as a small minority that is kicked out of the cabaret clearly becomes a group that represents the bulk of the Kit Kat Klub's patrons by the end of the film.

Director Bob Fosse also uses dramatic cuts between scenes in the cabaret to scenes of Nazi-led brutality on the streets of Berlin to highlight the growing violence. These contrasts also highlight the apparent misjudgment of the danger posed by the Nazis, or the tacit approval of the Nazi campaign against Communists, Jews, and so on, by the populace.

Steven Belletto's 2008 article "*Cabaret* and Antifascist Aesthetics" examines the political messages of the movie, including those that are not necessarily as obvious as the cut-to shots of Nazis harassing people or as harrowing as the singing of "Tomorrow Belongs to Me" by a member of the Hitler Youth. In particular, Belletto points to the importance of Joel Grey's master of ceremonies character. As Belletto writes, "Ultimately,

Cabaret offers an especially canny example of antifascist aesthetics, a complicated phenomenon rooted not in Sally's famous songs about sex and decadence, but in the Emcee's numbers, which are characterized by ambiguity, irony, and uneasiness" (Belletto 2008, 609).

Ultimately, Sally Bowles fits into the category of those who failed to confront the reality of the Nazi threat. She goes happily along with her life, seemingly completely unaffected by events around her, be they personal or the political and social upheaval that accompanied the Nazis rise to power. She becomes a symbol of how the decadent focus on the pleasure of the Roaring Twenties and the early 1930s helped to allow the Nazis to succeed. Similarly, Maximilian's view that the Nazis were just a bunch of thugs who could easily be controlled once they helped rid Germany of Communists proved to be naïve. This makes him a symbol of how the failure to speak out against evil or to tolerate it because one thinks that the ends justify the means, can allow that evil to expand in size and scope until it becomes uncontrollable.

Musically, some of the highlights include the opening "Willkommen" sequence, one of the more famous scenes from *Cabaret*, "Maybe This Time," which is a technical *tour de force* for Minnelli, "Two Ladies," in which the master of ceremonies and two female dances explore the possibility of a threesome, and the cut-to images of Nazi atrocities that immediately follow the song "Money Money."

The original Broadway production of *Cabaret* won multiple Tony Awards and the film won eight Academy Awards for Best Director (Bob Fosse), Best Actress in a Leading Role (Liza Minnelli), Best Actor in a Supporting Role (Joel Grey), Best Cinematography, Best Film Editing, Best Original Song Score or Adaptation Score, Best Art Direction, and Best Sound. The film did not win the Academy Award for Best Picture, which went to *The Godfather*; however, one could easily imagine that *Cabaret* could have won that award too had it not been up against one of the most iconic dramatic films of all time. *Cabaret* was a challenging movie that fundamentally differed from the stereotype of what a movie musical was supposed to be in its content and its structure. Its political and social themes such as xenophobia, fascism, public apathy, and issues of sexuality continue to resonate well into the 21st century. In addition to the recognition that *Cabaret* received from the Academy of Motion Picture Arts and Sciences at the time of its release, it has been recognized by the American Film Institute, which named *Cabaret* the No. 5 best movie musical of all time on its 2006 list (American Film Institute 2006), and ranked the movie's title song as the No. 18 greatest movie song of all time (American Film Institute 2004).

CHICAGO

Based on a play from the 1920s and set in the Chicago of that era, *Chicago* was first produced as a highly successful stage musical in 1975. The music was by John Kander, lyrics by Fred Ebb, and the book was by Ebb and Bob Fosse. The 2002 movie version starred Renée Zellweger as Roxie Hart, a woman who fantazies of becoming a star on the Chicago stage, Catherine Zeta-Jones as Velma Kelly, and Richard Gere as lawyer Billy Flynn.

Chicago is centered around a theater; however, it is anything but a typical show-within-a-show musical about musicals. The musical numbers are introduced by the pianist and bandleader, played by Taye Diggs, whose role is in some ways similar to that of the master of ceremonies in *Cabaret*. The plot revolves around two murderers, Velma Kelly, who killed her sister, and Roxie Hart, who killed her lover. Billy Flynn serves as the attorney for both women. The women compete against each other for Flynn's attention. However, a major wrinkle appears later in the story when Kitty Baxter, played by Lucy Liu, trumps Hart and Kelly by murdering her husband and his two mistresses. Queen Latifah also plays a significant role in the film as "Mama" Morton, the prison matron.

Chicago includes several elaborate dance sequences, including "All That Jazz" and "Cell Block Tango." The latter makes particularly effective use of the film medium to cut between the dance scenes, the murderous events described in the lyrics, interviews with reporters, scenes from the prison mess hall, and so on. Throughout the film, John Kander's score exhibits the influence of the jazz and show music of the 1920s, while sounding engaging for the late 20th-century and early 21st-century audience. There is also a consistency in Kander's melodic writing that is worth noting, whether one is watching the film or stage production. For example, "Mr. Cellophane" and "All That Jazz" share some melodic contours. In addition, Kander uses chromatic harmonies in similar ways in these two songs.

Although it featured what was arguably one of the more unlikely casts for an early 21st-century movie musical, *Chicago* was largely successful. In fact, the American Film Institute ranked *Chicago* No. 12 in its listing of the 25 greatest movie musicals of all time (American Film Institute 2006). The Institute also ranked "All That Jazz" No. 98 on its list of the 100 greatest movie songs of all time (American Film Institute 2004). But it was at the Academy Awards that *Chicago* earned its strongest recognition. Martin Richards, the film's producer, won the Academy Award for Best Picture, the first time that a musical had won the Best Picture award since *Oliver!* won in 1968. Catherine Zeta-Jones won the Academy Award for Best Supporting Actress; Collen Atwood won for Best Costume Design; Martin Walsh won the Oscar for Best Film Editing; and Michael Minkler, Dominick Tavella, and David Lee won the Academy Award for Best Sound. It is interesting to note that the movie, on the whole, was honored, as was one of its songs, one of its actors, and several members of the production team in different technical areas. In addition to this wide-ranging recognition, *Chicago* was a commercial success. Because the film captures the spirit of an iconic era so well and does so with humor, it continues to seem fresh.

DREAMGIRLS

The 2006 film *Dreamgirls* was based on the 1981 stage musical of the same name. Although the show cannot help but be understood as a fictionalized story of the Supremes and the Motown scene and the business world of the early 1960s through the early 1970s, particularly in the film version, in which the location was changed from Chicago to Detroit, the musical speaks more broadly about musical changes occurring from the late 1950s into the 1970s and the glamour and harsh realities of the entertainment industry. However, perhaps the best aspects of *Dreamgirls* are how the songs by composer Henry Krieger and lyricist Tom Eyen capture the style and spirit of the story's era and the vocal performances by the stars, particularly Beyoncé Knowles and Jennifer Hudson.

Writer and director Bill Condon adapted *Dreamgirls* from the original stage version. Condon's film principally starred Jamie Foxx as Curtis Taylor Jr., a car salesman turned artists' manager and record company owner; Beyoncé Knowles as Deena Jones, a member of the Dreamettes and the Dreams, whose career from the early 1960s through the early 1970s roughly parallels that of Diana Ross; Eddie Murphy as the R&B singer Jimmy Early; Jennifer Hudson as Effie, the original lead singer of the Dreamettes; Danny Glover as Marty Madison, Jimmy Early's original manager; Anika Noni Rose as Lorrell Robinson, a member of the Dreamettes and the Dreams; and Keith Robinson as C. C. White, Effie White's younger brother, who becomes a principal songwriter for Rainbow Records.

The story begins with Curtis Taylor Jr. discovering the Dreamettes at a Detroit talent show as they perform "I'm Lookin' for Something." Like most other songs in the film, "I'm Lookin' for Something" closely resembles the songs of the day, in this case, the early 1960s. As the Dreamettes sing "Move," another early song in the film, Effie White's lead vocals have more in common with soul singers such as Aretha Franklin than with the smoother sound of the Supremes and the other girl groups they are supposed to represent. In fact, this song establishes Effie as a decidedly self-assured highly emotional singer and character.

Although he is early in his music management career, Taylor takes on the group and arranges for them to sing backup for the R&B singer James Thunder "Jimmy" Early, a character whose performance style resembles an amalgamation of James Brown and some of the other leading male R&B singers of the early 1960s. Early and the Dreamettes' performance of "Fake Your Way to the Top," in fact, has something of a James Brown show production and performance quality to it, albeit with backing female vocals.

In an effort to leverage the early-1960s popularity of songs about cars, Taylor has Jimmy Early and the Dreamettes record "Cadillac Car." One of the curious aspects of the recording session scene is that the Rainbow Records studio is located in the car dealership where Taylor works. In real life, the garage doors would offer very little in the way of sound insulation; however, the setting illustrates the low-budget nature of the company at its inception. Soon after the release of "Cadillac Car," the song is covered by a white group that turns it into a ballad, which becomes a hit on pop charts. It should be noted that cover versions of songs had existed years before the time period depicted in *Dreamgirls*. Although at one time covers represented a way in which multiple record companies could capitalize on a popular song, in the rock era of the mid- to late-1950s, the scenario played out in the film was most associated with a racial divide in the music industry in which it was rare for black performers to enjoy success on the pop charts. Perhaps the best-known recording artist associated with cover versions, Pat Boone seems to be the white artist parodied in the film.

"Steppin' to the Bad Side" accompanies Taylor's attempt to control black music and take it to the pop charts by offering payola to DJs. The song starts off on the street, like a conventional musical theater production number, then it becomes the underscoring for the scenes of Taylor procuring the money to give to the DJs. "Steppin' to the Bad Side" then transitions into a live performance of the song by Jimmy Early, his band, and the Dreamettes. Interestingly, the musical style is more in tune with the late 1960s than the period depicted in the plot. "Steppin' to the Bad Side" is used both as a hit song for Early and as a commentary on Curtis Taylor's step "to the bad side" by resorting to illegal activities for promoting his artists and their material. Songwriters Howard Krieger and Tom Eyen (as well as Krieger with other collaborators on the songs that were newly written for the film version of *Dreamgirls*) used the technique of having the songs performed live and/or recorded by Rainbow's artists related directly to the action and/or the characters' inner feelings throughout the musical.

Because one of the major themes of *Dreamgirls* is Curtis Taylor's attempts to put black music on the pop charts, *Dreamgirls* has a structural problem, particularly to the extent that the film—even more than the 1981 original stage version of the musical—is often understood as a fictionalized story of Motown, its founder Berry Gordy Jr., the Supremes, and other Motown artists. Effie's solo recording of the song "Love You I Do" comes after the release of an album with Rev. Dr. Martin Luther King Jr.'s "I Have a Dream" speech in 1963. The real-life Motown had already enjoyed more than just a few pop chart hits by that time, and the black Brill Building girl groups had also placed singles well up in the pop charts. If one considers *Dreamgirls* as an entirely fictional account of a fictional singing group and record company, this slight technical issue might go unnoticed.

As Taylor continues to refine his formula for breaking his artists on the pop charts, he replaces Effie as the Dreamettes lead singer with Deena Jones and rebrands the group as the Dreams. Part of the emotional tension of the film comes from Effie's diminishing status, despite her physical relationship with Taylor. Just after Taylor switches the vocal roles of Deena and Effie, however, C. C. White, Effie's younger brother, opens the singing of his song "Family," a piece that establishes the idea that in its early days Rainbow Records functioned like a close-knit family, with its members focused on a common goal. This view of the company plays an important role throughout the film, particularly as Taylor becomes increasingly dictatorial.

It is at the debut of the rebranded Dreams with Deena Jones singing lead that her hair and makeup increasingly resemble those of Diana Ross. As the film progresses, other characters also become more—and some viewers might find, too—obviously related to the real-life Motown stars of the 1960s and early 1970s. In the case of Deena Jones, from this point in the film through its conclusion, Deena's appearance changes over the years mimic the different looks of Ross from the point she became the focus of the Supremes to the start of Ross's solo career and her early work as a movie actress.

After Effie becomes increasingly agitated about her diminished role in the Dreams, her performance suffers, she walks out and returns, and Taylor finally decides to replace her in the group. However, just before Effie learns that she has been replaced by Michelle Morris, a Rainbow

Records secretary who also happens to be a singer, there is a brief scene in which she is seen at a doctor's office. The audience later learns that she is pregnant by Curtis with her daughter, Magic.

When Effie realizes that Curtis has replaced her in the Dreams, Effie, Curtis, and the members of the Dreams get into an argument, set in an R&B version of the near-operatic recitative style. *Dreamgirls* contains several other similarly structured sequences demonstrates that composer Henry Krieger and lyricist Tom Eyen went well beyond writing a show based solely on recreating the sound of the popular songs of the storyline's time period.

The recitative-style argument leads into one of the musical's best-known showpieces, "And I Am Telling You I'm Not Going." In this highly emotional song, there is a sense that Effie is singing out of desperation with the knowledge that—despite the song's foreground lyrics—she fully realizes that Curtis really does not love her and that they have no future together. This is even more poignant to the extent that audience members equate Effie's mysterious visit to the doctor, comments about her gaining weight, and her aside about being "alright now" just before she discovered that Curtis had replaced her in the Dreams with her pregnancy. Soon thereafter, the audience sees Deena viewing a promotional film that completely writes Effie out of the history of Deena Jones and the Dreams.

As Deena feels increasingly over-controlled in her career and life, she confronts Curtis and tells him that the problem is that he treats her the way he did when she was a struggling teenager. In response, Curtis sings the love song "When I First Saw You" to Deena. Jamie Foxx's performance is one of the most understated in the film.

In an ironic turn of events, Deena is forced by Curtis to star in a movie about Cleopatra while Effie ends up unemployed. The song "Patience," which Rainbow artists including Jimmy Early and the Dreams record without permission from Curtis Taylor, is an antiviolence message song that accompanies Effie's bus ride back to Detroit in which she passes scenes of destruction leftover from the real-life 1967 Detroit Riots. This was one of the new songs that Howard Krieger composed for the film version of *Dreamgirls*, with lyrics by Willie Reale. During the rehearsal and recording, Jimmy Early wears a skull cap similar to that worn by Motown star Marvin Gaye in the early 1970s. When the principals share the recording with Taylor, he rejects it as a "message song," which parallels Berry Gordy's rejection of potentially controversial material being recorded and released by Motown. Stylistically, and in its antiviolence message, "Patience" resembles some of the songs on Marvin Gaye's iconic message album *What's Going On*.

One of the realities of *Dreamgirls* is that, through much of the film, the major vocal showpieces are performed by Effie. One of these is "I Am Changing" that signals her return to singing and a sense of empowerment. I find this to be an especially important song, given the extent to which much of the film is so closely aligned with the story of Diana Ross and the Supremes. The song paints Effie as a survivor—which ultimately figures significantly in the film's conclusion—unlike the real-life Florence Ballard, who tragically died at age 32.

When Taylor refuses to allow Jimmy Early to redefine himself musically (e.g., recording message songs and later moving into funk), Early makes a spectacle of himself at Rainbow's 10th-anniversary live-television broadcast concert (which seems to be based roughly on the Motown 25th anniversary celebration). Early, rejected by Taylor and the company, succumbs to a heroin overdose. Because this turn of events immediately follows the Dreams' performance of "Family," the fact that Rainbow has ceased to be the family it once was stands out in sharp relief.

Sister and brother Effie and C. C. White, who had been estranged ever since Effie was replaced in the Dreams, reconnect at Early's wake. C. C. gives Effie his new song, "One Night Only," which Effie records. Upon hearing Effie's soulful ballad-style recording, Taylor releases a disco version by the Dreams and pays off DJs to try to kill off Effie's version. Incidentally, the disco version of the song perfectly captures the style and feel of Donna Summer's hits of the disco era. In resorting to this action, Curtis Taylor demonstrates that he is no better than the record executives who had taken R&B songs to the pop charts by having them covered by white artists, the very thing that had motivated him and the birth of Rainbow Records in the first place.

Because she felt that her career was being too closely dictated by Curtis, Deena agrees to star in a film without Curtis's knowledge. Immediately after Curtis confronts her, we see him in the recording console area as Deena records the new song "Listen," new in the sense of the plot but also one of the new songs Howard Krieger wrote for the film version of the musical, with lyrics by Scott Cutler and Anne Preven. The song tells of the deterioration of the relationship between Deena and Curtis, particularly in the line "I'm not at home in my own home." Soon thereafter, Deena leaves Curtis. "Listen" is Deena's major vocal showpiece in the film. It is in this soulful song that she finally sings with the emotional intensity and the dramatic vocal technique that up until that point had been associated with Effie. In short, in breaking away from Curtis Taylor's control, Deena Jones finds her voice.

The film concludes with the Dreams' farewell concert. For the finale of the concert, Deena Jones brings Effie up to the stage to sing lead on "Dreamgirls." As Effie sings and directs some of her performance directly to her daughter Magic, who is sitting in the front row of the auditorium, Curtis Taylor begins looking at the girl in a puzzled way and quickly realizes that she is his daughter.

Musically, *Dreamgirls* is built around a balance between traditional musical theater pieces in which the characters sing to each other, songs that are presented as parts of rehearsals, recording sessions, television or live performances, and hybrids in which person-to-person pieces transition into recording session or live performances. Some viewers might find that this approach gives *Dreamgirls* a fluid structure, while some others might find that the approach makes the film too difficult to define (e.g., is it a traditional musical, or is it a work in which the songs are always directed at an audience?).

Dreamgirls was a popular film and won the Golden Globe Award for Best Motion Picture, Musical or Comedy. Perhaps the most significant accolade, however, was for Jennifer Hudson, who won the Academy Award for Best Actress in a Supporting Role in her acting debut.

EVITA

The 1996 film *Evita*, which starred Madonna as Eva Duarte Perón and Antonio Banderas as Ché (often identified as Che Guevara in productions of the stage musical), was a movie musical that was an especially long time in the making. *Evita* began as a 1976 concept album for composer Andrew Lloyd Webber and lyricist Tim Rice. The staged musical was produced two years later. During the years that followed, the rights to turn *Evita* into a film went through several ownerships, and several potential producers and directors came and went. Finally, the team of producer Robert Stigwood, screenplay writers Alan Parker and Oliver Stone, and director Parker produced the highly anticipated film. In addition to Madonna and Banderas, the movie starred Jonathan Pryce as Argentina's president, Juan Perón.

Structurally, *Evita* is similar to Lloyd Webber and Rice's *Jesus Christ Superstar*, which had also progressed from a concept album to stage musical to film. In particular, both shows/movies use very little dialogue: they are essentially rock operas. One of the more notable aspects of the film is the role of Banderas's character, Ché, as a narrator and commentator who functions throughout the film to advance the action. Although the Ché of the film does not necessarily have to be understood as the personification of the revolutionary Che Guevara, some sequences, such as the riots in the lengthy "A New Argentina" sequence, suggest the possible connection to Marxist revolutionary. This is despite the fact that the real-life Che Guevara did not undertake revolutionary activities until years after the marriage of Juan and Eva Perón and Juan Perón's election as president of Argentina.

Although the film's focus is on the life of Eva Perón, a major theme is the exploration of the nature of her husband's political success and the nature of Peronism as a movement. For example, in sequences such as "A New Argentina," the apparently contradictory nature of what would soon become identified as Peronism are brought to life through Tim Rice's lyrics and the film's visual imagery. This and other sequences raise the question, was Peronism a movement of the people—of the proletariat, as it were—or was it a South American version of fascism? One of the notable techniques used in the film to suggest the view of Perón as a man of the people in the sequences that follow Perón's release from prison, including the "New Argentina" and the scenes that follow the song, is a focus of Perón's frequent removal of his jacket. Although the connection of the character's jacket removal clearly shows Perón's connection to the common people of Argentina, it is perhaps too obvious.

The show's big hit "Don't Cry for Me Argentina" takes on several meanings. In the scenes approximately 73 minutes into the film, the song is, at least in part, an acknowledgment of Eva Perón's need to rise out of the lower classes to find herself dressed in a fancy dress. As Madonna sings "I never left you," the meaning seems to be that in her heart she never left her lower-class roots. The song solidifies Eva Perón's standing with the masses. Because the film opens with scenes that concern her death just a half-dozen years after Juan Perón came to power, the film's introductory material, which ends with the voice of Eva singing "don't cry for me Argentina," refers to her illness and death from cancer. Because this connection is made in the introductory scenes, the song continues to remind the audience of Eva Perón's illness and death and her connections to the working class, even as she successfully breaks free from her socioeconomic roots.

One of the interesting aspects of the musical—which is shown well in the film medium—is the role that Eva Duarte—later Perón—played in galvanizing trade unions and the common people in support of Juan Perón. This makes Eva Perón's later excesses stand out in sharp relief. As the musical tells the tale, her need to be simultaneously a sort of uber example of and savior of the working class emerges. As she sings, "I'm their savior, that's what they call me," it is clear that she has a firm idea of how she thinks the populace perceives her.

As the film moves toward its close, Juan Perón's troops move against unionists, unemployment soars, and the common people begin to turn against Eva. The contradiction of emotions and political conflicts of the early 1950s in Argentina are brought into focus as the film version of the musical comes to a close. The production suggests that Eva Perón's illness and her death ultimately allowed her to be viewed as "a saint," despite the political and social upheaval that engulfed the country. In the dance sequence in the slaughterhouse (and other venues used in the sequence) between Eva and Che, it becomes clearer that Che symbolizes the purest form of the social and political revolution that both he and Eva had imagined years before, and that Eva had become more concerned with her image than with political and social change. Even though she had tried to work on many fronts for the betterment of Argentine society, her cancer and her need to be the focus of attention had triumphed over her desires to impact the society for the long term. In the end, then, Eva Perón is shown to have been a person of conflict. The film—and the earlier stage version and the concept album—allow her to be viewed by the audience as a heroine, to be sure, but as a heroine with personal flaws that perhaps ultimately made her short life as much a question mark as a statement.

One of the most moving scenes in the movie occurs near the end of Eva Perón's life when her husband carries her up a couple of flights of stairs almost effortlessly. This suggests the extent to which she had wasted away near the time of her death.

One of the disappointing features of the film is that it condenses so much time. For example, Eva Perón's illness seems to manifest itself immediately on the heels of Juan Perón's election as the President of Argentina. One of the more interesting sequences in the movie is Eva's visit to the United Kingdom. when she is met by a crowd of frowning British elite. After the elites disappear, Che emerges with the working class and questions if Eva's only true allegiance is really just to herself, the question that runs through the entire film. Additionally, Eva's foundation, which distributed large sums of money and goods to the poor of Argentina, is portrayed by narrator Che as nothing more than a publicity stunt to cement Eva in the national consciousness as a political and pop culture figure. In this series of scenes, the audience can sense that, try as she may, Eva Perón could not before her final illness be embraced without suspicion by the upper classes or by the working class.

The final reprise of "Don't Cry for Me Argentina" accompanies Eva's illness and impending death. It is in this scene in which Eva Perón becomes almost a saint in the eyes of the common people. The final scenes suggest the direction that Webber's music would later take in his *Requiem*. Interestingly, Che has the last word in describing the culmination of Eva Perón's life as the "best show in town"; however, his facial expression illustrates the extent to which he, too, is conflicted about his feelings about Eva.

Ultimately, *Evita* elicited mixed reviews. Well-known television personality and movie reviewer Roger Ebert wrote that he "enjoyed [Evita] very much," commenting favorably on the believable nature of Madonna's "opaque" portrayal of the title character, as well as on Alan Parker's work as the director (Ebert 1997). In sharp contrast, *Rolling Stone*'s Peter Travers heavily criticized Madonna's posing—as opposed to acting—as well as the lip-synching of all the actors throughout the film (Travers 1997). In retrospect, Ebert's assessment of Madonna's portrayal is probably closer to the mark, particularly considering that, despite her fame during her brief time in the spotlight, Eva Perón was to a great extent a social climber who, like some of the reality stars of the 1990s into the 21st century, was famous for being famous.

To one of the points of Travers's review, the synchronization of the soundtrack and the mouth movements of the actors does leave much to be desired. On the other hand, the fact that the vocal tracks were recorded in the studio and not during the filming makes for a cleaner sound than what would have been possible. The album-like production and clarity of the movie's soundtrack led to a soundtrack album.

Although *Evita* shares some structural traits in common with Lloyd Webber and Rice's earlier rock opera—and another work that started out life as a concept album—*Jesus Christ Superstar*, Roger Ebert's review addresses one of the challenging parts of *Evita*: this is far less a musical with a long list of memorable songs. The opening of the film is dominated by several different guises of "Don't Cry for Me Argentina," the show's major hit, which also dominates at the end of the film.

Although *Evita*—the movie musical about the girl from humble beginnings who became a model, nightclub singer, actress, and eventually the first lady of Argentina—has not achieved the critical success of the concept album or the stage version of the musical based on the album, what even the most negative of reviews suggest is that the direction of Alan Parker and the cinematography of Darius Khondji was successful in how it portrayed Madonna's Eva and how location shots were incorporated.

FAME

In reference to the 1980 film *Fame*, well-known critic Roger Ebert wrote, "The movie has the kind of sensitivity to the real lives of real people that we don't get much in Hollywood productions anymore" (Ebert 1980). Comparing the original *Fame* to the 2009 remake, Ebert later wrote, "Why bother to remake *Fame* if you don't have [a] clue about why the 1980 movie was special? . . . The new *Fame* is a reflection of the new Hollywood, where material is sanitized and dumbed down . . ." (Ebert 2009). With Ebert's assessment as a backdrop, let us focus on the original film, recognizing that the 1980 movie not only inspired the less-than-well-received 2009 remake but also a television series than ran for about half a decade in the 1980s and a stage musical.

Because *Fame* was an MGM production, it illustrates the extent to which the musical had changed from MGM's heyday of the 1940s and 1950s to 1980. *Fame* is grittier than earlier MGM movie musicals and deals more frankly with sex, some of the characters' psychological and emotional issues, homosexuality, and other issues than its predecessors. Alan Parker produced and directed the movie written by Christopher Gore. Michael Gore provided the music and Dean Pitchford and Lesley Gore wrote the lyrics.

With a focus on a performing arts high school, *Fame* includes both old songs and instrumental numbers (e.g., the fourth movement of Ludwig van Beethoven's *Symphony No. 5 in C minor* comes up several times with the themes performed by a student on bank of Moog synthesizers, by a piano class, etc.), as well as new songs "Fame," "Out Here on My Own," "Hot Lunch Jam," "Red Light," and "I Sing the Body Electric." Although several of the characters sing in the movie, the principal featured vocalist throughout the film is Coco, played by Irene Cara.

Fame follows the students of the performing arts high school—instrumentalists, singers, and dancers—through their initial entrance auditions to their graduation four years later. Although it delves into some tough disturbing parts of the characters' lives, *Fame* includes numerous comic breaks, often in the form of one-liners. For example, one particularly naïve girl asks another about her nose ring by posing the question, "does that hurt or is it ethnic?"

The students are all well-defined and several, such as Bruno with his bank of Moog synthesizers, are decidedly off the proverbial wall. The film clearly suggests the creativity of the characters and makes them instantly recognizable. Some viewers might find some of the characters to be one-dimensional at times, while some might identify a few of them as stereotypes (e.g., the socially awkward Doris with her hovering mother or the always-on-the-make Leroy), but the storyline finds the principal students moving in enough different, and sometimes unexpected directions, over the course of their four years of high school that they avoid turning into cartoon-like characters.

Fame includes several major production numbers, including "Hot Lunch Jam," which takes place in the school's lunchroom. This is a particularly important sequence—even though this is not one of the best-remembered songs from the movie—because it establishes early on in the characters' experience connections between Coco, the singer, and Bruno, the keyboard player and expert on sound synthesizers and audio recording. The connection of Doris and Montgomery is also established during the "Hot Lunch Jam" number, a connection that provides some of the later dramatic tension in the film.

The second major production number is the film's title song. The premise is that Bruno's father, a cabbie who is very supportive of Bruno's work as a composer, parks his cab on the street in front of the high school. Modified with large speakers, the cab blasts out "Fame," which ostensibly is a composition by Bruno which has not been fully mixed and edited to a commercially releasable form. Not unexpected, performing arts students run out into the street and the piece turns into a major fantasy dance number. Adding some humor to the situation—as well as suggesting at least a hint of realism—is the fact that the police arrive on the scene to try to get traffic moving again, and that Bruno's father gets into a fight with an angry truck driver.

Not all of the new music for *Fame* was for major production numbers, however. Montgomery sings an introspective, James Taylor-like singer-songwriter-style song. Eventually, the audience—and Montgomery's classmates—learns that his homosexuality is at the core of his introspective nature. Montgomery's coming to grips with his sexuality is not the only issue that emerges in the film. It turns out that Leroy is illiterate but has managed to get by with not being able to read until he is at the high school. When his inability to read is exposed, he leaves class, goes out into the hall, and destroys a hallway bookcase. Eventually, on the cusp of graduation, in an awkward encounter with his English teacher, Leroy is confronted with the reality that the only person with whom he has any concern is himself.

Ralph Garci frequently plays the fool throughout his career at the school. The audience eventually learns that his father is in prison and that his rough family life includes a five-year-old sister who is attacked by a drug addict. We also learn that the reason for the incarceration of

Garci's father is that at some point the father had tried to attack Ralph and hit Ralph's little sister, who is now institutionalized because of brain damage caused by the injury. Ralph is infatuated with actor-comedian Freddie Prinze, who had committed suicide just a couple of years before the release of *Fame*. This infatuation leads Ralph to try stand-up comedy. After some initial open-mic success, however, the weight of Ralph's life turns him into a mean comic who becomes more adept at emptying houses than filling them.

Despite the gritty realism that the audience can feel in the in-school and outside-of-school struggles of some of the characters, *Fame* is not without its light moments. Perhaps one of the more memorable parts of the movie is when Doris decides to break out of her shell and change her name to Dominique. Doris/Dominique and a group of fellow students attend a showing of *The Rocky Horror Picture Show*, with Dominique smoking marijuana and getting high for the first time. She takes off her top and runs up on stage in the theater and sings and dances along with "The Time Warp," one of the most memorable songs from the movie.

As mentioned earlier, the principal singing star of *Fame* was Irene Cara, who, oddly enough, had originally auditioned for the movie as a dancer. Cara, as Coco, not only figures prominently in many of the ensemble numbers but also in the ballad "Out Here on My Own," sung by Coco to Bruno. Coco had written the song which helps establish a connection between the two performer-composers.

One of the interesting aspects of *Fame* is that the audience is kept on the edge at times about what is diegetic and what is non-diegetic music; there is a blending of the two forms at some points. This creates a musical flow that seems somewhat unconventional and unexpected the first time one watches the film.

The film's final production number, which apparently takes place at a year-end pregraduation assembly to which families are invited, is "I Sing the Body Electric." The verses are sung by various principals and some of the minor characters who the audience has not seen since the opening parts of the film.

Fame is not necessarily a movie musical that garnered a plethora of awards like some other films in the genre. It is a film, though, that focuses on high school life in a very different way than in other musicals. It can also be seen as the genesis of other films and television programs about high school musicians, actors, and dancers, a genre that emerged more fully in the early 21st century. The movie's theme song was a commercial success as a single for Irene Cara and was named the 51st greatest movie song of all time by the American Film Institute (American Film Institute 2004).

FIDDLER ON THE ROOF

With lyrics by Sheldon Harnick, music by Jerry Bock, and a book by Joseph Stein, the 1964 stage musical *Fiddler on the Roof* made an immediate impact on the world of musical theater. The show continues to be one of the most popular musicals for school groups and community theater troupes. For the film, Bock's score was adapted and conducted by John Williams; however, the casual viewer of the film might notice little difference between the Williams' adaptation and the original stage orchestrations and arrangements. In fact, perhaps the most noticeable difference is in the dance sequences, particularly in the bottle dance at the celebration of Motel and Tzeitel's wedding. Specifically, the klezmer-style clarinet obbligato is considerably flashier in the Williams version than what is published in the orchestral books available for rent from the licensing/rental company Music Theatre International (MTI). In addition, Isaac Stern's overdubbing of fiddler's music is also considerably more elaborate and filled with technical flourishes not printed in the score and books published for stage productions.

The location filming in Yugoslavia makes for what audiences probably perceive as a believable real-life Anatevka, the home village of Tevye and his family. As a director and producer, Norman Jewison makes strong use of the locations to give the film a feeling of authenticity that would be impossible on stage. However, some viewers may notice occasional continuity issues. Perhaps the most glaring of these—pardon the pun—takes place during Motel's wedding procession when in one shot the sun is near the horizon, followed by a shot in which the sun is noticeably higher above the horizon, only to disappear entirely below the horizon in the next shot.

The film starred Topol as Tevye; Norma Crane as Golde, Tevye's wife; Rosalind Harris as Tzeitel, Tevye and Golda's oldest daughter; Michele Marsh as Hodel, the second-oldest daughter; Neva Small as Chava, the third-oldest daughter; Molly Picon as Yente, the village matchmaker; Paul Mann as Lazar Wolf, the butcher; Leonard Frey as Motel Kamzoil, the tailor; Michael Glaser as Perchik, the Marxist teacher; Raymond Lovelock as Fyedka, a non-Jew who marries Chava; as well as an additional large ensemble cast. Norman Jewison, who had little previous experience with musicals, directed *Fiddler on the Roof*. After the success of the film, Jewison would go on to direct *Jesus Christ Superstar* in a couple of years, although he continued to focus on non-musical films.

Although the film has several highlights, including the sense of realism that can be missing from stage productions, arguably the best part of *Fiddler on the Roof* is the work of Topol as an actor and as a singer. Zero Mostel might have defined the role on Broadway, but Topol's film version of Tevye is believable in the mix and range of emotions that he lives throughout the story's timeline.

Fiddler on the Roof is not without some curious scenes and curious moments. One of the oddities of the film's production is how similar Fruma-Sarah looks in Tevye's Dream sequence to the Wicked Witch of the West in the 1939 film *The Wizard of Oz*. Arguably, this dream sequence is also one of the parts of the musical that could be more impressive on stage than in the way in which director Norman Jewison set it in the film.

Similarly, the dance sequence in the bar after Tevye and Lazar Wolf announce the engagement (soon broken) of Wolf and Tzeitel and the dance sequence after Motel and Tzeitel's wedding use enough close shots that these scenes might also be more impressive in stage productions than in the film. Arguably, however, the size of the cast involved in these scenes can be interpreted as more realistic than, say, when the entire town dressed in highly stylized bright clothing dance and parade in the film version of, for example, *The Music Man* just under a decade earlier.

One of the differences between *Fiddler on the Roof* and the 1960s film adaptations of musicals is that there is little overt evidence of stylized costuming, sets, and props. For example, *West Side Story*, despite the dark aspects of its depiction of youth gang violence and its outcomes, included shiny bright, apparently right-off-the-sales lot automobiles, not what one would probably see in that particular New York neighborhood in reality in the late 1950s.

Similarly, although *Fiddler on the Roof* contains an assortment of jokes and comic moments, there is always an undercurrent of poverty, oppression, and disenfranchisement that suggests the reality of the pre-Russian Revolution plight of the Jews. In fact, much of the humor includes references to the times and the situations. It is humor that is intricately tied to suffering.

One of the better, albeit subtle, ways in which the film version adds a layer of meaning to the story is in the song "Sunrise, Sunset," which takes place during Tzeitel and Motel's wedding. In stage productions, the lead vocals are often sung by Tevye and Golde as they watch the wedding of their eldest daughter. In the film, Tevye and Golde's lead vocals can be heard; however, the characters do not appear to be singing. This tells the audience more clearly than what is usually the case in stage productions of *Fiddler on the Roof* that the song represents Tevye and Golde's inner thoughts. This effect makes this scene work especially effectively. Director Jewison used the same technique in the Chava ballet sequence so that the entire sequence is clearly part of the wrestling that Tevye does in his mind as he ponders the unthinkable marriage of his third daughter to a Christian, Russian soldier.

Fiddler on the Roof is an effective example of one of the aspects that makes the best movie musicals stand out from numerous staged versions: the prominence of the vocals. Although one could site several strong examples in this movie, Motel's "Miracle of Miracles" is as good an example as any. Some listeners might find the vocal/instrumental balance to be unnatural, particularly compared with one might reasonably expect to experience at a live performance of the musical, and the balance covers up some of the orchestrational and arrangement details of John Williams's adaptation of the score. However, every word of every song is clear; therefore, all the contrasting moods are easy for the viewer to capture.

One of the ironies of the initial success of the movie version of *Fiddler on the Roof* is that the film seems to have become somewhat forgotten, perhaps because of the sheer number of stage productions of the show that continue to be mounted. Not only is it still popular for community theater troupes and high schools, a "Jr." version is available for production, thereby taking the basic story to the pre-high school level. *Fiddler on the Roof* has been revived on Broadway in the period from the 1970s to the 2000s, and most recently in 2015 and 2019. Similarly, *Fiddler on the Roof* has enjoyed numerous revivals in London's West End, and the late 2000s saw national tours of both the United States and the United Kingdom.

Pauline Kael, a reviewer for *The New Yorker*, described *Fiddler on the Roof* as "the most *powerful* film musical ever made" (Kael 1971). Of course, numerous powerful film musicals have been made in the decades since. However, as mentioned above, *Fiddler on the Roof* was produced with a sense of gritty realism that, despite the humor that runs through the first act, in particular, matches the harsh realities of the life of the Jewish residents of Anatevka to an extent greater than the more stylized movie musicals that preceded it. This realism also enhances the audience's appreciation of Tevye's inner battles as he is torn between his faith and its strong traditions and his unconditional love for his daughters. *Fiddler on the Roof* continues to resonate and receive high ratings on movie fan and critical review composite websites such as Rotten Tomatoes. Specifically, as of March 22, 2019, a composite of 40 reviews by critics gave *Fiddler on the Roof* an 83% favorable rating, while 92% of over 52,000 movie fans gave the film a favorable rating

(The Editors of *Rotten Tomatoes.com* 2019). Despite this, *Fiddler on the Roof* did not win as many awards as some other musicals covered in this chapter. The Academy Awards earned by the film centered on technical achievements—(1) Best Music, Scoring Adaptation and Original Song Score; (2) Best Cinematography; and (3) Best Sound. Topol won the Golden Globe Award for Best Actor, and the film won the Golden Globe for Best Motion Picture, Musical or Comedy.

42ND STREET

This 1933 Warner Bros. film starred Warner Baxter as Julian Marsh, a theatrical producer about to mount his final musical. As such, *42nd Street* can be viewed as one of the early important movie musicals about musicals. In fact, it is often cited as one of the first so-called backstage musicals, with a plot revolving around the backstage intrigues that lead up to the production of Marsh's final show. Some earlier movie musicals, such as *The Jazz Singer* in 1927, included show business as a central part of the plot; however, *42nd Street* took the focus on the entertainment industry and musical theater, in particular, to a noticeably higher level. To at least some extent, subsequent musicals about musicals owe a debt of gratitude to this film, including movies as diverse as *The Producers*, *All That Jazz*, *A Chorus Line*, and numerous earlier shows and movies from the 1940s and 1950s. In fact, one of the observations that is easy to make about movie musicals—even those that are not specifically about the world of musical theater—is that more than just a fair share present the audience with a stylized view, sometimes a glamourized view, and perhaps a stereotypical view of the entertainment business. These stereotypes and some stereotypical entertainment industry characters run through *42nd Street*. By and large, and with notable exceptions such as the 1954 version of *A Star Is Born*, it was not until some of the films and stage musicals of the 1970s—including *A Chorus Line* and *All That Jazz*—that the darker and more realistic side of the Broadway and film industries became more prevalent than the stylized version presented in *42nd Street*.

42nd Street was, however, much more than just the spiritual ancestor of later musicals about musicals. In addition to Warner Baxter, the film's stars included Ruby Keeler, Ginger Rogers, Bebe Daniels, and Dick Powell, well-known figures of the day. Harry Warren provided the film's music and Al Dubin wrote the lyrics. *42nd Street* included hits such as the title song and "Shuffle off to Buffalo." The American Film Institute ranked the movie's title song at No. 97 on its list of the 100 greatest movie songs of all time (American Film Institute 2004).

The film is also notable for Busby Berkeley's elaborate choreography and dance-number staging, which is particularly evident at the end of the movie when the show-within-a-show is finally staged. Berkeley's work as a director of grand production numbers had actually started shortly before *42nd Street*; however, this film, as well as several others in the first several years of the 1930s, established a production number style that persisted not only in the films he choreographed and/or directed but also in other musicals well into the 1950s.

The show-within-a-show's major production number, the extended version of the song "42nd Street," although perhaps not quite as extravagant as Busby Berkeley's grandest productions in films that followed, contains all of the iconic Berkeley touches, including numerous scantily clad showgirls, an elaborate stage, geometric patterns assumed by the troupe of dancers, and staging that just seems to keep expanding and expanding. One of the biggest ironies of Berkeley's work in *42nd Street* is the fact that the geometric patterns on the revolving stage that the movie audience can see in the overhead shots in "42nd Street" would have been nearly completely unappreciated by the audience of the show-within-a-show, given the elevation of the stage.

Arguably, one of the differences between stage shows—be they musicals or straight plays—and films made from the mid-1930s through the mid-1960s that might not be as noticeably perceived as aspects such as the use of close-up camera shots, the use of large backlot or location scenes, and so on, is the way in which film studios had to adhere to a moral code that was enacted after some of the risqué films of the 1920s as well as scandals among the Hollywood elite, such as Fatty Arbuckle, who had been tried for rape related to the mysterious death of actress Virginia Rappe.

The Motion Picture Production Code, informally known as the Hays Code, had been enacted in 1930 as a means of the movie industry policing itself with respect to certain kinds of references to sex, violence, drugs, and so on to avoid direct government censorship. In 1934, however, the movie industry began enforcing the Code more diligently. Because of its providence (post-Code, but pre-strict enforcement), the lack of censorship allowed some lewd references to come through in *42nd Street*. Ginger Rogers's character Annie, for example, is referred to as "Anytime Annie," the woman who "only said 'no' once." In another scene, the show-within-a-show's financial backer, Abner Dillon, tells star Dorothy Brock, that he will do something for her if she does something for him, with a sly look in his eyes. Although his request is resolved innocently, at the moment of his initial statement, the audience cannot help but assume that his request is for sex. There are other references that suggest casual sex and lust, and the song "You're Getting to Be a Habit with Me" can be interpreted as a play on the theme of drug addiction. In terms of the standards of films of later decades, *42nd Street* is tame; however, it is still routinely cited as an example of a film that included material that likely would not have been included had it been released a couple of years later.

It could be argued that part of the importance of *42nd Street* and part of the reason for its ongoing popularity and legacy was that it was produced early in the years of the Great Depression. Musicals such as *42nd Street* provided relief from the economic hardships of the time. The 1929 stock market crash and the subsequent Great Depression also play a role in the story, which makes the film topical. Specifically, it was because he lost his fortune in the crash that theatrical director Julian Marsh had to mount one final show, despite receiving news from his physician who suggested that doing so could easily lead to a heart attack. Although some aspects of the story, the spectacle of the show-within-a-show, and the lifestyles of some of the characters—most notably the show's financial backer Abner Dillon, the show's star Dorothy Brock, and Brock's one-time Broadway partner and love interest Pat Denning—provide an escape from the economic realities of the early 1930s, the specter of the Depression is part of the reality of the story, not only for Julian Marsh but also for musical theater novice Peggy Sawyer.

The storyline delves into various backstage relationships, intrigues involving the show's backers, the director, and underworld figures, and so on. However, just about everything is resolved when Julian Marsh's final great Broadway show, *Pretty Lady*, opens in Philadelphia. The film's audience is left with the sense, however, that even though Ruby Keeler's character, Peggy Sawyer, successfully steps in after leading lady Dorothy Brock breaks her ankle the night before the show's opening, Marsh's production is not a great artistic success and, in fact, might not even become the commercial success that he needs it to be to secure his financial legacy. In fact, in the movie's final scene, Marsh appears to be a completely broken man, not necessarily physically dead, but apparently finished artistically.

The three major Harry Warren (music) and Al Dubin (lyrics) songs "You're Getting to Be a Habit with Me," "Shuffle off to Buffalo," and "42nd Street" made an instant impact on popular culture. For example, although perhaps not as well remembered in the 21st century as the other two songs, "You're Getting to Be a Habit with Me" was a hit single just after it appeared in the movie for both vocalists Bing Crosby backed by Guy Lombardo and His Royal Canadians and for Fred Waring and His Pennsylvanians. After appearing in other films, "You're Getting to Be a Habit for Me" has been part of the repertoire of a number of jazz and pop musicians, including Doris Day, Frank Sinatra, Mel Tormé, Peggy Lee, Diana Krall, and others.

42nd Street was nominated for the Academy Awards for Best Sound Recording and Outstanding Production. Although the movie won no Oscars, it was a commercial success and helped establish the backstage musical as an important and popular movie musical subgenre—a subgenre that is still around in the 21st century. The Library of Congress selected *42nd Street* for inclusion in the National Film Registry in 1998, and the American Film Institute ranked *42nd Street* at No. 13 on its list of the 25 greatest movie musicals of all time in 2006 (American Film Institute 2006).

FROZEN

Although the renaissance of interest in and popularity of Walt Disney Studios' animated movie musicals occurred from the late 1980s through the 1990s, several of the company's 21st-century productions have been huge commercial blockbusters. The 2013 film *Frozen* was based on a tale by Hans Christian Andersen and represented a technical change from the early Disney animated films in that it was computer-generated and was released in 3D. Chris Buck and Jennifer Lee directed the film, which featured an orchestral score by Christophe Beck and songs by Robert Lopez and Kristen Anderson-Lopez.

The film opens with the work song of the ice processors, men who harvest ice that will be used during the warm season. Along with the burly men, the young Christoph, accompanied by his reindeer Sven, also works at harvesting ice, although Christoph childishly struggles with the process. Christoph becomes a central character as it is he who accompanies Anna years later in her quest to North Mountain. The processing of ice, the minor-key vaguely Scandinavian-sounding work song, and the depiction of the Northern Lights defines the scene as Scandinavia.

With the exception of "Let It Go," many of the songs of *Frozen* seem to be too specific to certain characters, scenes, or situations to be big memorable Disney hits in the manner of "A Whole New World," the big hit tune from *Aladdin*. "Do You Want to Build a Snowman," for example, is a thoroughly engaging tune and fits the childhood fantasy world of the sisters, Anna and Elsa, perfectly; however, it is strongly tied to the scene in which the sisters build Olaf, the snowman. Similarly, Olaf's main song, "In Summer," finds the snowman imagining life in the sun, on the beach, and so on, without concerning the probability of melting. It may be a cute song, but it was not destined to be a hit outside the context of the film.

Anna's "For the First Time in Forever," in which she declares her independence after being locked away and separated from her sister—for her own safety—for years, is a memorable song and probably has sufficient lyrical and melodic hooks to make it a hit; however, the song's brief references to ending "this winter" places it so firmly within the context of the storyline in a literal sense that it might be difficult for some listeners to fully appreciate the reference in the metaphorical sense.

Anna's "Love Is an Open Door" represents her reaction to her first encounter with Prince Hans. She sees Hans—and Elsa's coronation—as her twin opportunities to finally be herself and have her freedom. At this point of the story, Prince Hans appears to be the proverbial and stereotypical (in fairytale tradition) knight in shining armor. Ultimately, it turns out that Prince Hans was only feigning interest in Anna in an attempt to take advantage of her and gain power and influence in Anna and Elsa's kingdom.

In the story, both Anna and Elsa had led extremely sheltered lives after Elsa's magic had accidentally seriously injured her sister. Although Elsa retained her magic, she had to wear gloves that would keep the magic hidden. Anna, on the other hand, had her memory of her injury and Elsa's magic, as well as any magic she might possess eliminated by Pabbie, a troll with his own powerful magic. "Let It Go," in which Elsa removes the gloves that have covered her hands for years to keep her ability to magically create winter under wraps, is the most pop-like and accessible song in the movie. It is also a song with lyrics that are general enough that the song can function well outside the context of the film.

In *Frozen*, "Let It Go" represents Elsa's rejection of the gloves but also her acceptance of the fact that she possesses magic. Perhaps because of the tie between the song and Elsa's declaration of acceptance of who she really is, the song has generated a degree of controversy. Although arguably there is nothing overt in "Let It Go," some conservative Christian groups characterized—and condemned—it as an LGBTQ-friendly coming-out song. Several reports shortly after the release of *Frozen* documented the efforts of such groups to boycott the movie and Walt Disney Studios (see, for example, Petersen 2014).

On the day of her coronation, after Elsa removes her gloves, she begins freezing virtually everything in sight. The minor-key music during this sequence, in which the populace suddenly becomes frightened of the new queen, suggests the style of Hans Zimmer's music for the films Zimmer scored for the *Pirates of the Caribbean* series. In fact, some of the later action underscoring in *Frozen* also brings to mind the music of the *Pirates of the Caribbean* franchise.

In considering *Frozen* as a story and a film, that is, putting the music aside for a moment, it is interesting to note that generally the fairytale plays out fairly conventionally, except for the fact that what at first appears to be a love made in heaven between Anna and Hans turns out to be an entirely evil ploy by Hans. Additionally, the fact that it is ultimately the sisterly love between Anna and Elsa that breaks a magic spell is not part of the standard storylines that one finds in previous Disney animated movies. The one awkward aspect of the story is the condensation of time in the early part of the movie, particularly the death of Anna and Elsa's parents. This happens so suddenly and without explanation that some viewers might find that it seems like something of an afterthought.

Although the computer-generated animated people of *Frozen* look more humanoid than perhaps the hand-drawn human characters of earlier Disney animated movies, they still move in fantastical ways not possible for real people. One of the aspects of the film that some viewers might notice is that there is a certain resemblance to the stereotypical big-eyed-children "art" that has been widely parodied in popular culture since the late 20th century. Some commentators and reviewers have remarked about what they perceive to be stereotypes in the portrayal of female characters—principally Anna and Elsa—in the movie. Although in many respects they represent female empowerment, they are given the big-eyed-child treatment, even as the characters mature.

Despite the big-eyed-child treatment of Princess Anna and Queen Elsa, there is much to *Frozen* that speaks to the empowerment of the female characters. This emerges not only in songs such as "Let It Go" and "For the First Time in Forever" but also in some of the plot twists. Perhaps the clearest example comes when Anna, Christoph, and Sven are making their way to North Mountain (where Elsa moved after she lost control of her magic and transformed the entire kingdom of Arendelle into a perpetual and unrelenting winter). During their journey, Sven and Christoph sense that they are being pursued by wolves, and, as seems often to be the case in fairytales, the wolves are the proverbial "bad guys." Apparently intent on dining on the two humans and the reindeer, the wolves attack; however, their attack is thwarted primarily by Anna.

After Elsa freezes Anna's heart—a mortal curse—and Elsa sends Marshmallow, a vicious giant snowman, to force them to leave, Christoph, Sven, and Olaf take Anna to Christoph's "love experts," the trolls who Anna and Elsa's parents had consulted years before. The ensemble of trolls sings the production number "Fixer Upper," which segues into Pabbie's pronouncement that Anna needs to experience an act of pure love to be saved from becoming completely frozen. Without going into too many details of the story, Christoph assumes that this means that Anna needs to be kissed by Prince Hans, to whom Anna had pledged her love on Elsa's coronation day.

During the action that follows, it emerges that Hans is anything but Anna's knight in shining armor. The storyline is set up in such a way as to make the audience assume that it is really Christoph who needs to kiss Anna to break the spell. As mentioned earlier, however, this plot twist would only be a minor break from the stereotypical fairytale plots that had defined the Disney musical franchise decades earlier. Ultimately, it is the sisterly bond and love between Elsa and Anna that breaks the spell.

Once the spell has been broken and the seasons return to Arendelle, Elsa provides Olaf with a personal localized winter that follows him around and keeps him appropriately frozen. With that, and with the characters who were out for their own personal gain banished, the story concludes. It should be noted that although *Frozen* has been particularly popular among girls, it is a movie that contains numerous one-liners that might better be appreciated by their parents and grandparents.

The musical's most memorable song, "Let It Go" is used during the final credits. Hearing the song out of the context of the storyline during the credits brings to the fore how closely it resembles some of Taylor Swift's songs from 2009–2011 in melodic and arrangement style. I mention that not to suggest that "Let It Go" is necessarily derivative of Swift but to highlight the extent to which the song fits in with at least one part of the world of popular music of the general period.

It should be noted that this attribute of "Let It Go" is something of a double-edged sword and one that may suggest some incongruities to audiences. The film mixes conventional early 21st-century pop ballad style, up-tempo pop, a vaguely Scandinavian-sounding work song, Disney thriller underscoring, and so on. The music may appeal on many levels, but the songs and orchestral score do not necessarily represent a wholly coherent view of a mythical kingdom long ago.

Although Disney movies have been intimately tied with various forms of marketing for decades, in some respects *Frozen* took movie marketing to an even higher level. According to reporter Binyamin Appelbaum, in November 2014, "Disney said earlier this month that it had already sold three million *Frozen* dresses in North America, which, as it happens, is roughly the number of 4-year-old girls in North America. In

January [2015], 'Frozen' wedding dresses go on sale for $1,200. Next summer, Adventures by Disney is offering tours of Norwegian sites that inspired the film's animators at prices starting north of $5,000" (Appelbaum 2014). In addition to clothing and tours, Disney's marketing of the movie included the customary plush toys, non-plush toys, and so on. At the time of this writing, approximately half a decade after the initial popularity of the film, Adventures by Disney is still offering Scandinavian cruises and tours of sites in Norway; however, the *Frozen* connections do not seem to be emphasized to the extent that they were for the first couple of years after the film's release.

When considering *Frozen* and merchandising, it should also be noted that on its first day of release, the Blu-ray and DVD edition of the film sold 3.2 million copies (The Editors of *The Hollywood Reporter* 2014). By early December 2014, it was widely reported in the press that the film had racked up the largest DVD sales of any release for the year and was well on its way to becoming the biggest-selling DVD/Blu-ray release of the 2010s (Brown 2014). At the time of this writing, *Frozen* is reputed to be the best-selling Blu-ray disc of all time (see, for example, The Editors of *The Numbers* 2019).

In addition to its having been a commercial success both in its theatrical release and in the home video market, *Frozen* received industry recognition. This included the Golden Globe Award for Best Animated Feature and the Academy Awards for Best Animated Feature and Best Original Song (for "Let It Go"). *Frozen* continues to live on outside the context of the original 2013 film. The original movie spawned the 2017 short film sequel *Olaf's Frozen Adventure*, a full-length stage version has subsequently been produced, as has a *Frozen Jr.* for youth theater, and there is anticipation that Disney will release a feature-length sequel in November 2019.

FUNNY GIRL

A 1968 film based on the stage musical of the same name, the story of *Funny Girl* was inspired by the life of the early 20th-century comedienne Fanny Brice. Both the 1964 stage version and the film were important vehicles for their star, Barbra Streisand. The film also starred Omar Sharif as a professional gambler and entrepreneur Nicky Arnstein.

Funny Girl is an unusual film in that the overture is played over a black screen—most movie adaptations of stage musicals include some sort of visuals during the overture. By not running the opening credits during the overture, director William Wyler at least partially recreates the feel of the live stage musical experience for the audience. The over-ture includes arrangement cues from the 1920s, the time period on which most of the story focuses. This includes the emphasis on the saxo-phone section; however, the arrangement also includes touches that seem to fit the 1950s and 1960s more than the time period of the storyline. This mixture of the old and the new continues throughout the movie. For example, Streisand—as Brice—sings "Second Hand Rose," "My Man," and "I'd Rather Be Blue," songs that had been associated with the real-life Brice. The musical arrangement of "Second Hand Rose" is not entirely removed from what one might have experienced back in the 1920s; however, the movie's finale, "My Man," takes an old song and treats it perhaps more dramatically that what might typically have been the case back in the 1920s.

Lyricist Bob Merrill and composer Jule Styne wrote the show's orig-inal songs, which included "I'm the Greatest Star," "People," "Don't Rain on My Parade," and "You Are Woman, I Am Man." Generally, Mer-rill and Styne's songs are more melodically and formally complex than the bulk of the Tin Pan Alley songs that were popular during the time period depicted in *Funny Girl*. "People" uses the verse-chorus structure commonly found in earlier showtunes; however, the chorus is more com-plex than many earlier songs in the genre. One might even hear Jule Styne's work as a composer in *Funny Girl* as a sort of bridge between the early 20th-century Tin Pan Alley tradition and the midcentury heyday of the movie music with the even more complex music that follows *Funny Girl* in the work of composers such as Stephen Sondheim. Despite the differences, Merrill and Styne's style and songs such as "Second Hand Rose," "My Man," and "I'd Rather Be Blue"—the ones that were part of the repertoire of the historical real-life Fanny Brice—the old and the new integrate well together.

Funny Girl also seems to bridge the old movie musical tradition with the grittier, more realistic films that followed it visually. The street scenes, for example, stand in stark contrast to the immaculately kept streets and parked automobiles of *West Side Story*. At the same time, Barbra Strei-sand's wardrobe in some of the street is so much brighter and carefree that it calls to mind some of the costumes of *The Music Man* and other earlier films.

A large amount of the humor and the dramatic tension in *Funny Girl* comes from cultural clashes. Brice turns around stereotypes of Jewish female identity, which can be seen in the way in which her life conflicts with those of the women of her mother's generation. Another source of dramatic tension is the always-simmering conflict between Brice's world of musical theater and Nicky's world as a professional gambler and not-particularly-successful entrepreneur. Throughout the film, Brice also confronts the typical ways in which women were used by some stage musical directors. The social commentary of Fanny Brice and the way in which she was depicted in *Funny Girl* has been the subject of academic study. For example, in her book *The Musical: Race, Gender and Performance*, film studies scholar Susan Smith includes a section that details "Subverting the idea of woman as spectacle in *Funny Girl*" (Smith 2005, 55). Specifically, Smith points to Brice's appearance in a Florenz Ziegfeld production that featured women dancing in elaborate white wedding dresses. When Brice is shown in profile, she appears to be obviously pregnant. Although the episode can be seen as a simple joke playing on the wearing of supposedly virginal wedding white, Smith points out that the joke also parodies the image of women that Ziegfeld typically portrayed in his *Ziegfeld's Follies* and other shows he produced. It can also be understood as poking fun at the similar focus on the female body in Busby Berkeley's productions; the scene in the movie version of *Funny Girl* appears to be a direct parody of the famous choreographed scenes in the film musicals that Berkeley produced and choreographed. It is also important to note that the sequence also spotlights the comic genius of Fanny Brice, a sense that made it impossible for Ziegfeld to fire her after she changed the entire nature of the bridal scene in his show—it was a hit with the audience. So, Brice's adherence to her working-class roots and a working-class sense of humor wins over the very personification of the upper echelon of New York show business.

In addition to her comic modification of the bridal scene in the Ziegfeld show, *Funny Girl* highlights other ways in which Fanny Brice created audience-pleasing humor. Particularly effective is the scene from another show-within-a-show of Brice interrupting what was meant to be a well-choreographed roller-skating routine with an inept display of skating that brings down the house and literally brings down some of the other skaters.

In considering *Funny Girl* as a document of the life and career of the real-life Fanny Brice, it is important to note that the film was produced by Ray Stark, who was Brice's son-in-law. The movie ignores Brice's and Nicky Arnstein's past relationships and marriages. It also ignores Arnstein's early incarceration, during which time Brice regularly visited him and provided fodder for Arnstein's then-wife to file for divorce. However, the film suggests how through studied work, improvisation, and happenchance Fanny Brice became a leading figure in musical theater during the early 20th century.

One of the notable features of *Funny Girl* is that the movie's star, Streisand, had also starred in the Broadway musical. In perhaps two of the songs originally associated with the real-life Fanny Brice, "I'd Rather Be Blue" and "My Man," Streisand demonstrates a vocal dynamic range and a dramatic range that would be effective on stage. Unlike some other Broadway stars whose singing style or whose acting style did not translate well across the stage-film divide, Streisand's work in *Funny Girl* does successfully bridge the gap. To put it another way, Streisand demonstrates that she can sing for the microphone as well as for the theater.

As evidence of the movie's and its leading star's success, Streisand won the Academy Award for Best Actress, and the film was nominated for Best Picture, Best Actress in a Supporting Role (Kay Medford, who portrayed Fanny Brice's mother both on stage and in the film), Best Cinematography, Best Film Editing, Best Score of a Musical Picture, Original or Adaptation, Best Original Song, and Best Sound. The movie was recognized by the American Film Institute, which ranked *Funny Girl* at No. 16 on its list of the 25 greatest movie musicals of all time (American Film Institute 2006). The Institute also earlier named "People," which became one of Barbra Streisand's signature songs, No. 13 on its list of the 100 greatest movie songs of all time and "Don't Rain on My Parade" No. 46 on the list (American Film Institute 2004). In 2008, *Entertainment Weekly*'s Steve Daly ranked *Funny Girl* at No. 20 on his list of "25 Greatest Movie Musicals of All Time" (Daly 2008). Finally, in 2016, the Library of Congress added *Funny Girl* to the National Film Registry.

As Streisand, playing Brice, sings the movie's final song, an adaptation of "My Man," the ending of *Funny Girl* seemed to be designed to lead to a sequel. The sequel, *Funny Lady*, appeared in 1975 with Barbra Streisand reprising her role; unfortunately, the sequel was not nearly as successful as the original.

GENTLEMEN PREFER BLONDES

This 1953 film starred two of the most popular female Hollywood sex symbols of the era: Jane Russell as Dorothy Shaw and Marilyn Monroe as Lorelei Lee. The movie is based on the stage musical of the same name; however, while the stage musical contained songs written by Jule Styne and Leo Robin, the movie also included songs from the pens of Hoagy Carmichael and Harold Adamson. *Gentlemen Prefer Blondes* also starred Charles Coburn as Sir Francis "Piggy" Beekman, the owner of a diamond mine; Tommy Noonan as Gus Esmond, Lorelei's fiancé; Elliott Reid as Ernie Malone, a private detective hired by Esmond's father to try to dig up dirt on Lorelei; Taylor Holmes, as Mr. Esmond Sr.; Norma Varden as Lady Beekman; and the young George Winslow as Henry Spofford III. Howard Hawks, better known for his work on non-musicals, directed the film.

The movie's opening musical number, "A Little Girl from Little Rock," establishes Dorothy Shaw and Lorelei Lee as singing and dancing show-girls from the proverbial wrong side of the tracks who are looking for men. It turns out that Shaw is primarily interested in physically attrac-tive men, while Lee is primarily interested in wealthy men. It is Lorelei Lee's near-obsession that drives much of the plot which culminates in Monroe's famous performance of "Diamonds Are a Girl's Best Friend" later in the film.

Commentators and film studies experts have noted that director How-ard Hawks was particularly known for strong female characters and actors in his pre–World War II movies. According to Germaine Greer (2006) and others, even in Hawks's films, the female characters of the late-1940s and early-1950s movies were not as strong, and strong female stars such as Barbara Stanwyck and Katharine Hepburn gave way to stars such as Marilyn Monroe. In watching *Gentlemen Prefer Blondes*, however, it is important to observe how Lorelei and Dorothy are able to manipulate the male characters. Their techniques may be quite different than those employed by characters in Hawks's pre–World War II films; however, Hawks drops hints throughout the movie that Dorothy Shaw and Lorelei Lee are not necessarily solely the sex symbols they seem to be. One of the more interesting moments comes near the end of the film. Lorelei tries to convince Mr. Esmond Sr. that he should allow her and Gus to marry, Esmond tells Lorelei that he had heard she was less than fully intelligent (to put it more generously than Esmond does in the dia-logue), to which Lorelei replies, "I can be smart when it's important, but most men don't like it . . ."

In making her declaration, Lorelei confirms that she is forced to play the role of the proverbial stereotypical dumb blonde, but there is some-thing about the scene that suggests an element of social commentary. Lorelei seems to not be particularly happy to have to act dumb, but she does so because of the constraints that the society of the time put on women. I would argue that this subtext comes not so much from the words of the dialogue themselves but from Howard Hawks's direction of the scene and the way in which Marilyn Monroe delivers the lines. The scene also suggests the shallowness of the men who are physically attracted to Lorelei.

Interestingly, the interest of men in the physical attributes of women—as opposed to their minds—is confirmed throughout the movie. Certainly,

"Piggy" is immediately drawn to Lorelei upon their first meeting because of Lorelei's physical beauty and sexiness. The wolf whistles that Dorothy and Lorelei receive when the members of the Olympic team first see them and the subsequent encounters that Dorothy and Lorelei have with the Olympians clearly suggest that the male athletes are not most impressed by the showgirls' minds. Even the young Henry Spofford III is something of a parody of the focus of men on women's physical attractiveness and overt sexiness.

So, when Lorelei delivers her line about being "smart when it's important," it can be interpreted as an indictment of virtually all the men (and the young boy) that she encounters throughout the film, with the exception of Gus Esmond, her fiancé; the younger Esmond is the one male character who appreciates Lorelei for her mind and not just for her physical attractiveness.

Despite the above subtext that one might detect in Hawks's direction of the film, this is a movie musical with not a whole lot of serious depth, particularly on the surface. In fact, much of the humor tends toward the sophomoric. One example would be when the members of the U.S. Olympic team first meet Lorelei and Dorothy. One Olympian asks another which woman he would save from drowning if the ship sinks; the other Olympian responds that neither of them would drown, a sly entirely politically incorrect and sexist reference to the buoyancy of the two well-endowed showgirls. Another example of the kind of humor that runs through much of the show is the off-put response that Lorelei gives when one of the Olympians says that he is "the only four-letter man on the team." Lorelei's offended look suggests that she thinks the Olympian is referring to the use of the four-letter profanities. There are numerous other examples of Lorelei's portrayal as the stereotypical dumb blonde being the source of one-liners and other gags. The fact that there are so many of these heightens the impact of Lorelei's line about being "smart when it's important."

The songs of *Gentlemen Prefer Blondes* are catchy and engaging. "Bye Bye Baby," which is sung by Russell, is an elaborately arranged jazz number. The ensemble backing vocal arrangement suggests the influence of some of the popular small groups of the late 1940s, such as the Andrews Sisters. "Ain't There Anyone Here for Love," one of the Hoagy Carmichael and Harold Adamson songs added to the original version of the show for the movie, is another highlight and is also sung by Russell. The big-band arrangement includes riffs, unexpected rhythms, and several double-time figures that suggest the influence of bebop jazz. The song's choreography has the Olympic team members including calisthenics and gymnastics as part of the dance routine. "When Love Goes Wrong" is another elaborate song that includes the participation of two Algerian children, and numerous musical shifts, including tempo and stylistic changes that give the piece the feeling of being significantly more complex than the typical—or stereotypical—Tin Pan Alley song.

After various hijinks that culminate in "Piggy" Beekman giving Lorelei Lee his wife's diamond tiara—and then telling Lady Beekman that Lorelei stole it—Dorothy and Lorelei are cut off financially during their trip to Paris by Gus Esmond's meddling father. As a result, they become part of a cabaret show at Chez Louis. The show at the cabaret includes hints of the old elaborate Busby Berkeley dance choreography of the earlier days of movie musicals, almost in parody form. It is within this Chez Louis show that Dorothy performs her most important solo song. Easily the most iconic musical performance in *Gentlemen Prefer Blondes* is Marilyn Monroe's rendition of "Diamonds Are a Girl's Best Friend," a performance that was ranked at No. 12 by the American Film Institute on its list of the 100 greatest movie songs of all time (American Film Institute 2004). However, one of the other musical highlights is Jane Russell's performance of "Diamonds Are a Girl's Best Friend" in the courtroom where she is disguised as Lorelei. Almost a parody of Lorelei/Monroe's performance in the floor show at Chez Louis, Russell exaggerates Lorelei's sexy dancing and singing style. In considering the Monroe/Lorelei version of the song, it is important to note that "Diamonds Are a Girl's Best Friend" is often cited as a movie musical song that included overdubbing by ghost vocalist Marni Nixon. Nixon's contribution seems to be limited to the operatic-style introduction that precedes the song itself. For movie fans who listen for how Nixon interpreted or mimicked the stars, it is interesting to note that she captures the speed and width of Marilyn Monroe's vibrato; however, in operatic style, Nixon includes vibrato throughout the introduction, in contrast to Monroe who in all her songs in the movie generally only moves from a straight tone to vibrato at the end of phrases.

Viewed today, *Gentlemen Prefer Blondes* may raise some issues of gender bias and female subjugation in its subtext, but the movie is best remembered as an entertaining comic musical romp.

GIGI

In terms of Academy Awards, the 1958 Vincente Minnelli film *Gigi* was one of the most widely recognized movie musicals of all time, winning nine Oscars: Best Picture, Best Director, Best Adapted Screenplay, Best

Musical Score, Best Original Song, Best Film Editing, Best Cinematography, Best Costume Design, and Best Art Direction, Set Decoration. Alan Jay Lerner adapted the screenplay from the novella *Gigi* by the French writer Colette, and his songwriting partner Frederick Loewe provided the music. The famed pianist-composer-arranger-conductor André Previn conducted the film's score.

Gigi starred Leslie Caron as the title character; Louis Jourdan as Gaston Lachaille; Maurice Chevalier as Gaston's uncle, Honoré Lachaille; Hermione Gingold as Gigi's grandmother Madame Alvarez, among others. Uncredited was Betty Ward, who dubbed Gigi's singing in songs such as "Say a Prayer for Me Tonight" and "The Parisians." The story is set in Paris, and the movie includes a sufficient number of cues to suggest that it was filmed on location. One of the unfortunate aspects of *Gigi*, however, is that in some outdoor scenes it appears that obvious backdrops are used. This is most notable in the early stages of the film in which Gaston and Honoré sing "It's a Bore" as they ride in a carriage, as well as in the scene in which Honoré and Madame Alvarez sing "I Remember It Well" at the seaside with a far too red sunset in the background.

The story revolves around Gigi, a girl on the cusp of coming of age; Gigi's grandmother, with whom she lives; Gigi's never-seen mother (who is only ever heard in the background singing operatic warm-up exercises rather badly); Gigi's great aunt, who trains Gigi on all the rules of etiquette for the high society world in which she hopes Gigi will enter; Gaston, a playboy and friend of Gigi's family; and Honoré, Gaston's uncle. Maurice Chevalier's Honoré is a particularly interesting character in the structure of the film. Not only does he appear as a friend of Gigi's family, Gaston's uncle, and one-time lover of Gigi's grandmother he also plays the role of a narrator, directly addressing the audience at the film's opening, which leads up to the movie's best-remembered song, "Thank Heaven for Little Girls," and at other points. When Honoré sings "I'm Glad I'm Not Young Anymore," it is also directed to the audience.

The fact that the songs "Thank Heaven for Little Girls" and "I'm Glad I'm Not Young Anymore" are directed at the audience is significant and is part of a larger aspect of the film that sets *Gigi* apart from the majority of earlier movie musicals. In addition to Chevalier's character speaking and singing directly to the audience at several times, Jourdan's character, Gaston, sings a small part of "Gigi" directly to the camera. This suggests that he is letting the audience in on his new feelings of love for Gigi as he himself comes to the realization. It should also be noted that this is a film in which relatively few of the songs are part of the dialogue between characters. For example, Gigi sings "Say a Prayer for Me Tonight" to her cat, Gaston sings "Gigi" largely to himself, except for the small part in which he sings to the audience, Gigi's "The Parisians" is sung to herself. In fact, the most memorable uses of songs as dialogue in the movie are "It's a Bore," in which Honoré and Gaston debate the excitement of various opportunities afforded to rich people such as Gaston, and "I Remember It Well," in which Honoré and Madame Alvarez sing to each other their contrasting remembrances of the last evening they spent together as lovers years ago.

Although the movie's first song, "Thank Heaven for Little Girls," develops out of Honoré's spoken commentary to the film's audience in which he sets the stage, time, context, and location, it is "It's a Bore" that most strikingly demonstrates one of the characteristics that tie all of Lerner and Loewe's songs for the film together. Before singing "It's a Bore," Honoré and Gaston begin talking in rhymed verse, which segues into the singing. Each subsequent song mixes singing and speaking. This gives the entire movie a greater feeling of connection and continuity than is experienced in some musicals. In fact, arguably, the only time that *Gigi* has anything like the stereotypical now-it's-time-for-a-song moment in which the action stops for the obligatory song is for "Say a Prayer for Me Tonight." It should be noted that Lerner and Loewe did not invent this technique in *Gigi*—for one thing, it can be found in the songs performed by Professor Higgins in *My Fair Lady*, a show musical from a couple of years before *Gigi*.

One of the other notable techniques of the movie is the use of stop-action in the scenes that take place in Maxim's. In the first Maxim's sequence, all the action and the orchestral underscoring comes to a sudden and dramatic halt when a new couple enters the room. The high-society diners then rise and make unison comments on the couple. Near the end of the film, there is another such halt when Gigi enters and meets Gaston. As Gigi and Gaston make their way through the restaurant, groups of diners rise as if to comment on the couple; however, the action and the orchestral underscoring continues and the diners are not provided an opportunity to comment on Gigi and Gaston.

Gaston reaches the proverbial critical juncture in his feelings about Gigi when Honoré tells him that a young woman such as Gigi "can keep you entertained for months," implying that she will simply be a lover for a brief time in one of Gaston's ongoing affairs, a reinforcing the stereotype of the ephemeral nature of relationships for a French playboy. After hastily taking Gigi back to her grandmother and spending a brief amount of time alone with his thoughts, Gaston returns to Gigi's grandmother's apartment and asks for Gigi's hand in marriage. The film concludes with Chevalier singing the concluding phrases of "Thank Heaven for Little Girls" to the audience as Gigi and Gaston's wedding carriage departs the park.

Some critics commented on the similarity of the basic premise of the story to that of Lerner and Loewe's *My Fair Lady* of just a few years before. It should also be noted that at popular film rating sites such as Rotten Tomatoes and the Internet Movie Database, *Gigi* has not fared as well as many other movie musicals (see, for example, Internet Movie Database 2019). In part, this may be because of the similarities between the basic premises of *Gigi* and *My Fair Lady*. *Gigi* is also a musical that includes engaging songs, such as "I'm Glad I'm Not Young Anymore," "Thank Heaven for Little Girls," "I Remember It Well," and "The Night They Invented Champagne," but a large part of what makes those songs so successful is their context and their performance in the film. In other words, *Gigi* is not filled with as numerous and as hook-filled showstopper-type songs as other musicals (not necessarily films) that appeared at around the same time and that could be taken out of their original contexts, such as some found in *The Music Man*, *West Side Story*, and *The Sound of Music*. In terms of immediately accessible and memorable tunes, *Gigi* also pales in comparison to Lerner and Loewe's *My Fair Lady*, one of the more tuneful musicals to come out of the 1950s. The fact that those stage musicals from the 1950s were adapted into highly successful movies in the first half of the 1960s probably moved *Gigi* down several notches on the public's list of favorite movie musicals. Another aspect of *Gigi* that can cause the movie to pale in comparison to many of its predecessors and certainly to some later film adaptations—such as *The Music Man*, *My Fair Lady*, and *West Side Story*—is that Gigi is a movie almost entirely devoid of dancing. The sole exception is a brief sequence in which Gaston and Gigi join the dance floor at Maxim's. There simply are no big production numbers in the movie. Although this gives a *Gigi* a sense of intimacy and something approaching realism—compared with, say, the extravagant Busby Berkeley-produced movie musicals of the past couple of decades—it also means that *Gigi* is missing some of the sense of spectacle of other movie musicals.

That being said, it must be remembered that *Gigi* won Academy Awards like no other musical before it had done. In 1991, the U.S. Library of Congress Film Preservation Board added *Gigi* to the National Film Registry for its historical significance. The American Film Institute ranked Alan Jay Lerner and Frederick Loewe's "Thank Heaven for Little Girls" at No. 56 on its list of the 100 greatest movie songs of all time

(American Film Institute 2004). Film and theater scholar Thomas S. Hischak wrote that "for some, the film was the climax as well as the end of a Golden Age" for movie musicals (Hischak 2017, 264). Indeed, *Gigi* can be understood as part of the continuum of grand musicals, particularly grand MGM musicals, and visually perhaps one of the high points, given the film's use of Paris as a backdrop. In the late 1950s, the musical was changing and some of the more suggestive sides of the storyline can be understood as pointing the way to the far edgier movie musicals that would follow. The use of Maurice Chevalier's character as simultaneously part of the story and as a commentator for the audience at least in small part anticipated the role of the master of ceremonies in *Cabaret*. More recently, one probably cannot help but think that Lumière's performance of "Be Our Guest" in the 1991 animated version of *Beauty and the Beast* was inspired by Chevalier's performance of both "Thank Heaven for Little Girls" and "I'm Glad I'm Not Young Anymore" in *Gigi*. The integration of speaking and singing—although not always entirely seamless—moved *Gigi* away from the stereotypical structure of musicals of the past. Although the film no longer seems to receive the same level of recognition or popularity that it had when it garnered nine Oscars at the 1959 Academy Awards, it deserves to be revisited as an example of the *movie* part of the movie musical.

GREASE

Arguably one of the most beloved American movie musicals about teenage life, *Grease* was released by Paramount in 1978. Robert Stigwood and Allan Carr produced the film, and Randal Kleiser directed it. Like the stage musical on which it was based, *Grease* featured a large ensemble cast; however, the film principally starred John Travolta, Olivia Newton-John, and Stockard Channing.

The initial release of the film was met with generally good reviews, particularly the performances by cast members. For example, *The Hollywood Reporter*'s review stated, "Dominating the film is John Travolta, in effect repeating his Fever performance, but demonstrating again that his is a particularly charismatic screen personality. Under choreographer Patricia Birch's inventive supervision, his dancing is better this time out. So is his singing, often in tandem with Olivia Newton-John" (The Staff of *The Hollywood Reporter* 2015). *The Hollywood Reporter* staff review, as well as others, also pointed to the strength of Newton-John's performance, the effectiveness of Bill Butler's camera work, and the youthfulness and high energy of the entire film. Mention of the energy and youthfulness are important to note, especially in relationship to the principal cast members. John Travolta was in his early 20s when *Grease* was filmed; however, Olivia Newton-John was in her late 20s and Stockard Channing, who portrayed Betty Rizzo, the leader of the Pink Ladies, was in her early 30s. The actors who portrayed the other members of the Pink Ladies and the T-Birds ranged in age from approximately 20s to their early 30s. In short, this is a movie about high school students with a cast in some cases well removed from high school.

The connections to *Saturday Night Fever*, which was also produced by Bee Gees manager Robert Stigwood can be found not only in John Travolta's starring role but also in the film's theme song. "Grease" featured lead vocals by Frankie Valli, who sang lead with the Four Seasons, perhaps the dominant vocal harmony group of the first half of the 1960s; however, the song came from the pen of Bee Gees member Barry Gibb, who wrote or cowrote many popular disco hits from the *Saturday Night Fever* soundtrack. In fact, the instrumentation and the rhythmic style of "Grease" reflect the disco style of the Bee Gees of the 1970s more than it does the musical styles associated with the 1950s or pre–British Invasion 1960s.

"Grease" was not the only song that was especially written for the movie version of the musical. The production of the film followed in the tradition of numerous past movies based on stage musicals in including a contractual clause for songs to be added/substituted for a star. In this case, John Farrar, Olivia Newton-John's producer, wrote "Hopelessly Devoted to You" and "You're the One That I Want" for the movie. Ironically, "You're the One That I Want" was a huge commercial success and one of the most memorable songs from *Grease*, so much so that subsequent productions of the stage version tend to include it rather than the song it replaced. "Hopelessly Devoted to You" was also commercially successful and enjoyed radio airplay on stations with several formats, having made it onto the pop, country, and easy listening singles charts.

Although both "Hopelessly Devoted to You" and "You're the One That I Want" were contemporary-sounding enough that they were significant radio and record hits, they also included enough stylistic cues to be effective within the context of a fantasy film about the late 1950s/early 1960s. In particular, "Hopelessly Devoted to You" might bring a country feel to *Grease* that contrasts with the original score; however, it is close enough to early-1960s commercial country music that it is believable. To put it another way, the song reflects enough stylistic, formal, melodic, and harmonic cues that suggest songs such as the Willie Nelson's composition "Crazy" (immortalized by Patsy Cline in 1962). In contrast to "Crazy," which reflects Tin Pan Alley-era pop-song form and contains little in the orchestration to suggest country music, "Hopelessly Devoted to You" includes prominent pedal steel guitar. Interestingly, the use of the steel guitar in the song might suggest to the listener the country genre and ties back to the famous 1959 Santo and Johnny instrumental hit "Sleep Walk." These two stylistic references are important in that the references to country music connect the song to some of Olivia Newton-John's earliest hits in the United States and the connection to "Sleep Walk" might suggest to some listeners even some tenuous ties to surf rock, thereby connecting the song to the Southern Californian setting of the film.

Some of the songs—or, rather, some of the performances of the songs—of *Grease* exhibit some interesting quirks. When one considers the entire locational premise of *Grease*—the story takes place near the beach in Southern California, apparently before the greasers gave way to the surfer craze—"Summer Nights" is particularly curious: the members of the T-Birds sound more like they are from Brooklyn than from California. In the context of a fantasy movie, this actually works; however, viewers who think of *Grease* as an at least somewhat semi-realistic look at Southern California high school life may find some incongruities.

Grease contains several entertaining dance sequences and several scenes that are particularly effective in the movie medium. Particularly impressive and creative is how the automobile is used as a prop in "Greased Lightning," as well as some of the dancing technique in the *National Bandstand* dance-off scene. Also highly effective—and very unstage-like—is the use of close camera angles in songs such as "Summer Nights." Another effective and humorously naughty scene comes late in the film, in which Newton-John's Sandy is shown against the backdrop of the drive-in movie intermission short. As various couples make out in their cars, the intermission short shows a phallic-looking hotdog jumping into a bun. Although a scene such as this could be created on stage, the scale would be entirely different. In short, *Grease* makes effective use of the movie medium such that it clearly is not just the stage musical captured on film.

Granted, there is very little plot to *Grease* and very little depth to the story. In fact, it can be understood as almost a parody or a 1970s fantasy piece on the old beach movies of the early 1960s. That Frankie Avalon makes a cameo appearance as Teen Angel singing "Beauty School Dropout" confirms the fantasy nature of the film, as does the fact that Tony and Sandy fly off into the sky in an automobile at the movie's conclusion.

To the extent that the viewer is familiar with the stars and even some of the actors in smaller roles in *Grease*, the film is as much about the actors themselves as it is about plot, songs, dance numbers, and atmosphere. For example, Alice Ghostly as the shop teacher, Sid Caesar as Coach Calhoun, and Eve Arden as Principal McGee all appear in character roles that reflect other stereotypical roles that they had played in television and film. At the *National Bandstand* dance-off, the real-life band Sha Na Na appears as the fictional Johnny Casino and the Gamblers; however, they are still very much recognizable as Sha Na Na, the retro-1950s band that performed at the Woodstock music festival of 1969 and had a syndicated television variety show around the time of *Grease*.

There are also clear ties between John Travolta's portrayal of Danny and his work in *Saturday Night Fever*. In fact, viewers might even detect cues in Tony's costume in the *National Bandstand* dance-off sequence in *Grease* that reflects the outfits that Travolta wore as Tony Manero. No, Travolta does not wear a white suit in *Grease*; however, his shirt in the dance-off sequence, as well as some of the dance moves, are not entirely foreign in the context of his famous breakthrough movie of the previous year.

What perhaps is the most intriguing in retrospect, however, are the ties between Olivia Newton-John and her character, Sandy. If one considers Newton-John's career pre-*Grease* and post-*Grease*, then one can consider her role in the film to be something of a career metaphor. Specifically, Newton-John first came to prominence as a singer of country-flavored pop songs. "I Honestly Love You," "Have You Never Been Mellow," "If You Love Me, Let Me Know," and others had a broad appeal across generations and exhibited an innocence in their lyrics aligning with the *Grease* character of Sandy throughout the bulk of the film. As Newton-John moved into the 1980s, however, there were more rock and dance music twinges in her hits. In some respects, though, the release of her controversial 1981 hit "Physical" made the same kind of impact on a music world still accustomed to "Have You Never Been Mellow" and "I Honestly Love You" (e.g., from "I honestly love you" to "Let me hear your body talk") that Sandy makes in *Grease* when she appears in skin-tight leather in the lead-in to and during "You're the One That I Want." In both cases, the transformation of Sandy and the musical transformation of Olivia Newton-John represented an abrupt shift from simple innocence to overt sexuality.

All in all, *Grease* is a feel-good fantasy movie, and the film's stars recognize the movie for what it is. For example, on the occasion of the 40th anniversary of *Grease*, *Entertainment Tonight*'s Paige Gawley quoted John Travolta as saying, "This is a film that's so timeless that keeps on giving to each new generation. . . . When people watch this, they just get happy. They want to become the characters they're watching. They want to sing along with it, they want to dance, they want to be part of this film" (Gawley 2018).

The American Film Institute ranked *Grease* at No. 20 on its list of the 25 greatest movie musicals of all time (American Film Institute 2006). The Institute also ranked "Summer Nights" No. 70 on its list of the 100 greatest movie songs of all time (American Film Institute 2004). The iconic nature of *Grease* and its embedded place in popular culture are also suggested by the fact that in March 2019, NBC's *Today Show* used references to the film as a teaser for an upcoming interview with Olivia Newton-John. Newton-John's medical issues and focus on health was the main theme of the interview; however, *Grease* was also part of the interview over four decades after the film was made and despite the fact that Newton-John's numerous non-*Grease* U.S. Top 40 singles and her popular albums were scarcely mentioned.

GUYS AND DOLLS

The stars of the 1955 film version of *Guys and Dolls* represented some of the popular elite of mid-1950s Hollywood. Frank Sinatra (Nathan Detroit), for example, had been a star singer since the early 1940s and had previously starred in well-known films such as *Anchors Aweigh*, *On the Town*, *From Here to Eternity*, and several others; Marlon Brando (Sky Masterson) had made a huge impact on American cinema in the several years leading up to *Guys and Dolls* in films such as *A Streetcar Named Desire*, *On the Waterfront*, and *The Wild One*; and although perhaps not as well known in the United States, Jean Simmons (Sister Sarah Brown) had been a movie star in her native Great Britain since the mid-1940s. There were also significant casting ties to the original stage musical as Stubby Kaye (Nicely-Nicely Johnson) and Vivian Blaine (Miss Adelaide) reprised their Broadway roles from five years before in the film.

The movie largely follows the stage version, with a few notable exceptions. The original musical's songwriter, Frank Loesser, provided a new piece for Frank Sinatra's character, "Adelaide"; replaced "My Time of Day" with "(Your Eyes Are the Eyes of) A Woman in Love," sung by Marlon Brando's character; and substituted the newly written "Pet Me Poppa" for "Bushel and a Peck." "Pet Me Poppa" is a good stylistic match for the Hot Box club scene in which it is performed by Miss Adelaide and the other scantily clad female dancers. In fact, the lyrics are more sexually suggestive than those of the song it replaced. Interestingly, the new songs performed by Sinatra and Brando are not as successful.

The ballad style of "Adelaide" and "(Your Eyes Are the Eyes of) A Woman in Love" stands in fairly stark contrast to the music of the rest of the songs. "A Woman in Love" is also a bit problematic in that it does not segue into the subsequent dialogue nearly as well as "My Time of Day" does in the stage version of the show.

When compared with many MGM musicals of the 1940s and 1950s, the choreography of *Guys and Dolls*, a product of Samuel Goldwyn Productions, is worth noting. The film's primary production numbers—"Pet Me Poppa" and "Take Back Your Mink" performed at the Hot Box, "Luck Be a Lady" and "Sit Down, You're Rockin' the Boat" performed, respectively, by Marlon Brando and the gamblers and Stubby Kaye and the gamblers—are not nearly as grandiose as those in other movie musicals of the time. In fact, either intentional or otherwise, the showgirls in "Take Back Your Mink" are far less precise than what one sometimes sees in many stage productions of *Guys and Dolls*. Some of the most impressive choreography is in the film's opening extended sequence, in which various nefarious characters cheat and steal from the more respectable citizens on the streets of New York, as well as in the fight sequence in Havana.

Some of the film's musical highlights are Jean Simmons's performance of "If I Were a Bell," Vivian Blaine's performance of "Adelaide's Lament," Stubby Kaye and the gamblers' performance of "Sit Down, You're Rockin' the Boat," the "Luck Be a Lady" sequence, and gamblers' performance of "Guys and Dolls."

Compared with the sense of realism—or something closer to realism—that came into the settings and scenery of some later movie musicals, *Guys and Dolls* is very much a product of the Hollywood musical style of the 1950s. The street scenes are filled with vibrant colors. For example, the ubiquitous "Yellow" cabs of New York are multicolored, and all the automobiles boast shiny, just-from-the-factory paint jobs. Likewise, some of the minor characters and extras in the crowd scenes sport bright colors. This aspect of the film links it with musicals such as *The Music Man*, and even *West Side Story*, the former presents a stylized view of life in the Midwest in early 20th century, and the latter of which included scenes with brightly colored automobiles that lent an air of stylized unreality to a storyline that reflected at least in part the harsh realities of youth gang warfare of the 1950s. In the case of *Guys and Dolls*, the brightly colored cars and clothing of some of the extras help to make Nathan Detroit, dressed in the beginning of the film primarily in black and white and shades of gray, and Sky Masterson blend into the city's background. Additionally, Nathan Detroit's mismatched pinstriped suit and polka-dotted bow tie make him a particularly cartoonish gangster.

The costuming, the use of color in the backgrounds, and the instrumental underscoring tell the audience that this is a humorous musical about Damon Runyon's exaggerated, nearly cartoon-like gangsters and not, say, a gangster film noir. This sense of unreality comes in handy at the end of the film when the story resolves in the happy ending of the wedding of the two principal couples, Detroit and Adelaide and Masterson and Sister Brown, in the streets of the Broadway theater district of New York.

The stage version of *Guys and Dolls* remains a popular show for high schools and community theater troupes, perhaps only marred by the fact that the cast requires more than just a few strong male actors. The 1955 movie version was ranked at No. 23 in the American Film Institute's list of the 25 greatest movie musicals of all time (American Film Institute 2006). The Institute also named "Luck Be a Lady" the 42nd greatest movie song of all time (American Film Institute 2004). Interestingly, although "Luck Be a Lady" was performed in the movie by Marlon Brando's character, Sky Masterson, the song became one of Frank Sinatra's signature tunes.

HAIRSPRAY

The 1988 John Waters film *Hairspray* has been only sporadically available since its theatrical release; however, it became something of a cult classic. In 2002, *Hairspray* was turned into a stage musical, with a film version of the musical appearing in 2007. The movie musical includes a score by Marc Shaiman, lyrics by Shaiman and Scott Wittman, the book by Thomas Meehan and Mark O'Donnell, and screenplay adaptation from the stage version by Leslie Dixon. Adam Shankman provided the choreography and directed the film.

Both the original John Waters non-musical film and the stage musical included a fair amount of campiness, some of which was reduced for the movie version. One of the elements that were retained, however, was the casting of Edna Turnblad in a drag role. Played by Divine in the 1988 Waters comedy film and Harvey Fierstein in the original 2002 stage musical, John Travolta played Mrs. Turnblad in the movie version. For audiences familiar with Travolta's starring roles in two of the great musical/dance films of 1970, *Saturday Night Fever* and *Grease*, his appearance in *Hairspray* was a surprise; however, it also allows for comic connections back to the early part of his career. Specifically, one of the great lines that Edna Turnblad utters in the film is her observation that "nobody has asked me to dance in years."

Among the other featured well-known and immediately recognizable actors in *Hairspray* are Christopher Walken as Wilbur Turnblad, Edna's husband and Tracy Turnblad's father; Michelle Pfeiffer as Velma Von Tussle; and Queen Latifah as Motormouth Maybelle Stubbs, the host of the monthly "Negro Day" on *The Corny Collins Show* and mother of Seaweed J. Stubbs. In terms of capturing the spirit of the music of the 1960s—the story takes place in 1962—Queen Latifah is a major component in the film's musical success. Although Aretha Franklin's main contributions to soul music came later in the 1960s, Queen Latifah practically channels the spirit of Franklin's combination of gospel and R&B soulfulness in every song she sings in the film. Queen Latifah also provides Maybelle Stubbs a powerful personality that puts her in control of every scene she is in.

Much of the movie's energy, however, comes from the younger singer/dancer/actors, including Elijah Kelley as Seaweed J. Stubbs, one of Tracy's schoolmates and a talented dancer; Zac Efron as Link Larkin, an Elvis Presley–like featured singer and dancer on *The Corny Collins Show*; and James Marsden as Corny Collins, whose fictional Baltimore television program is akin to a local version of Dick Clark's famous *American Bandstand*. Nikki Blonsky, as the movie's lead character, Tracy Turnblad, was perhaps the most remarkable cast member in the film, as *Hairspray* represented her film debut. Blonsky more than held her own as an actor alongside such well-established and well-known stars as Pfeiffer and Travolta.

To a great extent, Marc Shaiman's music for *Hairspray* closely resembles the popular genres of the late 1950s and early 1960s. In fact, much of the music easily could have been from 1962, the time of the story, with the possible exception of the funk music listened to and danced to in the detention classroom by the school's black teens, and eventually danced to by Tracy Turnblad. Shaiman's music in the detention room sequences tends to sound more like the soul and funk of the late 1960s.

Shaiman and Scott Wittman's lyrics are filled with one-liners, clearly tied to the comic narrative of the film, as opposed to reflective of 1962. The songs contain so many one-liners and lengthier comic elements that they invite repeated listening. From a purely musical standpoint, however, "I Can Hear the Bells" suggests the full orchestrations and productions of early 1960s records that Phil Spector produced for artists such as the Ronettes, and the song "Welcome to the '60s" resembles the 1963 Martha and the Vandellas hit "Heat Wave."

Tracy sings "Good Morning Baltimore" in a setting that makes full use of a street scene. Subsequently, the audience is introduced to one of the story's themes: the racism of Baltimore in the early 1960s. Specifically, African American pop music is referred to as "race music," a term once commonly used in the music industry, but by the time period depicted in the musical, long-since replaced by rhythm and blues, aka R&B, as the moniker for African American pop music. The use of the older term suggests that the white members of the generation of Tracy's parents are still at least partially stuck in the racial attitudes of earlier decades. Throughout the rest of the show, the racist mantle is largely taken up by Michelle Pfeiffer's Velma Von Tussle and her daughter Amber Von Tussle, played by Brittany Snow.

The one song that reflects back even farther in history than the rest of the numbers is "(You're) Timeless to Me." Perhaps because this piece is sung by Tracy Turnblad's parents, Wilbur and Edna, and not by members of Tracy's generation, the song's scheme and style suggest the possible influence of "You're Awful," which was sung by Frank Sinatra and Betty Garrett in *On the Town*. The possible 1940s inspiration fits the characters particularly well, even though "(You're) Timeless to Me" is not necessarily one of the more popularly recognized songs from *Hairspray*.

One of the interesting aspects of *Hairspray* is the extent to which the movie is able to expand individual songs into large, extended production numbers. The entire "Welcome to the '60s" sequence, for example, takes the basic structure of a pop R&B song and keeps expanding it as the characters move from location to location for about two to three times the duration that a song from the early 1960s would have lasted. Perhaps the best example of this expansion and extension comes in the film's biggest production number—and one of its most well-known songs—"You Can't Stop the Beat." Not only is this a singing and dancing *tour de force*, "You Can't Stop the Beat" is important metaphorically in the show, with "the beat" appearing to represent the progress that was being made in race relations and toward equal rights for blacks and whites in the Baltimore of the story's era. It is in this song that finally black and white teens—and some parents—finally dance together on the set of the fictional *Corny Collins Show*.

Another important aspect of "You Can't Stop the Beat" is that because it is from a show-within-a-show (*The Corny Collins Show*), the production number exhibits the continuing influence of musicals about show business going all the way back to *42nd Street* and other musicals of the 1930s. As such, this production number helps to paint *Hairspray* as part of a continuum of movie musicals, both reflecting whimsically back to an early time and involving the entertainment industry as part of the milieu.

Hairspray was also part of a disparate series of musicals that reflected on the prepsychedelic-era 1960s, some movies and some works for the stage, including *Forever Plaid, Grease, Dreamgirls, Little Shop of Horrors, Jersey Boys*, and others. Of these musicals, *Hairspray* is perhaps the most whimsical, although the film is missing some of the campiness of the earlier stage version, and certainly missing some of the campiness of the 1988 film.

Hairspray is one movie musical where it pays off to watch the entire closing credits in the theater or on the in-home DVD. These credits include the music for songs that were in the stage version of the show but not included in the film. These include "Come So Far (Got So Far To Go)," "Cooties," and "Mama, I'm a Big Girl Now," the latter of which resembles the old Dion hit "Runaround Sue." From the musical standpoint, this song, in particular, with its use of the so-called oldies chord progression (I-vi-IV-V), could have come right out of the era depicted in the musical. In fact, Dion's "Runaround Sue" dates back to 1961, the year before the fictional time period of *Hairspray*.

In 2016, NBC produced *Hairspray Live!*, which was a telecast of a live performance of the stage musical. Although not nearly as critically or commercially successful as the 2007 film, the 2016 telecast suggests that the story, Marc Shaiman's music and lyrics, and Mark O'Donnell and Thomas Meehan's book for the 2002 musical are still popular. In fact, one could reasonably argue that *Hairspray* is one of the easiest 21st-century musicals to watch not just because it includes some of the social issues of the story's time period but is just plain fun.

A HARD DAY'S NIGHT

A group that evolved out of John Lennon's skiffle band the Quarrymen, the Beatles were formed in the early 1960s. After manager Brian Epstein fired the original drummer, Pete Best, and brought Ringo Starr—already a friend of other group members, and a musician who had sat in with the band from time to time during residencies in Hamburg, Germany—into the group, the Beatles released their first official recording as a band in 1962. Stardom in the United Kingdom quickly followed, then pandemonium erupted over the group in Europe, and in early 1964, the Beatles kicked off what became known as the British Invasion of the United States.

The 1964 film *A Hard Day's Night* fictionalizes what might be understood as a typical situation in the lives of the real-life Beatles during the high point of Beatlemania: a trip to London to appear on a television program. Writer Alun Owen was from the Beatles' home city of

Liverpool and managed to capture the general spirit of the time and the place. Director Richard Lester was perhaps another natural for the film, as Lester was known to the Beatles and their manager, Brian Epstein, as the maker of *The Running, Jumping & Standing Still Film*, which starred Spike Milligan, one of the Beatles' favorite comedians. Walter Shenson produced *A Hard Day's Night*. The title of the film is based on a statement made by the Beatle's Ringo Starr after a lengthy recording session. As fellow Beatle John Lennon put it, the phrase "was one of those malapropisms, a Ringoism—not said to be funny—just said" (The Beatles 2000, 128).

Although the film appears to capture the personalities of John Lennon, Paul McCartney, George Harrison, and Ringo Starr, Lennon described *A Hard Day's Night* as "a comic-strip version of what was actually going on" (The Beatles 2000, 128). Owen's script also seems to take a limited number of attributes of the real-life members of the band and use them to define Lennon, McCartney, Harrison, and Starr in a way that is digestible to the fan, but that fails to capture the full personalities of the band members. In fact, it could be argued that *A Hard Day's Night* and publicity that surrounded the Beatles during the Beatlemania period tended to cement a limited set of stereotypes of the four Beatles in the minds of fans. Lennon and the other Beatles admitted, however, that many of the situations in the film's storyline suggested parts of what they experienced in their daily work and as a result of their fame.

The basic premise of the film is that the Beatles travel from Liverpool to London for a live television appearance. Paul McCartney, however, is joined by his fictional grandfather, John McCartney, played by veteran actor Wilfrid Brambell. The elder McCartney demonstrates a penchant throughout the film for playing various characters off against one another. He also deviously acquires an invitation to a gambling club which he visits with humorous effect. The other most notable actor in the film is Victor Spinetti, who plays the beleaguered television producer.

Although *A Hard Day's Night* provides some surface-level insight into the lives of the Beatles when they were the biggest thing in show business, the real meat of the musical is in the quirky humor—some of which was improvised by members of the group—and the eight original compositions of John Lennon and Paul McCartney that formed the bulk of the soundtrack. In addition to these songs—"A Hard Day's Night," "I Should Have Known Better," "If I Fell," "Can't Buy Me Love," "And I Love Her," "I'm Happy Just to Dance with You," and "Tell Me Why"—the soundtrack included several of the band's earlier recordings.

Most of the previous—and many of the future—rock and roll films either included performance scenes of artists playing themselves (often for just short segments in the film) or found their stars playing roles that had little or nothing to do with their real lives. For example, Elvis Presley starred in movies in which he was a doctor, a convict, a Hawaii-based tour guide, a racecar driver, a Native American rodeo performer, and so on. In the 1956 film, *The Girl Can't Help It*, there are plenty of appearances by the likes of Little Richard, Fats Domino, Eddie Cochran, Gene Vincent, and others all performing as themselves, but they really are more like cameo roles. Despite the surface-level portrayal of the real-life Lennon, McCartney, Harrison, and Starr, the four Beatles—the stars of *A Hard Day's Night*—essentially played themselves, at least to a far greater extent than the paradigm that was set up by the numerous Elvis Presley and other rock and roll films of the 1950s and early 1960s.

Because the film focuses on how the Beatles were essentially prisoners of their own commercial success and fame, much of the hijinks involves their trying to escape from hotel rooms, press conferences, and theater dressing rooms. One of these escapes allows for other, already well-known Beatles songs to be used in the soundtrack. The scene of the band members in a discotheque finds them and the other clubbers dancing to snippets of previous Beatles releases "I Wanna Be Your Man," "Don't Bother Me" (the sole George Harrison composition heard in the movie's soundtrack), and "All My Loving."

An instrumental arrangement of "This Boy" accompanies Ringo Starr's brief exodus from the backstage turmoil concocted by Paul's grandfather. Although an instrumental version of "A Hard Day's Night" is also used in the film, the bulk of the musical material is from the Beatles themselves. The set that the Beatles perform in the supposed live television broadcast includes the aforementioned "Tell Me Why," "If I Fell," and "I Should Have Known Better," as well as the 1963 hit "She Loves You."

Including the songs that appear in the final television broadcast scene, all the new songs are mimed by the Beatles with the exception of "Can't Buy Me Love," which, most notably, accompanies director Dick Lester's Beatles version of his earlier work with Spike Milligan, *The Running, Jumping & Standing Still Film*, and the movie's title song, which accompanies scenes of British teenagers mobbing the band in the film's opening and which also accompanies the final credit sequence.

A Hard Day's Night is also notable as it contains a number of what might be termed mildly adult humor, very much in the British comedic tradition of acts such as the Goons. One such example occurs early in the film in the train ride sequence in which John Lennon can be seen attempting to snort a bottle of Coke ("coke" being used in drug culture for cocaine), another can be found in John McCartney's comment to a well-endowed female patron of the gambling club that she "must be a good swimmer," and another can be found in a dressing room scene in which the band's fictional manager (played by Norman Rossington) tells the fictional road manager (played by John Junkin) to take off a wig he is wearing because it "becomes [him]." The film also references the generation gap between the Beatles (as symbols of the carefree Baby Boomers) and an older World War II veteran (Veteran: "I fought the war for your sort"; Ringo Starr: "I bet you're sorry you won"), also found in the train ride sequence.

At the time of its release and still well over half a century later, *A Hard Day's Night* is one of the classic rock and roll musical films. Compared with some of the less memorable and more unbelievable films of Elvis Presley in the 1950s and 1960s and many of the other rock and roll films of its era and those that preceded it, *A Hard Day's Night* was appreciated by audiences and by critics. For example, in a 2011 update to *TIME* magazine's original 2005 listing of the 100 greatest movies of all time, critic Richard Corliss continued to include *A Hard Day's Night* as not just one of the best musical films but as one of the greatest films of all time (Corliss 2011).

HELLO DOLLY!

The 1964 musical *Hello Dolly!*, with music and lyrics by Jerry Herman, was based on a 25-year-old play by Thornton Wilder (*The Merchant of Yonkers*) and Wilder's subsequent adaptation (*The Matchmaker*) and was a hit. The musical won numerous awards, enjoyed a long run on Broadway, and remains one of the most popular Broadway musicals of the era. Interestingly, the title song became a significant hit for New Orleans jazz trumpet player and distinctively voiced singer Louis Armstrong. In fact, the Armstrong single remains famous as the record that knocked the Beatles out of the No. 1 position on the U.S. pop charts at the start of the British Invasion. "Hello Dolly!" became one of the most iconic recordings of Armstrong's long and illustrious career. When the film version of *Hello Dolly!* was produced five years later, it was only natural that Armstrong makes a cameo appearance singing a couple of choruses of the theme song.

Louis Armstrong's cameo was only the topping on the proverbial cake of this film, which starred Barbra Streisand as Dolly Levi, Walter

Matthau as Horace Vandergelder, Michael Crawford as Cornelius Hackl, Marianne McAndrew as Irene Molloy, E. J. Peaker as Minnie Fay, Joyce Ames as Ermengarde Vandergelder, Danny Lockin as Barnaby Tucker, and Tommy Tune as Ambrose Kemper. Movie musical legend Gene Kelly directed *Hello Dolly!*.

The movie's opening is notable for the action rippling out from what looks to be a sepia photograph of New York City in 1890. As Dolly Levi distributes her business cards in the opening song, director Kelly uses stop-action. Curiously, however, the production tricks are limited to the opening sequences in the movie. Another curiosity of the film is the fact that the sound and visuals are not as well synchronized as in other movie musicals from the same era, for example, in another Streisand hit from the late 1960s, *Funny Girl*. Another curious aspect of *Hello Dolly!* is in the fact that Broadway legend Tommy Tune was so much taller than other actors that he tends to dominate the ensemble dance sequences, despite the fact he was not necessarily the featured dancer.

The focus of the film, however, tends to be on Dolly Levi and her role as a general fixer and matchmaker, and her exploits in getting Horace Vandergelder to marry her. Perhaps not to the extent that Julie Andrews became linked to the role of Maria von Trapp, Barbra Streisand's performance as Dolly (and the fact that films can reach audiences decades removed from their original production much easier than live stage productions or television shows) made Streisand the definitive Dolly Levi.

The story takes place in 1890 and is divided between Yonkers, New York, and New York City. For the most part, Jerry Herman's music for "It Only Takes a Moment" is in the character of the great midcentury musicals. Michael Crawford's (Cornelius) performance of the song late in the film is particularly effective.

One of the highlights of *Hello Dolly!* is how grandiose the production numbers are. For example, songs such as "Put on Your Sunday Clothes" and "Before the Parade Passes By" are given treatments that go well beyond what would be possible on stage.

There is one scene that is completely unintentionally worth watching, if just as an example of how context can change over time. During the dance competition scene, as Cornelius is trying not to let his employer, Vandergelder, see him, he holds a fan over half of his face. The irony is that Michael Crawford, who played Cornelius in the film, would star in the most famous role of his career, the title character in *The Phantom of the Opera*, in which he would wear the well-known half-face mask.

Structurally, *Hello Dolly!* differs from many musicals that preceded it in that the show's main songs are reprised briefly leading up to the final scene in which Dolly and Horace are wed. Despite the years that have gone by and despite the fact that *Hello Dolly!* is not one of the most-highly honored films of all time, it remains an example of a strong feel-good movie musical.

HOLIDAY INN

The 1942 film *Holiday Inn* starred Bing Crosby as Jim Hardy, a Broadway crooner who gives up the glamour and demands of the New York City entertainment scene to buy an inn in Connecticut; Fred Astaire as Ted Hanover, Hardy's one-time partner in a Broadway act; Virginia Dale as Lila Dixon, Hanover's original dance partner and his love interest; Marjorie Reynolds as Linda Mason, Hanover's later dance partner and love interest of Hardy; and Walter Abel as Danny Reed, Hanover's agent. The film was inspired by an idea by Irving Berlin, who wrote the music and lyrics for the songs and instrumental numbers. Mark Sandrich directed the film, which was released by Paramount, one of MGM's chief competitors in the movie musical market of the 1940s and 1950s.

The basic premise of the storyline is that Hardy bought the inn thinking that Dixon would marry him and that the two would give up the entertainment industry and move to Connecticut. When Lila decides to remain a dancing partner with Hanover (whom she eventually leaves to marry a man who allegedly is a millionaire), Hardy eventually comes up with the idea of turning the inn into a performance venue that would only be open on holidays, the days that Broadway theaters typically would be dark. Another theme that runs throughout the film—driving much of the plot—is that Hardy and Hanover always compete for affections of the various women with whom they worked. In the end, as performance partners and romantic couples, Hardy and Mason and Hanover and Dixon eventually end up together.

Although several of Irving Berlin's songs for *Holiday Inn* were successful, "Easter Parade" and "White Christmas" are the two best remembered. In fact, "White Christmas," which was introduced in the movie, is arguably one of the most recorded songs in the history of the sound-recording era, and—although accurate sales accounting figures are not available—Bing Crosby's recording of the song is reputed to be one of, if not the, best-selling recordings of all time. It is also a song that is firmly etched into the repertoire of the Christmas season and into popular culture. In recognition of its importance and enduring popularity, the American Film Institute ranked "White Christmas" at No. 5 in its 2004 list of the 100 greatest movie songs of all time (American Film Institute 2004).

The movie plays on the public perceptions and stereotypes of its stars Bing Crosby and Fred Astaire. This is most noticeable in the early number "I'll Capture Your Heart," which includes Crosby delivering his well-known "ba-ba-ba-boo" scat singing and Astaire incorporating the tap and ballroom dance styles that defined much of the public's perception of his screen work. Particularly, in the case of Crosby/Hardy's use of scat singing, this style was so closely associated with Crosby as a singing star, the audience is torn between hearing this as a Jim Hardy number and as a Bing Crosby number. One of the delightful things about *Holiday Inn* is that the audience is torn (in a fun way) between seeing Crosby as himself or as Hardy and between seeing Astaire as himself or as Hanover.

The film also provides an opportunity for Astaire to parody his fame as both an elegant ballroom and a technically impressive tap dancer. Hanover/Astaire first appear at Hardy's Holiday Inn in a drunken state after having been jilted by Lila Dixon. The stumbling Hanover dances with Linda Mason for the first time. While Mason dances elegantly, Hanover exaggerates his moves in a very un-Astaire-like fashion, finally falling down passed out at the end of the number.

Other musical highlights include Hardy and Mason's first performance of "White Christmas," Hardy's performance of "Easter Parade," and Hanover's singing and dancing in "Be Careful, It's My Heart." Perhaps the most iconic dance sequence in the film, and one featured in retrospectives of Fred Astaire's work, is Hanover/Astaire's solo tap dance with pyrotechnics in the Independence Day sequence.

As Don Tyler wrote in *The Great Movie Musicals: A Viewer's Guide to 168 Films That Really Sing*, "*Holiday Inn* certainly reflects the era, but it hasn't aged. It ranks as one of the best movie musicals to come out of the Forties" (Tyler 2010, 148). Arguably, however, the one part of *Holiday Inn* that has not aged well is the blackface sequence for the song "Abraham," which Jim Handy performs for Lincoln's birthday. There may be multiple ways to interpret this sequence, particularly in light of film's release during World War II; however, on the most obvious level, the use of blackface is offensive as an entertainment form. Particularly jaw-dropping in the song when one experiences it in the 21st century is when Louise Beavers, as Jim Handy's maid and cook, Mamie, performs a phrase of "Abraham" for her children in which she sings that Abraham "set the darkies free."

Despite the groaner of a line sung by Mamie, "Abraham" is largely missing the overt racism of the lyrics associated with the blackface minstrel shows of the 19th and early 20th centuries. In the broader context of the film, the emphasis on freedom resonates with the World War II era in which *Holiday Inn* appeared. In fact, this—freedom—is the theme of the Independence Day piece "Song of Freedom," which Jim Hardy sings against a backdrop of filmed scenes of defense plants, the weaponry of World War II, and images of U.S. President Franklin Roosevelt. "Abraham" might, then, be understood as an example Irving Berlin equating the freeing of African American slaves under Lincoln with the war efforts against Hitler's Germany and its persecution and attempts at extermination of the Jews. If one understands "Abraham" in that way, then the song can be understood as reflecting back to Al Jolson—as Jakie—singing "My Mammy" in blackface in *The Jazz Singer*. Although some viewers interpret "My Mammy" as an extension of the blackface minstrelsy of the 19th and early 20th centuries, scholar Desirée J. Garcia writes that "through the allegory of the black experience, the song recounts the journey that Jakie has made during the course of the film" (Garcia 2014, 30). It might be quite a stretch to interpret "Abraham" as an allegorical work that connects the plight of African Americans under slavery and the plight of the Jews in Europe during the 1930s and first half of the 1940s; however, the possibility is there.

Some of the other songs, although not necessarily racially insensitive, have also not aged well. In the case of "Washington's Birthday," corny lyrics might lead some viewers to place it on their B or C lists of Irving Berlin songs. The piece does work on one level as a comedy number, particularly as Hardy's band abruptly shifts from a pseudo-18th-century style to jazz in Hardy's effort to sabotage Hanover and Mason's first public performance as a dance team. Likewise, although "You're Easy to Dance With" is tuneful and provides Hanover/Astaire with an opportunity to highlight the kind of elegant ballroom dancing the public associated with him, the song's form is more complex than the typical pop hit of the day and the piece is not as memorable as Berlin's best-remembered songs.

Although some aspects of *Holiday Inn* have not aged well, the film remains a Christmas season favorite and over the years has continued to be broadcast during the holiday season, albeit often with the entire "Abraham" blackface sequence removed.

JAILHOUSE ROCK

The movies of Elvis Presley included a generous helping of music. That fact cannot be disputed, regardless of whether viewers consider them "movie musicals" in the strictest sense. The plots may have been predictable and not particularly deep, but, generally, Presley's films were all about Presley and his way with a song. Although the bulk of Presley's films were released between his discharge from the U.S. Army in 1958 and his last film in 1969, two of Presley's pre-Army films, *Jailhouse Rock* and *King Creole*, are among his best. These movies, along with Presley's film debut, *Love Me Tender*, and his second film, *Loving You*, should be considered in the context of mid-1950s, rock-and-roll-era movies such as *The Girl Can't Help It, Don't Knock the Rock, Blackboard Jungle*, and others.

The early rock and roll films tended to include the then-popular artists playing themselves. Such was the case with the 1956 movie *Don't Knock the Rock*, a film with a storyline that centered around the character Arnie Haines, played by Alan Dale. In the course of the film, the fictional Haines performs as part of a package tour that includes real-life stars of the day Bill Haley and His Comets, Little Richard and his band, the Treniers, and Don Appell and the Applejacks. The most prominent and memorable musical numbers were those performed by Haley's group and Little Richard.

The 1957 movie *Jailhouse Rock* was written around Presley's stardom as a singer. Presley plays the fictional character Vince Everett, a man who was convicted of manslaughter. Everett's cellmate, Hunk Houghton, played by Mickey Shaughnessy, teaches Everett to play rudimentary guitar, Houghton having been a professional musician before he was incarcerated. Sensing musical potential in Everett, Houghton signs him to a contract.

After serving his sentence, Presley's character is released and through a chance encounter with Peggy Van Alden, played by Judy Tyler (who died in a car crash before the film premiered), who worked in the music industry, he records a debut song, has it stolen, starts a new record company, becomes a star, is confronted by the later released Hunk Houghton, loses Van Alden, gets her back, and so on.

When Presley's character becomes a star, he is signed to perform in a television special. In this special, former cellmate Houghton's thoroughly country-flavored sequence is cut, a cue to Houghton that his old-school style is passé. Incredibly—or incredulously—Houghton accepts a significant reduction from the terms of the original Everett-Houghton contract and becomes, essentially, a part of Everett's staff. Although audiences at the time of the release of *Jailhouse Rock* could not have had a clue about the twists and turns of Elvis Presley's professional and private life in the 1960s and 1970s, the transformation of the Everett character upon his initial brush with fame eerily anticipates Presley's later years in which, allegedly, he was waited upon by the members of the so-called Memphis

Mafia. Although some of the Presley biographies differ on the details of Presley's later years (see, for example, Dunleavy 1977; Guralnick 2000), most biographers agree that Presley was isolated near the end of his life and was surrounded by the kinds of staff members and hanger-ons that surround his character, Vince Everett, in *Jailhouse Rock*.

Although characters Hunk Houghton and Vince Everett perform several songs over the course of the approximately 1-1/2-hour movie, the soundtrack contained two bona fide Presley hits: "Jailhouse Rock" and "Treat Me Nice," both written by the well-known Brill Building team of Jerry Leiber and Mike Stoller. Both songs fit in with the theme of the film, although they are not essential to the plot in the way that plot-advancing songs tend to be in traditional musicals. Some listeners might detect stylist and melodic similarities between Leiber and Stoller's "Treat Me Nice" and Otis Blackwell's "Don't Be Cruel," which had been a massive hit for Presley in 1956 ("Treat Me Nice" and "Jailhouse Rock" made the singles charts the following year).

As a song, Leiber and Stoller's "Jailhouse Rock" is remarkable in several ways. Perhaps the most unusual and interesting aspect of the song itself is the fact that the lyrics can be interpreted as suggesting homosexual attraction among the inmates. This aspect of the song and film has been the subject of academic study. For example, musicologists Philip Brett and Elizabeth Wood cite "Jailhouse Rock" as one of the early examples of a rock and roll song that included homoerotic references (Brett and Wood 2006, 363). Clearly, with prisoners remarking upon the cuteness of other inmates and about how "delighted" they would be with the cute inmate's "company," there are implications of prison homosexual activity. Regardless of whether Leiber and Stoller intended the lyrics to reflect the silliness of the songs that they wrote for the Coasters, or if they intended them to reflect the realities of all-male prison life, the inclusion of such suggestions is remarkable, particularly for the time period.

The other notable feature of the film's title song is the set and choreography that is part of the show-within-a-show that stars Vince Everett. This dance sequence, in which Elvis Presley lip-syncs the lyrics, is easily the most famous scene in the movie. In fact, whenever this movie is referenced in print, on television, or in documentary films, the image(s) that seem most to frequently accompany the references are from the "Jailhouse Rock" sequence. The American Film Institute ranked "Jailhouse Rock" the No. 21 greatest movie songs of all time (American Film Institute 2004). In addition to the recognition that the title song and its dance sequence have received, the movie itself was selected by the Library of Congress for inclusion in the National Film Registry in 2004.

THE JAZZ SINGER

Based on the Samson Raphaelson short story "The Day of Atonement" and Raphaelson's subsequent play *The Jazz Singer*, this 1927 film is credited as the symbol of a complete change in the nature of motion pictures: it signaled the start of the age of the "talkie." Not only were there several sequences in which the film's star, Al Jolson, speaks and sings in synchronization with the movements of his mouth, *The Jazz Singer* also featured an elaborate synchronized score composed by Louis Silvers. Silvers's score, which runs throughout the film—except for the song sequences—includes original material but also numerous quotations from orchestral literature, as well as popular songs of the early 20th century (e.g., George M. Cohan's "Give My Regards to Broadway") and earlier Tin Pan Alley hits (e.g., "The Sidewalks of New York").

The film is the story of Jolson's character, Jakie Rabinowitz, the descendant of a long line of synagogue cantors, who as a child leaves home to go into show business, vowing never to return. Jakie's father disowns his son, although Jakie's mother remains tied to him via letters that Jakie sends home that his mother secretly reads. Jakie takes the stage name Jack Robin, is discovered, becomes part of a touring company as "the jazz singer," and is summoned to Broadway in his native New York. Literally, on the eve of potential Broadway stardom, Robin is confronted with the reality that his ailing father will not be able to sing the Kol Nidre prayer at the Yom Kippur service, the first time in generations that a Rabinowitz cantor would not sing the traditional prayer. Ultimately, Jakie/Jack takes his father's place—with the premiere of the show in which he was scheduled to appear canceled. Rather than finishing off Jack Robin's career before full stardom had struck, as the show's director had threatened, the film concludes with Robin, now a star, singing "My Mammy" to a packed house that includes his mother in the theater's front row. Although some viewers might interpret "My Mammy" as simply an extension of the blackface minstrelsy of the 19th and early 20th centuries, scholar Desirée J. Garcia writes that "through the allegory of the black experience, the song recounts the journey that Jakie has made during the course of the film" (Garcia 2014, 30).

In addition to "My Mammy," *The Jazz Singer* includes several songs that clearly are sung by Jolson using the Vitaphone sound synchronization technology that helped make this film one of the most frequently cited movies of the early 20th century. The first song the audience hears the mature Jack Robin sing is "Dirty Hands, Dirty Face," which is hardly a jazz song, but would have been known at the time of the story. At the conclusion of singing this song in the club, however, Robin says to the applauding crowd, "Wait a minute, wait a minute, you ain't heard nothin' yet," before launching into "Toot, Toot, Tootsie." In both songs, it is clear that actor Jolson's voice is on the film's soundtrack (I use this term for the sake of convenience; the "soundtrack" of *The Jazz Singer* was not recorded directly on the physical film as would be the case with later true film soundtracks), as the sound of his voice, his lip movements, his sung and spoken adlibs, and his handclaps clearly are synchronized. The performance of "Toot, Toot, Tootsie," in fact, is so filled with adlibs and handclaps that it seems almost designed to show audiences not accustomed to this kind of synchronization just what would be possible with the new technology.

Jack Robin's performance of Irving Berlin's "Blue Skies" for his mother while seated at the Rabinowitz's household piano during an expected visit back to his home is another sequence that seems almost to have designed to exhibit the new technology. Not only does Robin sing the song but he engages his mother in a dialogue, although he does most of the talking. The camera shot of the two characters clearly shows that Jack's statements and questions and his mother's responses are integrated into the soundtrack and not distant dubs. This is also one of the rare places in the film in which recorded spoken dialogue is presented; throughout the bulk of *The Jazz Singer*, silent-movie style captions are used while Louis Silvers's orchestral score is heard.

Almost all the other songs included in part in the movie, including the 13-year-old Jakie Rabinowitz singing "Waiting for the Robert E. Lee" and "My Gal Sal," are obvious sound dubs as the actors' lips do not move in synchronization with the sound. Generally, too, the obvious dubs are distinguished by the use of the new synchronization technology by the lower quality of the sound (not dissimilar to the sound of a 78-rpm shellac disc).

In addition to Al Jolson, who dominates the film, the cast of *The Jazz Singer* included Warner Oland as Cantor Rabinowitz (Jakie's father), Eugenie Besserer as Sara Rabinowitz (Jakie's mother), May McAvoy as Mary Dale (an actress-dancer who helps Jack Robin make it to Broadway), Otto Lederer as Moisha Yudelson (a busybody who helps advance the plot at several key points), Richard Tucker as Harry Lee, famed cantor Yossele Rosenblatt as himself, and Bobby Gordon as the young Jakie Rabinowitz. Alan Crosland directed the film, easily the most important film of his relatively brief career, and Darryl F. Zanuck produced it. For their efforts in producing the groundbreaking talkie, Zanuck and the Warner Brothers studio received an Honorary Academy Award.

The Jazz Singer has spawned several movie and television remakes over the years. The 1980 Jerry Leider film, which starred Neil Diamond, Lucie Arnaz, and Laurence Olivier, is the remake that remains the most readily available, although generally, the movie was not particularly successful. The 1980 version, however, resulted in a hugely successful soundtrack album, perhaps one of the crowning commercial successes of Neil Diamond's long career as a recording artist.

JESUS CHRIST SUPERSTAR

The 1973 film *Jesus Christ Superstar* began its genesis as a concept album back in 1970. Songwriters Andrew Lloyd Webber (music) and Tim Rice (lyrics) had already enjoyed some success a couple of years earlier with their show *Joseph and the Amazing Technicolor Dreamcoat.* As they conceived of a musical based on the Passion Week story of Jesus and his crucifixion from the viewpoint of Judas Iscariot, they had to build up to a full show slowly, at least in part because of concerns about how such a show might be received.

After a reasonable amount of success from the initial "Jesus Christ Superstar" single and the 1970 *Jesus Christ Superstar* concept album, a stage version of the show was launched, followed by the 1973 film. Norman Jewison and Robert Stigwood coproduced the film with Jewison directing it. The film had a strong ensemble cast that featured Ted Neeley as Jesus, Carl Anderson as Judas Iscariot, Yvonne Elliman as Mary Magdalene, Berry Dennen as Pontius Pilate, Bob Bingham as Calaphas, Kurt Yaghjian as Annas, Josh Mostel as King Herod, and Philip Toubus as Peter. In general, this was a cast with little previous experience in the film medium, although Neeley, Anderson, Bingham, and Elliman had performed in the stage version of the show.

In the 2004 special edition DVD release of the movie, lyricist Tim Rice discussed the motivation behind *Jesus Christ Superstar*, stating that he and Andrew Lloyd Webber wanted to "bring out [Jesus'] humanity" as seen through the eyes of Judas Iscariot, who in the musical sees Jesus as an ordinary man "who had gotten out of control" (Rice 2004). In the stage musical and the film version, Judas focuses on the political implications of Jesus' ministry, especially on the dynamics of the tension between the Jewish leaders and the Romans. Judas is not, however, the only disciple who fears that Jesus' ministry has gotten out of hand with respect to the threat that it poses to Romans who ruled the region at that time. In "Could We Start Again Please?," a wide range of Jesus' followers express the desire to call a halt and go back to the simplicity and less politically threatening start of Jesus' ministry.

In fact, Judas and the other characters' concern with the messianic movement getting out of hand resonates with some of the social unrest of the time of the release of the original *Jesus Christ Superstar* concept album, the subsequent stage musical, and the film. Specifically, the various versions of *Jesus Christ Superstar* came from the same general era as the Kent State University shootings (May 4, 1970), when it appeared that the antiwar movement had gone so far as to make it possible for the government (in the form of the Ohio National Guard) to use lethal force to counter social and political protest, the subsequent Jackson State College shootings (May 15, 1970), and the killing of Meredith Hunter by members of the Hells Angels at the violent Altamont Speedway Free Concert (December 6, 1969) while the Rolling Stones performed "Sympathy for the Devil." Although the film itself saw release a few years after these events, the antiwar movement was still ongoing, as was the social and political unrest around the world, and events such as the Kent State University shootings were still very much part of the popular consciousness.

The film offers the audience several value-added features not found in the stage version. Perhaps most obviously, *Jesus Christ Superstar* was filmed entirely in Israel, offering landscapes that tie the story back to the time of the events depicted. The landscapes include ruins, however, an important point to consider when viewing the film. This aspect of the location filming, as well as the fact that the cast members arrive at the ruins in an old hippie-style school bus suggest to the audience that this is not as much a cinematic recreation of the Holy Week story up to Good Friday, but is a movie about a contemporary interpretation of the Passion Play. This is a story filled with high emotions, and the close-up camera work on the principal singers allows them to visually exhibit those emotions to a degree that would be difficult on stage. This is perhaps the greatest added value that the film gives to this particular musical.

Whether audiences debate historical or biblical accuracy (e.g., Jesus telling a group of infirmed and diseased people seeking healing to "leave me alone" in the film) or other points of controversy that have surrounded the musical ever since it was first released as a concept album in 1970 or when the title song was released as a single the year before, *Jesus Christ Superstar* can rightly make a claim to be one of—if not the—first true rock opera. Both the stage version and the film are essentially sung throughout, and the story represents a more coherent narrative than the Who's *Tommy*, or *Hair*, which preceded both *Jesus Christ Superstar* and *Tommy*. For example, the scene in the film version of *Tommy* with Ann-Margret and Heinz Baked Beans has little to do with the Who's original concept album. In fact, it seems to be inspired more by the cover art for the band's album *The Who Sell Out* as well as the brief fake audio commercial for Heinz Baked Beans on the album. Likewise, although popular and successful with critics, the 1979 film version of *Hair* included many songs from the original loosely-constructed, happening-like show, but used as a superstructure, a storyline that was at most only implied in the original stage work.

There are a few aspects of *Jesus Christ Superstar* that might detract from the film for some audience members, aside from concerns that continue to be raised by Jewish groups and conservative Christian groups about some aspects of the plot. Although some viewers might not be aware of the fact, some of the scenes are reminiscent of earlier rock-related movies. Specifically, the scene in which Judas is pursued by tanks—during the song "Damned for All Time"—was anticipated by a similar scene in the Monkees' 1968 film *Head*. The scene in *Head*, in turn, appeared to have been influenced or inspired by a similar scene in the Beatles' 1965 film *Help!*. In addition, some viewers might find some of the cinematography effects too obvious or gimmicky, such as the stop-action that occurs mid-song when Jesus is asked if he will die for his disciples.

The musical's overture demonstrates the kind of accessibility that has continued to mark Andrew Lloyd Webber's work as a composer into the 21st century. In Judas's opening song, "Heaven on Their Minds," the audience is introduced to the idea that Lloyd Webber's approach to composition in the late 1960s and early 1970s was in the rock style but is more complex than much of the rock music of the era. For example, this opening song is in 7/8 meter. Mixed meters and asymmetrical meters such as 5/8 and 7/8 can be heard in other songs throughout the film. Perhaps the best-remembered example is Mary Magdalene's "Everything's Alright," which is in quintuple meter. "Everything's Alright," is also an excellent and early example of the lyrical and melodic hooks that would help make Lloyd Webber and Rice's musicals among the most commercially successful stage and film musicals of all time.

If one considers *Jesus Christ Superstar* as a body of work in song, Lloyd Webber and Rice's writing demonstrates a wide stylistic range, particularly from the musical standpoint. The ballads "Everything's Alright" and "I Don't Know How to Love Him" are contrasted by the hard rock style that permeates virtually everything that Judas sings and the ironic-sounding British music hall style of "Herod's Song." The two ballads and "Herod's Song" are also musical highlights of the film.

One of the central themes that runs through Jesus' songs throughout the musical is that none of his followers can truly comprehend his truth and an acknowledgment that they are fixated more on what he can bring them and on the political situation with Rome than on eternal salvation. That is also born out in several scenes, perhaps most clearly during the reenactment of the Last Supper. Here, the 12 apostles sing that in retirement they will write the gospels so that they (and not Jesus) are remembered after they die.

Throughout the film, there is very little evidence of positive change in any of Jesus' followers. The one exception would seem to be Mary Magdalene, who expresses the changes that have occurred in her life since she began following Jesus in the famous song "I Don't Know How to Love Him." Still, as Jesus is flogged near the end of the film, even King Herod appears to be disgusted as he realizes the extent of the pre-crucifixion brutality that Jesus had to endure.

In addition to Ted Neely as Jesus, several other cast members gave musical performances that help in significant ways to define their characters, such as Yvonne Elliman, also one of the stage cast members in the original production of *Jesus Christ Superstar*, in her role as Mary Magdalene. Carl Anderson brings a great deal of vocal intensity to Judas Iscariot. In fact, Anderson's singing is even intense in an era in which intense funk, hard rock, and heavy metal were prevailing styles. Josh Mostel, son of the famous comic actor Zero Mostel, played King Herod. Mostel's performance of "Herod's Song" is one of the movie's highlights. This is perhaps one of the songs that is likely to receive a negative reaction from some audience members because of Herod's mockery of Jesus; however, the comic music hall setting that Lloyd Webber gives to Rice's lyrics clearly establishes the flippant attitude of Herod.

Arguably, one of the more poignant parts of the movie comes at the end after the Passion Play has concluded and the actors and stagehands file back to their bus. In this scene, which would be difficult to recreate on stage, the audience can see that collectively and individually the cast and crew of the Passion Play have been changed by the experience. The exuberance that they exhibited at the opening, the smiles, the seemingly lighthearted manner in which they had assembled, gotten into their costumes, and set up some of the props—including the cross—is replaced with quiet and almost reverence. Especially notable is the transformation in Carl Anderson, whether he is interpreted as portraying himself, if he is portraying the actor who portrayed Judas, or whether his appearance was meant to suggest a change in Judas Iscariot's view of Jesus. In any case, the audience is left with the feeling that the *actors* were changed, regardless of whether the *characters* they portrayed in the Passion Play were or were not.

THE JUNGLE BOOK

An important part of the Disney animated musical franchise over the years, the original 1967 Disney film—the last animated movie produced by Walt Disney before he died—was based on Rudyard Kipling's 1894 collection of stories of the same name. Directed by Wolfgang Reitherman, and with songs by Robert B. Sherman and Richard M. Sherman and Terry Gilkyson, and a score by George Bruns, *The Jungle Book* adapted Kipling's stories of the Indian jungle so that they could be enjoyed by children of the 1960s. The 1967 film was commercially and critically successful. In fact, it is one of the most successful animated films of all time. *The Jungle Book* contained several songs that have become standards and spawned a live-action version in 1994, the animated *The Jungle Book 2* in 2003, and another live-action version in 2016. The film has also influenced video games, and several of its characters have appeared in subsequent films, musical and otherwise.

The voice actors who made up the cast of the film included a variety of well-known and not-as-familiar entertainment industry figures. Certainly, Phil Harris, as Baloo the bear; Sebastian Cabot, as Bagheera the panther; and Louis Prima as King Louie, the orangutan, were well-known entertainment figures at the time of the film's production, and audience members familiar with Harris, Cabot, and Prima would certainly recognize their contributions. These were among the more distinctive voicings of the animated characters in the film; however, one of the aspects of *The Jungle Book* that is likely to stay with viewers, in general, is how well the characters' voices match the personalities, and how iconic some of the voicings are. Among the not-well-known was Bruce Reitherman, the son of the movie's director, who voiced Mowgli, the man-cub.

In considering *The Jungle Book*, it is interesting to note that, according to Walt Disney's daughter, Diane Disney Miller, Disney was "more hands-on than he had been in years" in the production of this animated film (Disney Miller 2014). As a result, *The Jungle Book* may represent Disney's vision more fully than many of the preceding animated films produced by his studio, particularly during the time he was more focused on the establishment of Disneyland and on his television program.

The film opens with the opening of a book, which can be taken by viewers as a reference to the title but can also suggest that the story that is about to unfold ties in closely with Rudyard Kipling's *The Jungle Book* of the late 19th century. In actuality, although the basic plot comes out of the Kipling tales of Mowgli, the Disney film is considerably more lighthearted than Kipling's original story.

Although the musical focus of some viewers might be on the songs, particularly on the popular Terry Gilkyson composition "The Bare Necessities," the most memorable song in the film, George Bruns's score deserves focus as well. Bruns sets the mysterious mood of Kipling's story of the Indian jungle with his opening theme. Much of his score, however, adds humor, particularly in the entire sequence with the military parade and exercises of the Dawn Patrol, the group of elephants. Orchestrator Walter Sheets also deserves credit for some of the musical humor of sequences such as the Dawn Patrol scene. Sheets's use of tuba and contrabassoon in the scoring of the musical depiction of the clumsy exploits of the elephants might be stereotypical, but it is effective. Similarly, the use of the woodwinds in the opening of the film might seem somewhat stereotypical, but the scoring helps set the mood and the viewer's sense of place.

Easily the best-known song from the film, "The Bare Necessities" is performed primarily by Baloo the bear. The sole Terry Gilkyson song in the soundtrack, this piece reflects elements of early 20th-century music hall and New Orleans–style jazz music in its melody, harmony, and rhythm, and, perhaps most importantly, in its instrumentation. In it, Baloo sings about needing "the bare necessities of life"—in other words, a life of carefree simplicity. Eventually, Baloo is brought to the realization that he has important work to do in helping Bagheera ensure that Mowgli avoids the dangers of Shere Khan, the human-hating tiger, and gets safely to the man-village. Despite nearly being killed by Shere Khan, Baloo returns to his carefree nature by the end of the movie; *The Jungle Book* concludes with Baloo and Bagheera walking into the jungle after successfully getting Mowgli to the man-village as they sing a reprise of "The Bare Necessities." Interestingly, the basic premise set up by "The Bare Necessities" in its first iteration early in the movie returned decades later in "Hakuna Matata" in *The Lion King*.

Another musical highlight of *The Jungle Book* is the work of Louis Prima, as King Louie the orangutan, performing the jump blues song "I Wan'na Be Like You." Robert and Richard Sherman provided Prima with a song that reflects both the jazz style with which Prima was associated, and calls to mind the work of Cab Calloway and Louis Jordan in the 1940s.

The song "Trust in Me" is sung by Sterling Holloway as Kaa, the obviously untrustworthy snake. Although the tune is not as memorable as those of "The Bare Necessities" and "I Wan'na Be Like You," the cloying request for trust from Mowgli (so that the man-cub can be eaten by the snake) fits the character. In retrospect, because Holloway was so closely associated with the animated Winnie the Pooh in several Disney films starting in 1966, some viewers might find his voicing of Kaa a little odd—or at least may hear Winnie the Pooh in a different, somewhat disconcerting light, if they make the connection with the seductive snake.

A quartet of vultures sings "We're Your Friends" in a barbershop quartet style. Although apparently connections to the Beatles and other popular British pop musicians was toned down in this sequence, there are strong hints of the Beatles, particularly in the Liverpool accents that come out particularly strongly from a couple of the vultures. The connection to British Invasion pop music is also confirmed by the fact that one of the vultures was voiced by Chad Stuart, part of the duo Chad and Jeremy, who enjoyed several well-known pop hits in the mid-1960s.

In retrospect, perhaps the one aspect of *The Jungle Book* that was not as thoroughly developed as it might have been was Mowgli, the man-cub's return to the man-village. He seems smitten with an unidentified girl, voiced by Darlene Carr after she sings "My Own Home," but it is difficult to understand how easily and quickly Mowgli decides to go to the village considering that he spent nearly all of his previous life among wolves, panthers, and a carefree bear.

The film concludes with Baloo the bear and Bagheera the panther walking back into the jungle singing a reprise of "The Bare Necessities." This emphasizes the fun and carefree feel that Disney brought to what were really much darker stories in Rudyard Kipling's original book. However, this is one of the aspects of the Disney animated musicals—particularly before the renaissance that the studio enjoyed in the late 1980s through the 1990s—that is often commented on: they tended to be nearly, if not completely, disarming, and always had a happy ending in which all was resolved.

THE KING AND I

The King and I has an interesting and ongoing history. Anna Leonowens, the English schoolteacher, tutor, and governess, and King Mongkut, ruler of Siam, were real historical figures. Leonowens wrote of her experiences in the 1870 book *The English Governess at the Siamese Court: Being Recollection of Six Years in the Royal Palace at Bangkok.*

Margaret Landon's 1944 novel *Anna and the King of Siam* (Landon 1944) fictionalized the story and was the literary source on which Richard Rodgers's and Oscar Hammerstein's 1951 musical *The King and I* and the subsequent film are based.

At the time of the coronation of the great-great-grandson of King Mongkut on May 1, 2019, the stage musical, the 1956 film, the 1999 remake, and Margaret Landon's fictionalized account of Anna Leonowens's experiences in Siam in the 1860s were all still banned in Thailand. Leonowens's original account is not only available in the country it has also been translated into Thai (Wongcha-um 2019). The ban on the fictionalized accounts would seem to be a result of the portrayal of King Mongkut, suggestions of a romance between Anna and the King, and possibly the suggestion that it was Leonowens—and not King Mongkut—who prompted the reforms that took place during Mongkut's rule.

The original production of *The King and I*, which starred Yul Brynner as King Mongkut and Gertrude Lawrence as Anna Leonowens, was a critical and commercial success. Brynner, who starred in the 1956 film, would later star in revivals of the stage version of the musical, playing the role of the King of Siam thousands of times. Deborah Kerr played Anna in the film, with her vocals in the songs provided by Marni Nixon.

When considering the 1956 film it is worth noting that it was truncated somewhat from the stage musical. Although this, and some dialogue changes, might be noticeable to viewers familiar with the stage version, the film continues to stand up on its own very well. Musical highlights include Anna's songs "I Whistle a Happy Tune," "Hello, Young Lovers," and "Getting to Know You." Richard Rodgers's score is also rich and betrays possible influences from the standard orchestral repertoire. Most notably in this regard is the fact that "The March of the Siamese Children" contains hints of Tchaikovsky's *Nutcracker* ballet music. At the same time, the "Small House of Uncle Thomas" sequence finds Rodgers writing faux-Asian music which might be considered stereotypical.

Certainly, one of the highlights of the film—and one of the scenes that is often used to represent *The King and I*—is the entire "Shall We Dance" sequence. The music is very much in the classic Broadway showtune tradition and Anna and the King use so much of the available space in their dance that this remains one of the biggest-feeling dance sequences on film, despite the fact that it involves just two characters. Although the scene can be understood as an indication of a growing relationship between Anna and the King, it is interesting to consider for another important subtext. The fact that King Mongkut is so adept at Western dance and that composer Rodgers sets the dance in the classic Broadway style suggests—without using words—just how intent the King was at bringing what he saw as the best of Western ways to his country.

One of the minor niggles that some audience members might have with the film is that it is clear in some cases when the actor on screen is not providing the vocals. In part, this may be because Yul Brynner's performance of "A Puzzlement" and "Song of the King" are so well-synced compared with some of the songs performed by Kerr/Nixon. The "We Kiss in a Shadow" sequence, which includes overdubbing for both actors, also suffers from some lack of synchronization. About the only song in the movie that has not aged particularly well is Terry Saunders's performance of "Something Wonderful" as Lady Thiang. Some viewers may find the performance to be too studied, too playing-to-the-back-of-the-house in nature, and to be as believable as the other non-over-dubbed performances (e.g., those by Brynner).

Despite concerns in Thailand about the portrayal of King Mongkut and the historical accuracy of the musical and the novel on which it was based, the story has held up well, compared with some other mid-20th-century musicals. The theme of women's empowerment runs throughout the film. Although it is the source of some of the movie's humor, there is also a seriousness to the fictionalized Anna's pursuit of her promised house outside the palace walls, her use of Harriet Beecher Stowe's *Uncle Tom's Cabin* to teach the evils of slavery to the King and his children, and so on. Not necessarily dwelt upon in the film, but certainly part of the storyline, is a form of human trafficking, in the form of the King of Burma's gift of Tuptim (portrayed by Rita Moreno) to the King of Siam.

The American Film Institute ranked *The King and I* at No. 11 on its list of the 25 greatest movie musicals of all time (American Film Institute 2006). The Institute also ranked "Shall We Dance" No. 54 on its list of the 100 greatest movie songs of all time (American Film Institute 2004). The ongoing popularity of the story and the musical, albeit outside of Thailand, is confirmed by the 1999 film *Anna and the King* (a non-musical) and the 1999 animated film *The King and I* based on the Rodgers and Hammerstein musical.

LA LA LAND

La La Land, written and directed by Damien Chazelle with music by Justin Hurwitz, starred Ryan Gosling, Emma Stone, John Legend, and Rosemarie DeWitt. The plot primarily concerns the relation between Gosling's character (Sebastian Wilder), a jazz pianist, and Stone's character

(Mia Dolan), an actress, struggles with prevailing musical attitudes, and the struggles between ambition and love. With its defense of the jazz idiom and old-fashioned storyline, *La La Land* suggests the musicals of the mid-20th century. Although some viewers might detect a sense of patronizing in a white character, Gosling's Sebastian Wilder, defending jazz (originally an African American genre), that aspect of *La La Land* only seemed to faze some movie critics. The title of Ruby Lott-Lavigna's *Wired* review, "*La La Land* Review: An Ambitious Musical Soured by Racist Overtones," reflects the reaction of some critics to the role of Gosling's character (Lott-Lavigna 2017). In stark contrast, however, *Rolling Stone*'s Peter Travers gave the film a thoroughly glowing review (Travers 2016) as did numerous other critics. *La La Land* received 14 Academy Award nominations and won the Oscars for Best Actress, Best Director, Best Cinematography, Best Production Design, Best Original Score, and Best Original Song for "City of Stars." Rather than interpreting Sebastian as a symbol of the great white savior of jazz, it might make more sense to view him as a lover of the genre and as the traditionalist he is. However, Sebastian's connection to the jazz of an earlier age presents one of the film's many points of irony. One of the more notable quotes from John Legend's character, Keith, perhaps says it best. When describing the impact of the jazz greats of the past as being rooted in the fact that they were musical revolutionaries, Legend's character asks Sebastian: "How are you going to be a revolutionary, if you're such a traditionalist?"

The retro nature of *La La Land* is presented to the audience at the very opening, in which the old CinemaScope of the 1950s and 1960s is referenced. Although the time period presented in the storyline clearly is the early 21st century—probably very close to the time of the film's release in 2016, there are other subtle and not-so-subtle visual touches that represent the connection between the age of the classic Hollywood movie musical, the 1930s–1950s, and the present. For example, in one scene Sebastian is seated in front of a mural on a wall that is painted in the style of old mid-20th-century location-based postcards. A classic Fiat automobile can be seen in several scenes on the Hollywood movie lot area near across the street from the coffee shop in which Stone's character works before becoming a successful film actress. The automobile connects the story back to the 1950s, although one might simply see it as a prop on the story's movie lot. In addition, the musical styles and dance styles throughout the film suggest a strong connection with the 1940s.

Part of the success of *La La Land* has to be attributed to the fact that the film plays with audience expectations and causes the audience to question what is supposed to represent reality and what is supposed to represent a fantasy world. The mixing of reality and fantasy is introduced to the audience immediately at the film's opening. The audience sees numerous cars at a standstill on a Los Angeles freeway. Among the drivers are Sebastian, who listens to a brief jazz piano lick on his cassette deck over and over, and Mia, who rehearses a script that is used later in the story in an unsuccessful audition the would-be actress takes. Suddenly, characters begin exiting their vehicles and start singing and dancing to the musical's opening number. The colorful clothing is somewhat reminiscent of mid-20th-century musicals—the colorful costumes in the large-scale dance scenes in *The Music Man*, for example. Finally, the motorists return to their cars and begin driving in stop-and-go traffic. This kind of sudden cut between believability and fantasy takes place many times throughout the rest of the movie.

Some of the juxtapositions are so jarring that they add to the humor of the movie. One that stands out is the song "Someone in the Crowd" performed by Mia and three of her would-be actress friends as they dance down the street to Mia's automobile on their way to a party. The musical style suggests ties to mid-20th-century jazz and the fantasy world created by the four singing and dancing down a street with absolutely no traffic around them also suggests the fantasy world of the mid-20th-century classical movie musical. This world of fantasy comes to a jarring halt as they step into a very much 21st-century Toyota Prius hybrid.

There is something enchanting about the non-slick singing and dancing of the movie's two principals, Gosling and Stone, that adds to the movie's interesting blurring of lines between fantasy and reality. It is also one aspect of the film that stands in contrast to the "real" classic movie musicals of the mid-20th century, a time period in which a ghost singer such as Marni Nixon provided vocals for the roles played by movie stars such as Audrey Hepburn, Natalie Wood, Janet Leigh, and Rita Moreno.

In the opening sequence of the film, a freeway in which traffic is at a literal standstill becomes a soundstage for an elaborate dance scene. In fact, colorful clothes are worn by what turns out to be all the motorists who eventually participate in the song

Another point of irony, liable to be lost on some viewers who do not have a thorough knowledge of jazz history, is that Keith's ensemble, which seems to mix jazz, R&B, and electronic pop, is called the Messengers. This was the name of a jazz group, originally called the Jazz Messengers, in the 1950s—1990 that originally represented fresh-sounding bop, hard-bop, and post-bop music, but continued to maintain ties to the jazz tradition even as other jazz ensembles—such as the Crusaders and Miles Davis's ensembles—incorporated new popular music trends into their sounds. The original Messengers—not Keith's group—also weathered such storms as the free jazz of the 1960s.

Some other subtle ties to earlier films include a party scene in which Emma Stone's character is seen talking to the host, a man who might immediately call to mind the character Tony Lacey (played by Paul Simon) in the 1977 Woody Allen film *Annie Hall*. The '80s cover band in which Sebastian plays keyboards in the party sequence is portrayed in a particularly effective humorous way. The songs "Take on Me," originally by A-Ha, and "I Ran (So Far Away)," originally by A Flock of Seagulls, are presented effectively as spot-on clichés of 1980s new wave pop, and about as far away from the kind of work that a jazz traditionalist such as Sebastian would want to play.

There is something vaguely familiar-sounding about much of the music that Justin Hurwitz composed for the movie. The song "A Lovely Night," for example, bears at least some resemblance to a major-key version of the classic song "Autumn Leaves," particularly in Hurwitz's use of sequential motives to build the melody.

The Griffith Observatory and planetarium flying dance scene is pure mid-20th-century movie musical fantasy. It should also be noted that the scoring in this particular dance sequence is full and uses the various orchestral instruments in a mid-20th-century style, as opposed to the more block scoring and rock band-influenced style of many movie musicals of the early 21st century.

The blurring of the lines between what is reality for Sebastian and Mia and what is part of the fantasy world that perhaps comes from the fantasy lands of the character's minds and imaginations mentioned earlier is also effective in setting up the final reality of the relationship of the characters as a surprise—if not a shock—when Mia and her husband leave Sebastian's jazz club and Sebastian and Mia catch one another's eyes. Clearly, the two characters maintain a tie, but ultimately their relationship was about encouraging and pushing each other to follow their dreams, specifically, their career dreams and ambitions.

New York Times reviewer A. O. Scott wrote, "*La La Land* succeeds both as a fizzy fantasy and a hard-headed fable, a romantic comedy and a showbiz melodrama, a work of sublime artifice and touching authenticity" (Scott 2016). Scott also writes about the retro nature of the characters and the entire conception and construction of the movie, and the filming techniques that were used to capture the feel of a mid-20th-century movie musical. Writer Anthony Carew (2018) places *La La Land* in the same milieu as Gene Kelly's favorite *Singin' in the Rain*: a meta-musical, or a musical about musicals. I would argue that *La La*

Land is not as much a musical about musicals, but a musical about deliberately jarring contrasts (love versus career ambition; fantasy world versus the harsh reality of life; a love for an artistic form that is very much alive in one person's life, but appears to be dying in the greater world at large; mid-20th-century aesthetics versus 2010s aesthetics; and so on).

Although Justin Hurwitz's songs and instrumental pieces are engaging, they reflect the forms and styles of a by-gone era. As a result, they have little connection to contemporary popular music. Hence, one can argue that the soundtrack does not contain bonafide, new-sounding hits that are likely to be standards years from now. The music is, however, immediately accessible, particularly to listeners familiar with the musical traditions from which Hurwitz draws. The music from the soundtrack was popular, however, outside the context of the film, with the motion picture soundtrack album making it to No. 2 on the *Billboard* 200, a notable achievement for a soundtrack album that contains a relatively heavy concentration of instrumental music, almost all of which has a decidedly retro feel.

THE LION KING

Part of the so-called Disney Renaissance of the late 1980s through the 1990s, *The Lion King* continued the pattern set by the movies *Beauty and the Beast* and *Aladdin* of Walt Disney Studios' production of animated musicals that were designed for a general—as opposed to a children's—audience. Although before the completion of *The Lion King* some writers might have wondered if this film could possibly achieve the cross-generational success of its immediate predecessors (see, for example, Welkos 1993), arguably *The Lion King* was an even greater success, particularly in the home video market.

The film included important contributions by some of the heavyweights of the movie and music world. Hans Zimmer provided the score, which referenced African music, as well as the dramatic style of 19th-century European orchestral music on the order of Richard Wagner's "Ride of the Valkyries" and Modest Mussorsky's "Night on Bald Mountain." Composer Elton John and lyricist Tim Rice wrote the film's original songs, which included "Circle of Life," "Can You Feel the Love Tonight," "I Just Can't Wait to Be King," "Be Prepared," and "Hakuna Matata." Voices for the various animal characters were provided by Matthew Broderick as the mature Simba; James Earl Jones as Simba's father, King Mufasa; Jonathan Taylor as the young Simba; Whoopi Goldberg, Cheech Marin, and Jim Cummings as the three principal hyenas; Jeremy

Irons as Mufasa's jealous, evil brother Scar; Robert Guillaume as Rafiki, the baboon; Ernie Sabella as Pumbaa, the warthog; Rowan Atkinson as Zazu, the hornbill who serves as King Mufasa's factotum; Madge Sinclair as Sarabi, Simba's mother; Nathan Lane as the humorous meerkat Timon; and Moira Kelly as Nala, Simba's friend and later his mate; as well as other vocalists who provided the singing voices for some of the characters. Roger Allers and Rob Minkoff directed the film.

The Lion King opens with the iconic sunrise scene, used in various print and electronic advertisements for the movie, and the song "Circle of Life." "Circle of Life" establishes the film's overarching theme, and it returns at the movie's conclusion as Rafiki presents the offspring of Simba and Nala to the animals of the Pride Lands as the future Lion King.

After the first iteration of "Circle of Life," Rafiki, the wise baboon, presents the cub Simba to the other animals, who genuflect to show their allegiance to the future king. Simba demonstrates his eagerness to become king in the future in the song "I Just Can't Wait to Be King." In part because of the style of Elton John's music on this song and in part because of the performance by singer Jason Weaver—who, incidentally, had portrayed the young Michael Jackson in the television miniseries *The Jacksons: An American Dream*—"I Just Can't Wait to Be King" exhibits some of the feel of early Michael Jackson and Jackson 5 recordings along the lines of the 1970 hit "ABC."

In addition to the oblique reference to the music of the Jackson 5, *The Lion King* connects back to other pop culture icons. Perhaps one of the clearest examples is the use of geometric patterns in the animated choreography during the production number of "I Just Can't Wait to Be King." This strongly suggests the continuing influence of Busby Berkeley's choreography and film direction in movie musicals of the 1930s and 1940s. The overhead shots of the animated animal dancers (in these geometric formations) also bear the touch of Berkeley. Part of the success of *The Lion King*, as well as Disney's *Beauty and the Beast* and *Aladdin*, is that these films, albeit animated, were not so much children's movies as they were musicals aimed at a wide-ranging age demographic. As mentioned earlier, *The Lion King* was successful in this regard, becoming one of the highest-selling home video releases of all time. It can be argued that part of the ability of the film to connect with older audiences came out of the seriousness of some of the subject matter (e.g., life and the inevitability of death and the pure evil of the character Scar) but also out of the pop culture references to the early 1970s and earlier decades.

Some audiences might be surprised at the effectiveness of some of the material written by Elton John and Tim Rice, particularly considering that John is most frequently associated with commercial pop music and Rice is most closely associated with darker songs that he wrote for several rock operas with composer Andrew Lloyd Webber. Scar's song "Be Prepared," for example, finds Elton John writing appropriately sinister-sounding music to match Rice's lyrics and Scar's evil intents. It should also be noted that "Be Prepared" also contains historical references that might be missed by younger audience members, but that could easily be understood by older viewers familiar with 20th-century authoritarianism: the goose-stepping of the hyenas who (at least during this song) are loyal to Scar immediately calls to mind scenes of military parades in the Soviet Union, Nazi Germany, and other authoritarian states.

Other songs, most notably "Can You Feel the Love Tonight," reflect the more conventional pop musical sensibilities of Elton John. This is also an interesting song structurally as it is built like a conventional Tin Pan Alley-era verse-chorus piece, with Timon's introduction serving as the verse. So the song connects a standard form associated with musicals from the first half of the 20th century with a pop music style suggestive of John's hit ballads of the mid-1970s such as "Don't Let the Sun Go Down on Me" and "Someone Saved My Life Tonight."

Despite the depiction of some of the harsh realities of life and death, including the murder of Mufasa by his brother, there are many comic elements to *The Lion King*, generally provided by the hornbill, the warthog, and the meerkat. In one scene, the caged hornbill sings part of the African American sorrow song "Nobody Knows the Trouble I've Seen" before being reprimanded by Scar. He then breaks into the iconic 1963 Disney song "It's a Small World," which causes Scar to admonish the hornbill to sing "anything but that!"

Although the bulk of the soundtrack consists of Hans Zimmer's score and Elton John and Tim Rice's songs, it includes more already-existing material than just "It's a Small World." The soundtrack also includes bits of other songs that are worked into the storyline such as "Hawaiian War Chant" and "The Lion Sleeps Tonight." In fact, among the controversies surrounding *The Lion King* was legal action that was undertaken by the estate of Solomon Linda, the original writer of "The Lion Sleeps Tonight," over Disney's use of the song in the film.

Although the storyline of *The Lion King* is easy enough to follow, there is at least one temporal oddity to the film. During Pumbaa and Timon's song "Hakuna Matata" Simba visibly ages from a cub to a mature young adult lion. This suggests that he lived with the meerkat and warthog for some time and absorbed their philosophy of letting whatever happens in the world to roll off your back. Later, this philosophy comes into conflict with Simba's sense of duty when he is called upon to return to the Pride Lands and rescue the animals from the devastation that they suffered under the leadership of Scar. In this respect, "Hakuna Matata" plays a similar role in *The Lion King* to "The Bare Necessities" in *The Jungle Book*. It should be noted that "Hakuna Matata" became another source of *The Lion King* controversy when a petition was circulated in Africa calling upon Disney to release its trademark on the African expression (Adeoye and Adeng 2018).

Another point of controversy surrounding *The Lion King* was the charge that a hidden message (e.g., the word "SEX") could be seen in the stars in one particular sequence. Some right-wing religious groups and conspiracy theorists included this on a list of various messages that they claimed Disney artists were using for subversive purposes (for coverage of the controversy, see, for example, Mikkelson 1996). Interestingly, Disney's artists did admit to including a hidden message; however, they claimed that the stars spelled "SFX," a tribute to the film's special effects crew.

The film also elicited controversy around issues of race, economic class, and immigration. For example, Robert Gooding-Williams (1995) wrote a study of *The Lion King* for *Social Identities* that suggested that the film could be understood as a metaphor for concerns of the upper socioeconomic classes about the urban poor (represented by the hyenas). Subsequently, writing in the same journal, John Morton (1996) argued that Gooding-Williams's argument was too firmly rooted in Marxism—particularly Gooding-Williams's view that Scar was a political revolutionary and that his portrayal as an evil character represented mainstream capitalistic society's suspicions about revolutionaries. Writing in *Aztlan*, Manuel M. Martin-Rodriguez (2000) suggested that *The Lion King* contained an anti-immigrant—particularly an anti-Hispanic immigrant—message. Martin-Rodriguez pointed to the fact that the hyena voiced by Cheech Marin sounded Hispanic and that the hyena voiced by Whoopi Goldberg sounded black as problematic. Even more to the point, the devastation that is caused to Pride Lands comes solely as a result of Scar's invitation to the hyenas to immigrate into the land from which they were once blocked. That critics and scholars argued about the possible presence of political or social messages in *The Lion King*, or whether the story was more of a morality play, suggests the importance of this film as part of the popular cultural landscape of the mid-1990s.

In a later era more concerned with cultural appropriation and stereotyping one could possibly pick apart *The Lion King* for depicting African stories through animals. A Marxist reading of *The Lion King* might suggest that animals were chosen because Disney thought—or wanted to depict—Africans as less than human. It should be noted, however, that the Disney franchise has a long history of telling stories using animals as metaphors for human beings, and indigenous mythologies from around the world often use animals metaphorically. It is, perhaps, well-known film critic Roger Ebert's review of *The Lion King*, which takes the story as a face-value, mythology-inspired metaphorical tale, that best captures the merits and the reason for the success of this movie (Ebert 1994).

The American Film Institute ranked "Hakuna Matata" No 99 on its list of the 100 greatest movie songs of all time (American Film Institute 2004). Despite the fact that the original version of *The Lion King* is a fairly recent film, the Library of Congress has added it to the National Film Registry.

Although originally released as a stand-alone film, *The Lion King* has become a franchise for Disney. The movie spawned the 1998 sequel *The Lion King II: Simba's Pride*, the 2004 prequel *The Lion King 1 1/2*, television programs, and a Broadway stage musical version. *The Lion King* was a rare film that was converted into a 3D version for re-release. In 2019, on the occasion of the 25th anniversary of the original film, Disney released a remake of *The Lion King*, the film made using computer-generated—and more realistic-looking—animation. The 2019 version of the story received mixed reviews; however, its opening was commercially successful. In fact, at the time of the film's release, analysts estimated that the box office revenue for *The Lion King* could be between $175 million and $200 million at its U.S. debut (Whitten 2019a).

LITTLE SHOP OF HORRORS

Perhaps one of the more unlikely musicals, Alan Menken and Howard Ashman's off-off-Broadway show *Little Shop of Horrors* was based on the low-budget 1960 Roger Corman film *The Little Shop of Horrors*. The basic premise of both the Corman film and the Menken and Ashman musical version revolves around a florist's assistant who raises a man-eating plant. Despite the title of the Corman film and the musical version, the story is very much more comedy and spoof than horror. For their original musical, Menken and Ashman wrote the songs in the style of the popular music of the early 1960s, thus preserving some of the period feel of the Corman film.

The 1986 film adaptation of the 1982 Menken and Ashman musical was directed by Frank Oz and starred Rick Moranis as Seymour

Kelborne, the nerdy florist's assistant; Ellen Green as Audrey; Vincent Gardenia as flower shop owner Mr. Mushnik; and others such as Steve Martin as the dentist Orin Scrivello; Bill Murray; John Candy; and Jim Belushi. Moranis was known primarily as a cast member and writer for *Second City Television* (*SCTV*) and for his popular comedy sketches with fellow *SCTV* cast member Dave Thomas as fictional Canadian brothers Doug and Bob McKenzie; however, he was perfect for the role of Seymour. The film's connections to the American and Canadian Second City comedy troupes are confirmed by the presence of Murray, Belushi, Candy, and Martin, who had ties to comedy television and to the Second City-related programs *SCTV* and *Saturday Night Live* of the late 1970s and early 1980s. Director Frank Oz's longtime connection to Jim Henson's Muppets is manifested in a cameo appearance by Henson's daughter Heather, not to mention the puppeteer-operated killer plant, Audrey II, the other "star" of the film.

For the movie version of *Little Shop of Horrors*, the dark ending was changed; instead of the leads succumbing to Audrey II, Moranis's Seymour, having learned a valuable lesson, manages to electrocute the plant; Seymour and the human Audrey apparently live happily ever after. Well, except that in the very closing fadeout the audience sees that in the perfectly manicured flowerbed of their stereotypically perfect suburban home grows a baby version of the Audrey II.

The period feel of the stage musical is also preserved in the movie, with a Black, "girl-group"-style trio, appropriately consisting of characters named Crystal, Ronnette, and Chiffon (after popular early-1960s black female vocal groups) functioning like a Greek chorus providing narration and commentary on the story. Portrayed by Tichina Arnold, Michelle Weeks, and Tisha Campbell, the trio captures not only the style of the Chiffons, the Ronnettes, and the Crystals but also the gospel-inflected soul sound that would become more prominent as the 1960s rolled on. Adding to the early-1960s tie in *Little Shop of Horrors* is the fact that Bob Gaudio, a one-time member of the Four Seasons, served as the movie and the soundtrack album's musical producer.

Even though the premise of the story seems like such an unlikely candidate for a musical comedy and a film adaptation, movie critics and film scholars generally had largely favorable reactions to *Little Shop of Horrors*. For example, in his book *Musicals in Film: A Guide to the Genre*, Thomas S. Hischak wrote, "The Off-Broadway musical was not an easy thing to put on film, but the filmmakers by and large pulled it off with a gleeful grin" (Hischak 2017, 354). In describing her favorite film, *The Guardian's*, Jessica Hopkins wrote "*Little Shop* is a love story. It's also a story about conquering your demons and discovering the best you can be—even if it takes a blood-guzzling talking plant to get you there. That said, for me it's not really about the story, it's about the experience" (Hopkins 2011). *New York Times* critic Walter Goodman praised the performances by Moranis and Green, as well as Levi Stubbs's voicing of Audrey II, the cameo appearances by Steve Martin and Bill Murray, and the Audrey II special effects (Goodman 1987).

Although the campy, and at times silly storyline, might not seem like the stuff of a must-hear movie musical, it seems clear that the songs and production numbers are what for some viewers, such as the afore-mentioned Jessica Hopkins, form the real entertainment meat of *Little Shop of Horrors*. In an article titled "18 Movie Musicals You Can Actu-ally Sing Along With," Tasha Robinson wrote of *Little Shop of Horrors*, that it is easier to sing along with than *The Producers*, "particularly on over-the-top goofs like 'Skid Row' and 'Suddenly, Seymour,' which seem to be satirizing classical musicals and channeling them at the same time" (Robinson 2006). The revisiting of the musical styles of the late 1950s and the early 1960s was not limited to *Little Shop of Horrors*. Other musicals, notably *Forever Plaid* (staged in 1989 and released as a film in 2008) for its somewhat macabre plot, also turned to the music of that earlier era, as had earlier musicals such as *Grease*.

Although Rick Moranis provides the lead vocals in several songs in the movie, his first performance of "Suddenly Seymour," which reprises later in the film, is worth consideration. Moranis brings out the nerdiness of his character in song as well as in his customary non-singing work as a comic actor. His singing is not studied—however, not entirely without technique—and is entirely believable as a representation of Seymour, a character who is always trying his best, despite the fact that things do not work out entirely smoothly for him. There is an element of humor in the song—not only because of Howard Ashman's lyrics—but also because of deliberate mismatch of an arrangement that includes several gospel music cues and Seymour's character.

In addition to "Suddenly, Seymour" and "Skid Row," a big pro-duction number from early in the show, other musical highlights in the film adaptation of *Little Shop of Horrors* include Steve Martin's performance as a sadistic, Elvis Presley-look-alike dentist in the song "Dentist!," and Levi Stubbs (one of the original members of the Four Tops)—voicing Audrey II—in "Mean Green Mother from Outer Space." The element of the music that cannot be ignored is the reoccurring pres-ence of Crystal, Ronnette, and Chiffon. These elegantly dressed—picture the 1964 and 1965 publicity photos and television appearances of the

Supremes—women stand in sharp contrast to the characters on the streets of the movie's Skid Row. This adds significantly to the sense of humor-through-incompatibilities that runs through the movie. However, the trio provides impressive vocals with a strong technique that stands in sharp contrast to the lead vocals of the much, much plain-sounding principal characters.

In comparing the original stage version of the musical to what was finally released as the film, it is important to note that the two versions end quite differently. Some audiences might find that movie's ending seems more consistent with the rest of the storyline than the darker ending of the stage musical, which was also supposed to be the ending of the film but was changed. The sight of Seymour and Audrey's perfect suburban house with a baby Audrey II growing in the flowerbed might suggest a sequel in the works; however, it also allows the audience's imagination to consider just what comes next in the saga of Seymour, Audrey, and the plant that we might dub Audrey III.

Another important point of comparison is in how the film medium allowed Frank Oz and the movie's technicians to create a more impressive Audrey II than what might typically be possible on stage. The movie version of the killer plant is most impressive beginning in the sequence in which it breaks free of its pot, manages to raid the cash register for a coin, and makes a phone call to Audrey. Likewise, the movie's climax—the battle between Audrey II and Seymour—is something that just could not be accomplished on stage, and is, in fact, part of the storyline that veers away from that of the stage show and the ending originally intended for the movie.

Although an unlikely premise for a movie musical, *Little Shop of Horrors*—in somewhat the same vein as *Rocky Horror Picture Show*—is an over-the-top, campy, unbelievable tale. It is also one of the funnier movie musicals of its era.

MAMMA MIA!

It has been this author's experience that people either love the music of the Scandinavian group ABBA or they hate it. Undeniably, however, ABBA was a huge commercial success in the world of pop music from 1972 to 1982 with hits such "Dancing Queen," "Mamma Mia," "Knowing Me, Knowing You," "Take a Chance on Me," and others. In total, the group, which consisted of Björn Ulvaeus, Benny Andersson, Agnetha Fältskog, and Anni-Frid Lyngstad, placed just over a dozen singles in the U.S. Top 10; however, generally, ABBA enjoyed even greater commercial and critical success around the world than in the United States. Catherine Johnson's 1999 musical *Mamma Mia!* builds a story around the compositions of Ulvaeus and Andersson—all of ABBA's major hits—becoming one of the most successful and longest-running musicals in London and New York.

The 2008 movie version included a strong star-filled cast. The principals were Amanda Seyfried as Sophie Sheridan, a bride-to-be; Meryl Streep as Donna Sheridan, Sophie's mother and the owner of Villa Donna, a hotel on a Greek island; Pierce Brosnan as Sam Carmichael, an architect and one of Sophie's possible fathers; Colin Firth as Harry Bright, a banker and another of Sophie's possible fathers; Stellan Skarsgård as Bill Anderson, an adventurer and travel writer and another of Sophie's possible fathers; Julie Walters as Josie Mulligan, a one-time member of Donna Sheridan's old singing group, Donna and the Dynamos; Christine Baranski as Tanya Chesham-Leigh, the other one-time member of Donna and the Dynamos; and Dominic Cooper as Sky, Sophie's fiancé. Ashley Lilley and Rachel McDowall, as Sophie's friends and bridesmaids, and Philip Michael and Chris Jarvis also played significant roles in the film.

The premise of the musical is that Sophie was raised solely by her mother who never told her who her father was. Sophie subsequently finds her mother's diary and tracks down her possible fathers to three men. Sophie tells her friends and bridesmaids Ali and Lisa about the men and her invitation to them to her wedding upon their arrival to the island; however, Donna remains unaware that her daughter knows the identities of the three men who may be her father and that she has invited all three men to her wedding. Donna's former bandmates, Tanya and Josie, also arrive for the wedding, which provides Donna and the Dynamos a chance for a musical reunion. Ultimately, after much humor, Donna's conflicting emotions once her three former lovers arrive on the island, and Sophie's collapse when she realizes that all three of her prospective fathers intend to walk her down the aisle, Donna and Sam's romance is rekindled; it is they who are married at the end of the movie. Sky and Sophie do not get married, but instead, start off on a travel adventure together. Sam, Bill, and Harry decide that they do not want to know who was really Sophie's father; instead, they will all share as fathers.

Compared with the stage version of the show, the film provides numerous opportunities to highlight location scenes, and the reality of the Greek island scenery makes *Mamma Mia!* stand out from the soundstage- and backlot-heavy movie musicals of the early and mid-20th century. In this regard, *Mamma Mia!* can be understood as a 21st-century descendant of *On the Town* and *Gigi*. Unlike those two earlier musicals, which had begun life as movie musicals, however, *Mamma Mia!* clearly retains ties to its original stage version: contrasting the sense of realism that the locations give the film, *Mamma Mia!* includes several production numbers (e.g., "Money, Money, Money" and "Dancing Queen") that reflect the earliest, prelocation, movie musicals.

One of the challenges of adapting a show that refers to specific time periods—such as *Mamma Mia!*—a decade after the premiere of the original show is that some of the references can create believability problems. In the case of *Mamma Mia!*, references to the "flower-power" era in the song "Our Last Summer" and even the use of ABBA songs to possibly represent the time period in which Donna and the Dynamos was in its heyday create problems. For one thing, ABBA was active from 1974 to 1982 after the flower-power era ("Our Last Summer" would have worked temporally as a reflection back to the late 1960s and early 1970s when ABBA released it on record in 1980); for another, if Sophie had been conceived during the flower-power era, the character would have to be significantly older than Seyfried appears to be; for another, if Donna and the Dynamos was part of the ABBA era, and that was the time period in which Sophie was conceived, then the references to the flower-power era do not make sense. In the late 1990s, when the original musical was being put together, these temporal issues would not have been quite as problematic, particularly from the standpoint of Sophie's age.

For the most part, the actors work well as an ensemble cast. Being musicals, however, movies such as *Mamma Mia!* present challenges with respect to casting that non-musical films do not. Although Meryl Streep was trained as a singer, and most of the other cast members adapt to the musical genre well enough, Pierce Brosnan's singing was widely panned by critics. For example, writing in *The New York Times*, A. O. Scott described Brosnan's singing as "bellowing" (Scott 2008). *Rolling Stone*'s Peter Travers was even more pointed, writing that "Brosnan bleats like a moose who just took a bullet" (Travers 2008).

The singing might have been a bit uneven, the plot may have been silly, some of the characterizations might have veered toward the cartoonish, but *Mamma Mia!* is largely about reviving ABBA songs that were popular around the world between the mid-1970s and the early 1980s. The songs written by Björn Ulvaeus and Benny Andersson (with some contributions from ABBA's manager Stig Anderson) are general enough in their subject matter that a plot (as unlikely as it might be) could be constructed around them, some of the timeline issues of "Our Last Summer" notwithstanding. Included in the movie are "Honey, Honey," "Money, Money, Money," "Our Last Summer," "Dancing Queen," "Lay All Your Love on Me," "Super Trouper," "Gimme! Gimme! Gimme! (A Man After Midnight)," "Voulez-Vous," "Take a Chance on Me," "The Name of the Game," "SOS," "Does Your Mother Know," "Slipping Through My Fingers," "The Winner Takes It All," "I Do, I Do, I Do, I Do, I Do," "When All Is Said and Done," "Waterloo," and "Thank You for the Music."

Although several of the songs are used as part of party scenes, most notably "Voulez-Vous," several others are more fully woven into the plot, such as "Money, Money, Money," which represents Donna's desire to have adequate money to fix her hotel and turn it into the establishment she had always dreamed it would be. Although not the main musical highlight of the film, "Money, Money, Money" is notable as a production number that incorporates a yacht at sea as part of the performance setting. In this sense, it represents an example of how the film medium can add value to a musical. One of the musical highlights is "When All Is Said and Done," a dramatic ballad that presents the audience—and Sam Carmichael—with the reality that, despite her relationships with Bill Anderson and Harry Bright, Sam was the love of Donna's life.

Like the original stage productions of the show, the film version of *Mamma Mia!* was a commercial success. Critics, however, were lukewarm about the movie. For example, writing in *The New York Times*, A. O. Scott suggested that "you can have a perfectly nice time watching this spirited adaptation of the popular stage musical and, once the hangover wears off, acknowledge just how bad it is" (Scott 2008). As a competitor to some of the best early 21st-century movie musicals, *Mamma Mia!* might not succeed through its plot; however, as an entertaining location-based jukebox musical that seems to have revived the right body of music at the right time, *Mamma Mia!* was a success.

Probably based on the commercial success of the film and the fact that two decades after its premiere productions of the stage version of the musical continue to draw audiences in droves, *Mamma Mia!* spawned a movie follow-up. The 2018 film *Mamma Mia! Here We Go Again* both extended the story of the original show but also reflected back to the days before Donna moved to the Greek island. *Mamma Mia! Here We Go Again* reprised some of the most well-known ABBA songs from the original musical and included several less-well-known songs by the group. The sequel was both a commercial and largely a critical success.

MARY POPPINS

The 1964 Walt Disney film *Mary Poppins* was based on the series of *Mary Poppins* books that P. L. Travers began writing in the 1930s. The movie music featured a score and songs by Richard M. Sherman and Robert B. Sherman, the writers behind such classics as "It's a Small World (After All)," "You're Sixteen," and the music for Disney and non-Disney films such as *Chitty Chitty Bang Bang*, *The Aristocats*, and *The Jungle Book*. The movie starred Julie Andrews as the title character, Dick Van Dyke as Bert the chimney sweep and jack of all trades (and in a couple of brief scenes as the banker Mr. Dawes Sr.), David Tomlinson as George Banks, Glynis Johns as Winifred Banks, and Karen Dotrice and Matthew Garber as Jane and Michael, the Banks children.

Mary Poppins opens with a traditional overture, which contains references to all the musical's big tunes. This type of overture ties the movie to the classic Broadway stage musical tradition. As the movie opens, the audience is introduced to Winifred Banks, who is active in the early 20th-century British movement for women's suffrage. The Banks family has gone through several nannies for their two children in quick succession. As the audience gets to know Mr. and Mrs. Banks, it becomes clear that the turnover in nannies that precedes Mary Poppins getting the job may have more to do with the parents than with the children.

Dick Van Dyke's character, Bert, plays a particularly interesting role in the film. In addition to being a principal part of the storyline, as a long-time friend of Poppins and experienced participant in her moments of magic that she brings into the lives of her charges, he also plays the role of a narrator. In this capacity, Bert sets the stage for the story and shares some insights about Mary Poppins.

One of the notable features of Mary Poppins is the way in which the live characters, particularly Poppins, Bert, and the Banks children, interact with animated characters. This was not, however, the first movie to integrate live characters with animation. Some of the famous predecessors include Gene Kelly dancing with Jerry the Mouse (of Tom and Jerry fame) in the 1945 film *Anchors Aweigh* and James Baskett—as Uncle Remus—performing "Zip-a-Dee-Doo-Dah" in the 1946 film *Song of the South*.

The integration of animation and live characters occurs in several places in the film, beginning with Mary Poppins and an animated robin interacting in "A Spoonful of Sugar" the first time the song is heard. Perhaps the most memorable integrated sequences, however, take place later in the film when Poppins, Bert, and the Banks children visit the park and are swept up into a fantasy world. Anecdotally, this author can confirm that perhaps the two most memorable scenes in the film—after seeing the movie for the first time as a child when it was first released—were Mary Poppins's first appearance riding the wind down to the ground using her umbrella, and the live-animation integration of Bert's dance with the animated penguins during the sequence in the park.

The score for *Mary Poppins* makes several references to the principal songs, sometimes in the underscoring, and at times in the singing. Perhaps the most firmly fixed tune in the movie is that of "Chim Chim Cher-ee." Although the most well-remembered version of the tune, with the "Chim Chim Cher-ee" lyrics, occurs later in the film, the tune is used during the first interaction of Mary Poppins and Bert, but with different lyrics. This interaction informs the audience that they have a history and that Bert is no stranger to the fact that Poppins brings magic into her itinerant roles as a nanny. The full song, as it occurs later in the movie, confirms the association of Poppins, Bert, and the mysterious nighttime world of the London chimney sweeps with "good luck." Whether intentional, the Sherman Brothers' score also contains a melodic similarity in places to some of Herbert Stothart's Wicked Witch theme music from *The Wizard of Oz*.

There are a few odd unexplained aspects to the film. Perhaps most strange is the fact that in so many of the street scenes there is no one out and about except for the principal characters. Another oddity is the entire Uncle Albert sequence, which includes the song "I Love to Laugh." In the context, P. L. Travers's *Mary Poppins* books, which include characters not found in the movie musical, Poppins's Uncle Albert is just one of the several magical characters associated with the nanny. The fact that other characters are missing makes Albert Wigg stand out. Uncle Albert's song, however, establishes the importance of laughter as a way of overcoming adversity. George Banks's employer, Mr. Dawes Sr., has a similar episode of laughing and becoming seemingly lighter than air near the conclusion of the movie, which establishes a link with Albert and places the Uncle Albert sequence into context.

The senior Mr. Dawes's episode of laughter and subsequent floating up into the air takes place after the Banks children inadvertently cause mass confusion resulting in a run on the bank. Their father is called into a board meeting at which the only explanation he can provide is the word "Supercalifragilisticexpialidocious." Banks leaves the meeting fully expecting to be fired; however, Dawes finds the humor in the word and Banks's use of it, begins laughing and floats up to the ceiling, as Uncle

Albert had done during "I Love to Laugh." Instead of being fired, ultimately Banks is offered a seat on the bank's board.

Before Mr. Banks's situation is resolved, however, Bert tells the children that their father and their family is going to need some help. This leads to one of the strongest song sequences in the film that includes "Chim Chim Cher-ee," as well as "A Spoonful of Sugar" used as marching music as Mary Poppins, Bert, and the children parade along the rooftops of London and climb a smoke staircase. The sequence culminates with "Step in Time," the major production number of the movie that features the whole of London's chimney sweeps. At the conclusion of this sequence, Bert lays out for the father that he has not provided his children with time and attention, and that they need and deserve more. Finally realizing the correctness of Bert's assessment, Mr. Banks and his children reconnect in the song "Let's Go Fly a Kite." It is after this reconnection with his family that Mr. Banks's employment situation is favorably resolved.

Like numerous iconic movie musicals, *Mary Poppins* experienced a renaissance in the form of an update. Unlike some of the other remade movie musicals of the past, the 2018 film *Mary Poppins Returns* was a sequel. In the film, Dick Van Dyke, who had played Bert, the chimney sweep, and Mr. Dawes in the original, appeared as Mr. Dawes Jr., now aged. Angela Lansbury, who had appeared in a 1979 Broadway performance of Mary Poppins, also appeared in *Mary Poppins Returns* as the Balloon Lady. As Lin-Manuel Miranda, who played Jack, the lamplighter, put it, "There are two moments in *Mary Poppins Returns* when the grown-ups watching really lose it: Dick Van Dyke's arrival and when Angela Lansbury starts singing. . . . Those are playing on a lifetime of heartstrings" (Alexander 2018, 2D).

The song "Supercalifragilisticexpialidocious" made an instant impact on popular culture; throughout the rest of the 1960s—and beyond—children made a memory game out of being able to spell the word. It is also recognized as one of the classic movie songs. The American Film Institute ranked "Supercalifragilisticexpialidocious" No. 36 on its list of the 100 greatest movie songs of all time (American Film Institute 2004).

Perhaps one of the better examples of pure cross-generational entertainment in the genre, *Mary Poppins* was ranked No. 6 in the American Film Institute's list of the 25 greatest movie musicals of all time (American Film Institute 2006). Songwriters Richard and Robert Sherman won the Academy Awards for Best Original Song—for "Chim Chim Cher-ee"—and Best Music Score, Substantially Original—for the entire *Mary Poppins*. In addition, Julie Andrews won the Academy Award for

Best Actress in a Leading Role for her portrayal of the title character, and the technical crew of the movie won the Academy Award for Best Visual Effects.

LES MISÉRABLES

If one considers that the majority of the most popular and well-known musicals and movie musicals have been comedies, then the gist of this story from the pen of the 19th-century French writer Victor Hugo might seem to be one of the least likely plots for what would become one of the most popular musicals ever. Hugo's novel *Les Misérables* was first published in 1862; however, it was based on events that transpired between approximately 30 and 50 years earlier. Composer Claude-Michel Schönberg and lyricists Alain Boublil and Jean-Marc Natel wrote the original stage musical based on Hugo's work. After a successful premiere in 1980, the musical was adapted into English by lyricist Herbert Kretzmer, and began lengthy runs in major cities, including New York and London. Approximately three decades after the premiere of the still-popular English version, Tom Hooper directed the film version.

The 2012 movie starred Hugh Jackman as Jean Valjean, Russell Crowe as Valjean's nemesis Javert, Anne Hathaway as the doomed factory worker Fantine, and Amanda Seyfried as Fantine's daughter Cosette, who was raised by Valjean as a surrogate father after Fantine's death. In addition to these first-billing actors, the strong ensemble cast also featured Sasha Baron Cohen as Thénardier and Helena Bonham Carter as Madame Thénardier. Given that several of the principals in *Les Misérables* were film stars not necessarily best-known for their singing abilities, most bring strong technique to the movie, with the possible exception of Russell Crowe, whose tone color and relative lack of vibrato tend to make him stand out unfavorably compared with an actor such as Jackman, and compared with Amanda Seyfried, whose vocal style tends to be closer to pop and folk music than what one might expect to hear in this famous musical.

The story opens in 1815, 26 years after the French Revolution. The first musical number, "Look Down," returns several times throughout the film. The piece is associated with the downtrodden, in the case of *Les Misérables*, with the people who supported the French Revolution around 1890 and eventually supported the 1832 June Rebellion. One of the notable features of the first appearance of the ensemble piece, as well as the later appearances of the piece, is that the mix of long shots and close-ups provides the audience with a combination of size and intimacy that would be impossible on stage. "Look Down" also provides the audience with the first opportunity to hear the extent to which the vocals are upfront in the texture, an advantage that the film medium has over the average stage production.

Although *Les Misérables* is sung almost completely throughout, it is not quite a work that is built in the mold of, say, a Wagnerian opera. Several times over the course of the film, abrupt musical changes interrupt what generally is almost a through-composed feel. One of the other features of Claude-Michel Schönberg's score that is particularly notable is that the ensemble numbers and several of the songs are quite accessible, but have a timeless melodic, rhythmic, and harmonic quality that never veers too close to the world of more transitory pop music.

One of the early major ensemble pieces, "At the End of the Day," occurs after eight years have elapsed and Jean Valjean—the man who remains wanted after breaking his parole—has become a pseudonymous respectable citizen. Just before and after this piece, there are several obvious camera cuts to Javert and other French soldiers suggesting the dominance of the military and continuing the ongoing interplay between Javert and other characters who return later in the story. More specifically, these shots show that Javert continues to pursue Valjean, perhaps unconsciously finding him at the factory even before realizing who Valjean is.

One of the aspects of *Les Misérables* that is easy to overlook, both because there is so much nearly continuous music and because the major solo songs and large ensemble numbers demand so much attention from the listener, is how much variety Schönberg achieves in the musical settings of dialogue sequences and the sequences in which characters share their inner thoughts with the audience. Perhaps one of the most memorable is the "there was a time" sequence, in which Fantina reflects on how emotionally dead she feels after her first experience as a prostitute. Most of the melody is quite simple and the accompaniment with sustained high-register strings is haunting. Ultimately, Fantina's self-reflection turns into a verse-like introduction to the verse-chorus form song "I Dreamed a Dream."

Close-ups, such as those used in "I Dreamed a Dream," can expose synchronization issues, as has been the case with a number of movie musicals over the years. The synchronization of Anne Hathaway's voice and visuals is quite good, perhaps part of the reason for the film's Academy Award for Best Achievement in Sound Mixing. "I Dreamed a Dream" is closer to the popular musical theater style of the time of the original stage musical's writing than the more recitative-like passages in the show. However, although the piece shares some structural traits with old Tin Pan Alley verse-chorus form, it is complex enough that it transcends much of pop music. Some listeners may consider "I Dreamed a Dream" to be similar in style to some of the famous ballads from Andrew Lloyd Webber's musicals of the late 20th century.

Much of the storyline of *Les Misérables* is decidedly dark. The principal figures who provide some humor are the sometimes unscrupulous and sometimes downright evil innkeepers, the Thénardiers, played by Sacha Baron Cohen and Helena Bonham Carter. The almost sing-song style "Master of the House" finds the Thénardiers picking the pockets of their patrons and engaging in other devious activity. The sing-song, music hall-ish nature of the piece calls to mind some other tension-breaking dark-humored pieces from earlier generally serious shows such as "Herod's Song" from *Jesus Christ Superstar*.

The "I Dreamed a Dream" theme returns when Valjean offers to take Cosette and raise her as his duty. In fact, this music, either instrumentally, with the lyrics used in its first iteration, or with different lyrics, weaves the hope for a better future throughout the story, especially at crucial points in the plot. In this way, the song becomes something of a musical *idee fixe*, in the manner in which 19th-century composers such as Hector Berlioz and Richard Wagner used musical materials to represent various characters or concepts in operas and programmatic symphonic music.

As mentioned earlier, Russell Crowe is not the strongest major-role singer in the movie. However, his performance of "Stars" works well in helping to define Javert and what drives the character. The song itself is part of a continuum of songs going back to Hoagy Carmichael's "Heart and Soul" of the 1930s that are built primarily around what came to be called the "oldies progression," the harmonic pattern I-vi-IV-V. "Stars" uses an expansion and variant of the chord progression in its verses. Songwriters over the years have used the progression in songs of a variety of moods, however, songs from the 1960s through the early 21st century, such as Orchestral Manoeuvres in the Dark's "If You Leave" and "Enola Gay," Ben E. King's "Stand by Me," Taylor Swift's "Tim McGraw," and numerous others, illustrate how effective the progression's move from the major tonic chord (I) to the minor submediant chord (vi) is in establishing a bittersweet mood. The musical setting, and particularly the bittersweet quality that the tonic major to submediant minor provides, enhances the lyrics.

As the action jumps ahead nine years to 1832, the ensemble piece "Look Down" returns. In this case, "Look Down" belongs to the downtrodden who have been suffering under the current government. The piece is also notable for one of the quirks of *Les Misérables*. One of the soloists in the piece is the young, somewhat stereotypical street urchin Gavroche, played by Daniel Huttlestone. It should be noted that the film included several actors with British accents; however, none is as extreme as that of the Cockney-sounding Gavroche. Although Gavroche's accent clearly paints him as part of the urban working class, some audiences might find that Gavroche's accent creates a somewhat disconcerting sense of loss of place, as the action supposedly takes place in the streets of France and not in the East End of London.

The audience sees a France possibly on the verge of another revolution, with some members of the upper classes and the lowest socioeconomic class ready to take violent action to affect a return to the republic. The music that leads up to the June Rebellion, such as "Red and Black" and "Do You Hear the People Sing," are close enough in style to political and social anthems of the past—albeit perhaps not dating all the way back to 1832—that they sound as though they could be authentic political rallying songs.

Although not as central to the overall plot as characters such as Valjean and Javert, one of the most memorable characters is Éponine. She first appears as a child earlier in the movie; however, it is the grown-up Éponine—played by Samantha Barks in the film—who delivers what is perhaps the most popular song from *Les Misérables*, "On My Own." The song finds the character expressing her unrequited love for the revolutionary Marius, who quickly falls in love with Cosette after seeing her only once. Especially because of some of the song's extended phrase endings, "On My Own" serves as a good illustration of how composer Claude-Michel Schönberg was able to combine easy accessibility with a musical complexity that goes beyond most pop music in the songs and major ensemble numbers.

Jean Valjean sings another of the show's major pieces, "Bring Him Home," a prayer for the safety and protection of the revolutionary Republicans. It is in this song—as well as in other ensemble pieces and solo songs—that Hugh Jackman performs as the post-1815 Jean Valjean in which his singing technique helps to establish the fact that Valjean has undergone a transformation into a man who aims only to do what is right and his duty.

As Valjean sits at the edge of death, the ghost of Fantina beckons him to follow her to a world in which there is no more pain or heartache. The film concludes as Valjean follows Fantina and sees all the deceased characters massed together performing "Do You Hear the People Sing." In the context of the ongoing battles between the Republicans and the loyalists to the crown, the masses seem to represent all those who died on the Republican side during the 18th-century French Revolution and during all the subsequent conflicts that continued through the 1832 June Rebellion. The message seems to be that eventually all the conflict and the deaths resulted in modern France, a republic rather than a monarchy.

The early productions of *Les Misérables* in French and in English were hugely successful and established this musical as one of the longest-running productions in history. The 2012 film version was nominated for eight Academy Awards. *Les Misérables* won in the categories of Best Achievement in Sound Mixing, Best Achievement in Makeup and Hairstyling, and Anne Hathaway won the Award for Best Performance by an Actress in a Supporting Role. The film won the Golden Globe Award for Best Picture, Comedy or Musical.

MOULIN ROUGE!

The 2001 release *Moulin Rouge!* was perhaps one of the most unique movie musicals to date. Cowritten by Baz Luhrmann and Craig Pearce and directed by Luhrmann, *Moulin Rouge!* was part of a trilogy of fantasy films that the Australian Luhrmann brought to life in the late 20th century and beginning of the 21st century. *Moulin Rouge!* starred Nicole Kidman as Satine, Ewan McGregor as Christian, Jim Broadbent as Harold Zidler, Richard Roxburgh as the Duke of Monroth, John Leguizamo as Henri de Toulouse-Lautrec, and a large ensemble cast. The inclusion of Toulouse-Lautrec, the famed French post-Impressionistic artist, and Zilder as characters is telling. Just as Toulouse-Lautrec championed the kind of nightlife associated with the famous Moulin Rouge nightclub, of which Zilder was one of the founders, and its decadence, the film is centered on that turn-of-the-century scene.

Where *Moulin Rouge!* differs from the nightlife-oriented paintings of Toulouse-Lautrec is that the film is significantly over the top in its pop culture references and cinematic techniques. In fact, one of the most distinctive features of the film is the way in which it integrates mid- to late 20th-century songs and song lyrics into the storyline. The sheer amount of pop culture references—all years or decades removed from the 1899–1900 period in which the plot supposedly takes place—makes for something of a love-it or hate-it reaction to *Moulin Rouge!*. For example, audiences that value historical context might be taken aback at songs associated with Rodgers and Hammerstein's *The Sound of Music* ("The Sound of Music" and "The Lonely Goatherd"), Nat King Cole ("Nature Boy"), David Bowie ("Heroes" and "Diamond Dogs"),

Madonna ("Like a Virgin" and "Material Girl"), Dolly Parton ("I Will Always Love You"), the Police ("Roxanne"), Elton John ("Your Song"), Labelle ("Lady Marmalade"), Nirvana ("Smells Like Teen Spirit"), and others not just being used, but being in some cases fully integrated into the score. On the other hand, other audiences find that Luhrmann's approach is highly creative, at times highly humorous, and helps early 20th-century filmgoers relate to a cultural scene that might have been closer to later subcultures and countercultures than one might at first imagine. The elements of surrealism that can be found from the beginning to the end also seem as though they could be polarizing; however, the techniques and the inclusion of social fringe characters, some of whom might be viewed as carnival freaks, might suggest to some film aficionados the possible influence of filmmakers such as Federico Fellini in the legendary Italian director's surrealistic films such as *8 1/2*.

The potentially polarizing nature of the film and its unrelenting quick pace has been mentioned in several reviews of *Moulin Rouge!*. For example, writing in *The Guardian*, critic Peter Bradshaw described *Moulin Rouge!* as being "too fast-paced for its own good" (Bradshaw 2001). *Variety*'s Todd McCarthy described *Moulin Rouge!* as "a tour de force of artifice, a dazzling pastiche of musical and visual elements at the service of a blatantly artificial story" (McCarthy 2001). McCarthy's sole qualm about the film was whether moviegoers in the 15–30 age group would appreciate the pop culture references. McCarthy's concerns are legitimate, as much of what makes the film work is the way in which the non-congruous pop culture references—many of which predated some members of that prime movie-going age demographic—resonated with older audiences.

Cowriter and director Baz Luhrmann revealed in an interview that the influences included the ancient story of *Orpheus and Eurydice*, as well as the texts *Camille* and *La Bohème* (Andrew 2001). It is interesting to note at least some of the connections to these works. In the first story, the talented musician Orpheus marries Eurydice, who subsequently dies. Heartbroken, Orpheus attempts to bring Eurydice back to life by undertaking an ill-fated journey to the underworld. Although Orpheus fails and dies, it is in death that he and Eurydice are reunited. In *Camille*, originally written by Alexander Dumas *fils* in the mid-19th century, the courtesan Marguerite, tries to work her way out of her social class, but fails and dies of consumption. The well-known *La Bohème*—perhaps best known in its form as an opera by Giacomo Puccini—or from its mid-1990s' adaptation into the rock opera *Rent*—similarly deals with class struggles and the tragedy that accompanies the life of impoverished bohemians. In considering these influences, it is interesting to note that Luhrmann produced a modernized version of *La Bohème* approximately a decade before cowriting *Moulin Rouge!*

As mentioned earlier, however, some viewers might find hints of the filmmaking techniques and style of Fellini in *Moulin Rouge!*. It is likely that audiences will also compare the movie with *Cabaret*. Not only do both films utilize a decadent cabaret scene as the primary setting (albeit one story is set in Paris in 1899 and the other in Berlin approximately 30 years later), both also incorporate dark humor and include filmmaking techniques that define them fully as movies, as opposed to musicals that could exist in pretty much the same form on stage. Unlike *Cabaret*, however, *Moulin Rouge!* began its life as a film; it was not adapted into a stage musical until over a decade and a half after the movie's premiere. Compared with its Berlin-based relative, *Moulin Rouge!* is considerably more over-the-top in the heavy use of filmmaking techniques that go well beyond what would be possible on stage.

It is also worth noting that, particularly during the sequence in which Christian, Toulouse-Lautrec, and the others in their circle try to sell the Duke of Monroth on their surrealistic show, *Spectacular Spectacular*, some viewers might detect traces of the popular Mel Brooks movie-turned-stage musical *The Producers*. This brings up an interesting aspect of what some audiences might experience during *Moulin Rouge!*. There are so many deliberate references to earlier songs, films, and stage works that after a while some viewers might find themselves actively listening and watching for any little kernel, any little hint of another reference, be it intentional or entirely in the mind of the audience.

Critics have credited *Moulin Rouge!* and *Mamma Mia!*—the stage version of which appeared shortly before the release of *Moulin Rouge!*—as seminal works in establishing the jukebox musical (see, for example, Brantley 2018). Although the two musicals were popular works—as were the movie version of *Mamma Mia!*, Julie Taymor's 2007 Beatles-focused film *Across the Universe*, the 2018 film *Mamma Mia! Here We Go Again*, and other post-*Moulin Rouge!* jukebox movie musicals—the concept of the jukebox musical, a work built around pre-existing songs, certainly did not originate at the start of the 21st century with *Moulin Rouge!* and *Mamma Mia!*. Even within the rock era, the 1978 Robert Stigwood film *Sgt. Pepper's Lonely Hearts Club Band* had a storyline built around Beatles songs. Venturing even deeper into the history of movie musicals, the classic 1951 film *An American in Paris* was built around the songs of George and Ira Gershwin and the instrumental compositions of George Gershwin. What the *Moulin Rouge!* and the *Mamma Mia!*

franchise did was to raise the level of popularity of the jukebox musical. What *Moulin Rouge!* did like no other jukebox musical was to explode the genre in terms of the amount of pre-existing material, the diversity of the material, and the creative way in which the cowriters and director wove seemingly incongruous snippets of popular music and pop culture in general into a storyline that supposedly portrayed an entirely different era, place, and society.

In addition to Craig Armstrong's score, *Moulin Rouge!* also contained new musical material in the form of David Baerwald and Kevin Gilbert's "Come What May," the most significant original song in the film. Although the song did not qualify to win the Academy Award for Best Song—since it had been written for, but not used in Baz Luhrmann's earlier film *William Shakespeare's Romeo + Juliet*—the American Film Institute ranked "Come What May" at No. 85 on its list of the 100 greatest movie songs in the first century of the movie industry (American Film Institute 2004).

The film itself, as well as composer Craig Armstrong, won or were nominated for numerous other honors, including Golden Globe Awards, British Academy of Film and Television Arts (BAFTA) Awards, and Australian Academy of Cinema and Television Arts (AACTA) Awards. Armstrong was selected as the American Film Institute's Composer of the Year for his original score for *Moulin Rouge!*. *Moulin Rouge!* received eight Academy Award nominations, winning in the categories of Best Costume Design and Best Art Direction. The film won the Golden Globe Award for Best Motion Picture, Musical or Comedy, and in 2006, the American Film Institute ranked *Moulin Rouge!* No. 25 in its list of the 25 greatest movie musicals of all time (American Film Institute 2006).

Moulin Rouge! uses so many cut-to, panning, close-ups, distance shots, special effects (e.g., transitioning from black and white into color), and so on that it has "film" written all over it. Because so many of the scenes are so vivid and memorable, this seems like a particularly challenging film to convert into a stage musical. Nonetheless, a live stage version was developed and opened in Boston in 2018 and on Broadway in July 2019. The Boston production won several awards from the Independent Reviewers of New England, including Best Musical and Best New Musical (McPhee 2019), suggesting that against all odds the transformation from a highly distinctive film to the stage might ultimately be successful.

THE MUSIC MAN

The 1962 Warner Bros. film adaptation of Meredith Willson's 1957 musical *The Music Man* was perhaps one of the best movie musicals of its time, although the movie has not made it onto some of the lists of the greatest movies of the first 100 years of American cinema that were published in the early 21st century. Although the story is intentionally corny at times, Willson's music and lyrics fit perfectly with the fanciful tale of an early 20th-century flim-flam man who unexpectedly manages to pull off what he promised simply in an attempt to rip off the residents of River City, Iowa. *The Music Man* is remarkably true to the original stage musical; however, it makes full use of the resources of the film medium.

The principals of the film, Robert Preston (as Professor Harold Hill) and Shirley Jones (as Marian Paroo) helped make *The Music Man* the commercial and critical success it was. However, the entire ensemble cast is strong, from the young Ronnie Howard (as Winthrop) years before he became known as Ron Howard and became a famous actor and film director, to the various members of River City society. One of the most notable accomplishments, however, was by Robert Preston. Not only does Professor Harold Hill get a considerable amount of screen time in *The Music Man* he has some challenging acting and singing throughout the show. Perhaps most importantly, however, Preston was one of the few Broadway stars of the era to successfully make the transition from the stage to the film. The norm at the time was, for various reasons, to recast a film adaptation of a Broadway show (e.g., Mary Martin playing Maria in the original Broadway production of *The Sound of Music*, but Julie Andrews playing the role in the film). Because of his success in several stage productions of the show and in the film, Robert Preston owned the role of Professor Harold Hill to the same extent that Yul Brenner owned the role of the King of Siam in *The King and I* and Barbra Streisand owned the role of Fanny Brice in *Funny Girl*.

Certainly not unique to the film version of *The Music Man*, one of the notable features of the film—in addition to the tunefulness of Willson's songs—is the fact that *The Music Man* contains several notable examples of partner songs. For example, "Pick-a-Little, Talk-a-Little" is paired with the barbershop quartet classic "Goodnight Ladies." Willson also essentially used the same tune with a different tempo and rhythmic setting as part of his way of connecting characters such as the songs "Seventy-Six Trombones" and "Goodnight, My Someone."

In the film, the costumes are visually stunning, even in the long shots, such as in the "Seventy-Six Trombones" dance sequence. The costuming in sequences such as this dance and the subsequent march through town is interesting when one considers that the brightly clothed characters are those who follow Professor Harold Hill in his march; the bystanders and those who express suspicions about Hill (e.g., librarian Marian

Paroo) are dressed in more subdued colors. It is this kind of costuming that seems to come directly out of the world of the stage musical. In the movie, it certainly makes strong use of the color technologies of the time and provides the audience with production numbers that are visually appealing. The flip side is that the costuming is so stylized that the movie offers little in the sense of visual reality—much like the storyline of Harold Hill's "think method" as a way to learn to play band instruments offers little in the way of plot reality.

This is not a musical with a great deal of depth; however, there are some probably unintended subtext issues that one might consider when considering *The Music Man*. Although the study does not deal with the role of the barbershop quartet in *The Music Man*, it is interesting to consider Richard Mook's article "White Masculinity in Barbershop Quartet Singing" if one is disposed to look for the significance of meaning in the movie (Mook 2007). The article explores the barbershop quartet and its history as a manifestation of whiteness, despite the fact that some aspects of the music had African American roots. This is particularly interesting to note in the context of the film version of The *Music Man*, as the River City which is largely, if not entirely, white. The quartet also symbolizes old-fashioned, conservative Midwestern values. Interestingly, Mook points out that early 20th-century barbershop quartet composer C. T. "Deac" Martin handwrote in one copy of his 1932 book *Handbook for Adeline Addicts*, "What this country needs is more . . . and much closer . . . harmony" (Mook 463). In *The Music Man*, Professor Harold Hill manages to use the connection between close harmony (in the sense of the chord structures commonly found in the barbershop quartet music of the early 20th century, and in the sense of comradery) to bring the four sometimes-bickering male town leaders together. He also uses this close harmony to deflect the men's probing into his—Hill's—past, questionable qualifications and dubious motives. Of course, the quartet is also featured in the stage version of the musical; however, the film emphasizes the whiteness of the populace and the way in which Hill uses the early 20th-century social context of Martin's metaphorical "close harmony" more clearly than is possible in stage productions, both because casting choices for a live production need not be as monochromatic as the casting for the film was and because the close-ups on the singers can be interpreted as another manifestation of their oneness. In the long run, however, *The Music Man* is more about pure entertainment and the fantastical exploration of life in the early 20th century than it is about deep meaning.

The Music Man was remade in 2003 in a television film version that starred Matthew Broderick as Professor Harold Hill. The 2003 version seemed slower-paced than the classic 1962 film. Because it used television's 4:3 aspect ratio of time, the 2003 remake lacks some of the widescreen visual impact of the original film. The Robert Preston and Shirley Jones film remains available on DVD at the time of this writing, and it is also available through streaming media services. Likewise, the made-for-television version that starred Matthew Broderick is also available at the time of this writing.

Although *The Music Man* received several Academy Awards nominations, the only Oscar won by the film was by Ray Heindorf for Best Musical Score (Adaptation or Treatment). Although it did not win additional Academy Awards and has not been recognized as one of the most important movies by the American Film Institute, it was selected for inclusion in the Library of Congress's National Film Registry. *The Music Man* defies time like few other movie musicals. Perhaps this is because of Meredith Willson's memorable songs, but it may also be because the film (and the stage musical) is a fanciful depiction of a time period in the United States that even at the time of the premiere of the musical was far enough in the past that the story and music was not subject to being a believable depiction of the time of its writing. Although the 1962 movie has been underappreciated, the stage musical received five Tony Awards, including Best Musical. *The Music Man* has also remained a staple of school and community theater troupes ever since the late 1950s. The stage version of *The Music Man* has also been revived on Broadway over the years, including a planned 2020 production scheduled to star Hugh Jackman as Professor Harold Hill.

MY FAIR LADY

Based on the 1956 Broadway musical, which in turn was based on George Bernard Shaw's 1913 play *Pygmalion*, the 1964 film version of *My Fair Lady* starred Audrey Hepburn as the Cockney flower seller Eliza Doolittle and Rex Harrison as the pompous professor of phonetics and elocution Henry Higgins. Harrison reprised the role after starring in both the original Broadway and London runs of the stage version. Other significant actors in the film included Stanley Holloway as Alfred P. Doolittle, Eliza's father; Wilfrid Hyde-White as Colonel Hugh Pickering; Gladys Cooper as Mrs. Higgins; Jeremy Brett as Freddy Eynsford-Hill, Eliza's suitor; Theodore Bikel as Zoltan Karpathy; Mona Washbourne as Mrs. Pearce, the Higgins' housekeeper; Isobel Elsom as Mrs. Ensford-Hill; and John Holland as the butler.

In addition to the book and lyrics by Alan Jay Lerner and music by Frederick Loewe, *My Fair Lady* included musical arrangements and conducting by André Previn; Previn won the Academy Award for Best Adaptation or Treatment Score for his work on the film, one of the eight Academy Awards won by the film.

It should be noted that the film is very close in structure to the stage version, even including an intermission with an orchestral entr'acte, although the intermission and entr'acte are placed slightly earlier in the film than in the stage version. The inclusion of the instrumental numbers usually associated with stage productions was not uncommon during this era, particularly in film versions of stage musicals dating back to the 1950s. What is especially notable about *My Fair Lady* is how the instrumental numbers highlight just how many memorable musical theater standards were in this show.

The story opens with Cockney flower girl Eliza Doolittle being studied by the self-professed expert on elocution and phonetics Professor Henry Higgins. Soon thereafter, Higgins and Colonel Pickering, a fellow expert on elocution and phonetics, make a bet, with Higgins wagering that within six months he can turn Doolittle into a woman who will be able to fool all in attendance at the Embassy Ball into thinking that she is a duchess.

This early part of the film includes the songs "Why Can't the English" and "Wouldn't It Be Lovely," sung, respectively, by Higgins and Eliza Doolittle. The Higgins number sets up a formula that runs through the film: all the songs that Rex Harrison performs freely mix singing and speaking. This carryover technique from the stage version of *My Fair Lady* was exploited even more dramatically in the 1958 film *Gigi*, which dated a couple of years later. In *Gigi*, Lerner and Loewe used this technique in virtually every song associated with a wider variety of characters; here, it solely defines Higgins.

In considering "Wouldn't It Be Lovely," it is important to note that most of Eliza's songs in the film were overdubbed by Marni Nixon, despite the fact that Audrey Hepburn had received vocal training as the film took shape. Nixon was one of the leading ghost vocalists of the movie musical genre, lending her voice to female lead characters in films such as *The King and I* and *West Side Story*; Nixon also sang Marilyn Monroe's high notes in "Diamonds Are a Girl's Best Friend" from the film of the same name. It is interesting to study the coordination of the audio and visual track in *My Fair Lady* with the overdubbing in mind. In "Wouldn't It Be Lovely," in particular, the coordination is quite tight, and Nixon's stylistic approach is casual enough to match the song to the character of a Cockney flower girl. This stands in contrast to some of the ghost overdubbing in the highly acclaimed *West Side Story*, which at times is too mannered to fit the characters and in which the audio and visuals coordinate as well as they did in *My Fair Lady*.

The one song that mixes Nixon and Hepburn's vocals is "Just You Wait." Hepburn sings the opening section, which is in a generally fairly narrow range and low tessitura, which Nixon sings in the higher-range and more melodically flashy chorus section. In this piece, the juxtaposition of the two voices works particularly effectively, as Hepburn conveys her character well. Nixon's use of a fast vibrato and close tone color to Hepburn suggests the lady that Eliza Doolittle has become in the fantasy part the song, the part during with Nixon provides Eliza's vocals.

Eliza has her breakthrough in speech and elocution at the transition into the song "The Rain in Spain." At the conclusion of this Spanish-style piece, which includes dancing from Doolittle, Pickering, and Higgins, the three are encountered by Higgins's housekeeper, who complains about the pounding sounds that she heard. This is interesting to note because it suggests the breaking down of the paradigm of action stopping for a song (and possibly a dance) in musicals. The housekeeper's complaint suggests that the song is part of the action. The "Rain in Spain" scene transitions into Eliza Doolittle singing "I Could Have Danced All Night," one of the show's best-remembered songs. The fact that "The Rain in Spain" and "I Could Have Danced All Night" is significant because it highlights just how rich *My Fair Lady* is in Lerner and Loewe songs that became and continue to be standards of the American popular songbook. In fact, as Don Tyler writes in *The Great Movie Musicals: A Viewer's Guide to 168 Films that Really Sing*, "There aren't many musical films that can boast of so many excellent songs that are still remembered after half-a-century (especially noteworthy are 'Wouldn't It Be Loverly,' 'The Rain in Spain,' 'I Could Have Danced All Night,' 'On the Street Where You Live,' 'I've Grown Accustomed to Her Face,' 'With a Little Bit of Luck,' and 'Get Me to the Church on Time')" (Tyler 2010, 213).

After Eliza's breakthrough, Higgins and Pickering take her to Ascot Racecourse as a test to see how well she does with her first encounter with the upper class. The entire Ascot sequence is one of the film's highlights. The opening of the sequence parodies the extreme understatement and focus on the propriety of the British upper class. Eliza meets Freddy Eynsford-Hill, Freddy's mother, and Higgins's mother at the horse races. She had briefly encountered Eynsford-Hills at the start of the movie, but she was not recognized as the former flower girl during the encounter at

Ascot. In a hilarious scene, Eliza talks properly with these members of the upper class, focusing on what were supposed to be two safe issues, the weather and one's health. Gradually, however, Eliza allows expressions such as "done her in" enter her vocabulary. Unfamiliar to the older members of the upper class, these are thought to be part of the "new small talk." In the next scene, as the crowd watches a race, Eliza's Cockney accent and vocabulary suddenly return and her roots are exposed.

Freddy Eynsford-Hill becomes smitten with Eliza at Ascot. He appears on the street where the Higgins house is located bearing a gift of flowers for Eliza. The song "On the Street Where You Live," sung by Eynsford-Hill, was dubbed by ghost vocalist Bill Shirley (BBC 2019). The studied approach to the song does not seem like quite the character match of Nixon's voicings of Eliza's songs; however, it is one of the dramatic highlights of the musical.

By the time of the Embassy Ball, Eliza successfully convinces all in attendance that she is a lady. In fact, Zoltan Karpathy, a Hungarian former student of Professor Higgins, is convinced that Eliza is not Pickering's niece—as Pickering had identified her when he, Doolittle, and Higgins entered the ballroom—but is instead a Hungarian princess. One of the musical highlights of the ball scenes is Loewe's "Embassy Waltz," as well as the underscoring that accompanies the sequences.

Upon the return of Doolittle, Higgins, and Pickering to Higgins's house, Higgins and Pickering congratulate each other on what they achieved largely because of the brilliance of Higgins. Clearly, Pickering and especially Higgins treat Eliza like a commodity as she receives no credit for the transformation. Rejecting Higgins, Eliza leaves with her suitcase.

As Eliza leaves Higgins' residence, she encounters Freddy who reprises "On the Street Where You Live" and declares his love for Eliza. Eliza makes her way to her old working-class neighborhood only to discover that her father has become a member of the middle class, thanks to a reference from Higgins that resulted in an American leaving him a fortune. As a new member of the respectable middle class, the former dustman Alfred Doolittle is preparing to marry Eliza's stepmother. This is the setting for "Get Me to the Church on Time," one of the film's production numbers.

Higgins comes to the realization that he misses Eliza, which forms the basis for the show's final major song, "I've Grown Accustomed to Her Face." When Eliza returns to Higgins at the end of the show, it is clear that she is willing to put up with his arrogance and a constant sense of superiority. The relationship is not what would be called healthy today, and it suggests a happy ending—or at least an ending with tolerance—which seems to run counter to Bernard Shaw's original intent. In light of the women's movement of the 1970s, subsequent movements for women's empowerment, and the social norms of the 21st century, Eliza's acceptance of male tyranny in *My Fair Lady* has not aged well.

Film historian Don Tyler (2010) commented on the fact that *My Fair Lady* was not the recipient of the kind of critical acclaim that it deserved at the time of its release. Nevertheless, the film eventually was recognized as more than just a collection of some of the best-remembered show tunes of the genre. Regardless of the degree of acclaim from critics that *My Fair Lady* did or did not receive, the movie did win Oscars for Best Picture; Best Director; Best Actor; Best Cinematography; Best Sound; Best Adaptation or Treatment, Score; Best Art Direction; and Best Costume Design at the 1965 Academy Awards.

In the early 21st century, the American Film Institute ranked *My Fair Lady* at No. 8 on its list of the 25 greatest movie musicals of all time (American Film Institute 2006). The Institute also ranked "I Could Have Danced All Night" No. 17 on its list of the 100 greatest movie songs of all time (American Film Institute 2004). In 2018, *My Fair Lady* was added to the National Film Registry by the Film Preservation Board of the U.S. Library of Congress.

OLIVER!

It is interesting to note that, in the 1950s and 1960s, several British-themed musicals were among the most popular and the greatest-award-winning works in the genre. In the United Kingdom itself, perhaps one of, if not the most popular, musicals from the era was the 1960 Lionel Bart show *Oliver!* The show was released in a film version in 1968. Incorporating Bart's music, lyrics, and book—based on the early 19th-century Charles Dickens novel *Oliver Twist*—the film had a screenplay by Vernon Harris, was directed by Carol Reed, and produced by John Woolf. The cast of *Oliver!* included several British child stars, most notably Mark Lester as Oliver Twist and Jack Wild as the Artful Dodger, as well as several more seasoned British actors, including Shani Wallis as Nancy, Ron Moody as Fagin, Oliver Reed as Bill Sikes, and Harry Secombe as Mr. Bumble. Just as the stage version of the musical has been a favorite in Britain for 60 years, the movie was well-received by audiences and critics alike; *Oliver!* won 6 Academy Awards, including Best Score and Best Picture. It was the last musical to win in the category of Best Picture until *Chicago* repeated that feat 34 years later.

Oliver! opens like a traditional Broadway/London West End musical of the mid-20th century with the "Overture," which feeds into the opening credits. In fact, throughout the film, viewers are likely to find numerous ties in Bart's songs to the golden age of musicals and movie musicals, in particular. Several songs contain structural references to early 20th-century verse-chorus form, and several of the choruses exhibit traditional Tin Pan Alley-style AABA form. Additionally, several songs reflect the influence of the early 20th-century British music hall style. Interestingly, at the same time, the storyline's focus on the struggles between the various socioeconomic classes and the violence that is part of the experience of the daily lives of the members of the struggling working class—all coming from Charles Dickens's original novel—give the musical a dark undercurrent. Part of the fascinating nature of *Oliver!* comes from this deliberate disconnection between upbeat, catchy tunes and the darkness that eventually reaches a high point in Bill Sikes's murder of Nancy, and Sikes's eventual death from a policeman's bullet.

The emotional pulls of the film can also be seen in individual scenes. For example, after the Artful Dodger first takes Oliver Twist to the thieves' lair, Fagin appears in a cloud of smoke as he emerges from the furnace in which he was cooking sausages. His emergence seems foreboding—Fagin appearing almost like Satan emerging from the smoke and fires of hell; however, Fagin's subsequent song "Pick a Pocket or Two" suggests a perky musical hall style that—at least from the musical standpoint—is disarming, even given the song's minor tonality. The dual nature of Fagin's character can later be seen in his near-violent reaction when he believes that Oliver has seen the secret hiding place for Fagin's most expensive stolen goods—a sharp contrast to the nearly fatherly way in which he had earlier tucked young Oliver in bed the first night he stayed with Fagin and the young thieves.

One particularly effective musical work that illustrates Fagin's dual nature is "I'll Do Anything." The song itself includes stanzas for Nancy, the Artful Dodger, etc., however, Fagin's stanza suggests the extent to which he controls all aspects of the boys' thievery and their lives. In contrast to that suggestion, however, rhythmically and melodically, this is perhaps one of the more disarming, music-hall-like songs in the entire score. "Be Back Soon," not nearly as well-remembered as "I'll Do Anything," also underscores the contrast between lighthearted music and dark lyrical and conceptual undertones.

One of the interesting structural aspects of the musical setting, easier to achieve and perceive in the film than in a stage production, is the way in which diegetic music of the pub transitions in the songs proper.

Especially effective is the transition into Nancy's song "It's a Fine Life." A similar transition from diegetic pub music to song can be heard later in the movie in "Oom-pah-pah." Another interesting aspects of Lionel Bart's score—however, one that is not unique to the film version of *Oliver!*—is how hints of "As Long as He Needs Me," Nancy's second act declaration of love for the thoroughly evil Bill Sikes, enter the background underscoring during the sequences in which Nancy appears in the film's first act. In the film's second act, immediately after Sikes murders Nancy, the score contains minor-key references to "As Long as He Needs Me," as Sikes takes Oliver back to Fagin's den of thieves. Incidentally, I intentionally use the terms first act and second act because the film, like the stage version of *Oliver!*, is divided into two acts and contains a full entr'acte that sets up the second part of the musical. In fact, even the DVD release of the movie splits the acts between sides of the disc, with the entr'acte opening side two.

Throughout the film, as in the stage musical and the Dickens novel before it, *Oliver!* has a central theme throughout the storyline, the visual imagery, and the lyrics of the songs focus on the economic and social class distinctions of early 19th-century Britain. This is clear in the film's opening song, "Food, Glorious Food," and throughout the rest of the film, these connections between members of the working class move into other aspects of everyday life. Although several later scenes—particularly when Sikes and Fagin prevail upon Nancy to play a major role in kidnapping Oliver—contain significant amounts of dialogue between musical numbers, viewers might sense during the "Food, Glorious Food" and "Oliver!" sequences that this musical is near-operatic in its focus on music.

Although identified as Jewish in Dickens's *Oliver Twist* novel, there is little overt reference to the ethnic or religious background of Fagin in the text of the musical. Fagin's identity is strongly hinted at, however, in his song "Reviewing the Situation." The minor key of the music, use of judicious klezmer clarinet in the instrumental accompaniment, and the general melodic and harmonic style of the piece betray Fagin's heritage. When one listens to the first appearance of the song and its reprise near the end of the film, one might notice some resemblance between the slow parts of "Reviewing the Situation" and Jerry Bock's music for the song "Sunrise, Sunset" in the 1964 musical *Fiddler on the Roof*. Similarly, some of the melodic, harmonic, and general stylistic material of the fast sections of "Reviewing the Situation" suggest that the song might have influenced Bock's "To Life," another well-known *Fiddler on the Roof* piece.

As Oliver Twist is expelled from the Workhouse and Mr. Brumble takes him out into the streets to sell him, the almost less-than-human nature of the poor and orphans is clear. Bart highlights this in Brumble's song "Boy for Sale." It is worth noting that the character of Mr. Brumble is voiced in a studied manner, complete with an almost stereotypical musical theater vibrato. The working-class characters and the street urchins sing with a less-than-studied sound. So, the singing style throughout the film's cast emphasizes the class distinctions between characters.

One of the best-remembered songs from the show is "Consider Yourself," first sung by the Artful Dodger when he first meets Oliver Twist. The song keeps expanding, however, with various groups of laborers joining in the singing and dancing. This production number—one of several that make strong use of the film medium—highlights the connectedness of the 19th-century British working class. Particularly notable are the dance sequences, including the scene with the butchers, the chimney sweeps, and the clear disconnection between the police and the common laborers. One of the purely musical highlights of the lengthy "Consider Yourself" sequence is the implied hemiola when the compound duple meter of the song intersects with the music of the carousel.

Although one could argue that much of *Oliver!* could be as effective on stage as on the big screen, several contrasting sequences make full use of the possibilities of film that just could not succeed as well on stage. For example, Fagin's interactions with the owl that lives in the derelict flat where Fagin lives with the young thieves are effective because of the close-up camera work, as is the later power shift that occurs among the thieves when Fagin hands over a £5 note to Sikes. The two largest production numbers in the film, the early "Consider Yourself" sequence and the second act "Who Will Buy," also make strong use of space. "Who Will Buy" is especially interesting in how the shots move from close-ups on individual singers (e.g., the flower girl who opens the song) to shots that show large groups of singers and dancers, even including a group of guardsmen and their accompanying musicians all outfitted in Busby hats. Like "Consider Yourself," the ever-expanding range and number of working-class characters in "Who Will Buy" suggests that a large number of people who populated the lower socioeconomic class of the London of the time of Charles Dickens, and, like the earlier song, suggests a connectedness that runs through the members of the working class. From a purely musical standpoint, "Who Will Buy" is also interesting for connections that listeners might make between it and African American work songs. This sense of connection might be felt because of the song's minor key and use of melodic syncopations.

Because *Oliver!* won the Academy Award for Best Score, it is interesting to focus on some of the underscoring and instrumental introductions to the songs. One of the notable uses of the various tone colors and textures of the orchestral instruments can be heard fairly early in the film in the introduction to "Where Is Love," as Oliver walks through the storage room filled with upright coffins. Another instrumental sequence that is worth noting is the underscoring to Oliver's journey to London. This sequence also incorporates a variety of instrumental tone colors and makes full use of the studio orchestra.

One of the other notable features of Lionel Bart's score is that the musical challenges of the songs are not left to the songs associated with the adult characters and actors. For example, the aforementioned "Where Is Love" contains a fairly wide melodic range and a number of wide intervals. Like many of the film's other songs, it is this kind of melodic material that makes the score so memorable.

As mentioned earlier, another interesting feature of Bart's songs, especially notable because of the film's release at about the same time as rock musicals were starting to appear, is the use of traditional Tin Pan Alley-era AABA song form. "Where Is Love" is an example. Similarly, "As Long as He Needs Me," a better-remembered song than "Where Is Love," includes a bit of early 20th-century verse-chorus form.

British Film Institute contributor John Oliver describes *Oliver!* as "one of the most successful British films ever made" based on its reception by critics and audiences. Oliver writes, "With its recreation of 19th-century London on the studio lot, from a bustling Covent Garden to a mammoth Bloomsbury Square, via the slums and gin houses of the Victorian underworld, the film is never less than stunning" (Oliver 2018).

ON THE TOWN

The movie *On the Town* has one of the more interesting and convoluted histories of all the movie musicals detailed in this chapter. The work started as the 1944 ballet *Fancy Free*, with music by the young composer-pianist-conductor Leonard Bernstein and choreography by Jerome Robbins. The ballet, with its story about three U.S. sailors on shore leave for a day in New York City, was expanded into the musical *On the Town* in 1944, with book and lyrics by Betty Comden and Adolph Green. When the 1949 film was produced, it contained the stage musical's famous ballet scene ("A Day in New York"), the song "New York, New York," but precious little else of Leonard Bernstein's original score. MGM replaced the bulk of Bernstein's music with what was deemed to be more commercially viable. Listeners familiar with the complexities of Bernstein's music will probably easily notice that the film version of

On the Town has a certain inconsistency with regards to musical style (particularly the country-style song "Count on Me"). However, despite the fact that so much of the original music vanished in the film, the movie is punchy enough in structure with appealing enough songs that it manages to capture the spirit of the stage musical, while allowing the film's stars—particularly Frank Sinatra and Gene Kelly—feature numbers that are more in keeping with the movie musical pop songs of the late 1940s than the more challenging music of Bernstein.

Despite the success of the stage version of *On the Town* and the relative lack of music by Leonard Bernstein in the film, Bernstein's "New York, New York" is recognized as a movie musical classic; the American Film Institute ranked the song the 41st greatest movie song of all time (American Film Institute 2004). The ballet sequence also provides the audience with a strong sense of how Bernstein could combine his classical and jazz sensibilities into a musical style that still perfectly captures the spirit of its time, much the same way in which Bernstein's music for *West Side Story* would do in the next decade.

On the Town is an excellent example of a movie musical that simply could not be nearly as visually effective on stage: in short, it is a musical that seems to be made for film. In particular, the movie makes full use of location scenes from around New York. In fact, it is one of the first movie musicals to do so. That numerous later movie musicals used either the locations from the storylines or locations that could believably be thought to be the actual locations in the storyline perhaps can be traced back to the successful integration of the city of New York into the filming of *On the Town*.

The ballet sequence known as "A Day in New York," the title taken from a performance advertising poster that Gene Kelly's character encounters as he walks through the city, is one of the more significant parts of the movie. For one thing, Leonard Bernstein's music was retained for this lengthy ballet. For another, the ballet plays a familiar role within the MGM musical style. As Jane Feuer wrote in *The Hollywood Musical*, "Dream ballets in MGM musicals emphasize either the wish of the dreamer (the Pirate ballet, the first dream ballet in Lili) or they represent a tentative working out of the problems of the primary narrative (*Yolanda and the Thief*, "A Day in New York" in *On the Town*, the *An American in Paris* ballet, the second dream in *Lili*)." The author continues, "Those ballets which recapitulate the plot retrace the narrative in symbolic form to its point of rupture. The resolution of the narrative comes on the heels of the ballet, implying the dream ballet has been catalytic in resolving the film's narrative" (Feuer 1982, 74).

Despite composer Leonard Bernstein's displeasure with how some of his work was removed from the finished film and replaced with songs that were thought to be more conventionally accessible, *On the Town* has continued to be recognized over the years as one of the best and most entertaining movie musicals ever. In 2006, the American Film Institute ranked *On the Town* at No. 19 on its list of the 25 greatest movie musicals of all time (American Film Institute 2006).

PURPLE RAIN[1]

In one of the more memorable scenes from a 1980s' pop music-related film, a crowd of racially and ethnically diverse young people in a Minneapolis nightclub slowly begins to sway and wave their hands over their heads as they become immersed in a new song, performed by "The Kid," as it debuts. This mysterious character, The Kid, had seen his family disintegrate, had seen his standing in the musical hierarchy of his community greatly diminished, and his new girlfriend and potential bandmate had broken ranks to form another rival band. To add insult to the injury, the now ex-girlfriend became romantically involved with The Kid's archrival. To top it off, The Kid was on the verge of losing his regular performance gig and seeing his band entirely disintegrate. The song that ended up saving the day was "Purple Rain." This concert scene was the grand finale of Prince's film *Purple Rain*. The film, the soundtrack album, and the single release of the title track were unqualified successes: Prince and the Revolution had the No. 1 album, film, and pop single in the same week. This put the group in a highly exclusive club because by that time only Elvis Presley and the Beatles had enjoyed a simultaneous No. 1 soundtrack album, film, and single from the film.

In his book *The Great Movie Musicals: A Viewer's Guide to 168 Films That Really Sing*, Don Tyler wrote, "Film critic Vincent Canby thought Prince was 'a riveting spectacle' in the film's performance sequences, but felt his off-stage screen presence was 'a pale reflection of the dynamic recording personality.' Although it may not be entirely true, the reason for *Purple Rain* seems to be the soundtrack album" (Tyler 2010, 249).

Tyler's assessment seems to suggest that the fact that Prince simultaneously had the nation's No. 1 album, film, and single revolved around the album. In retrospect, there are elements of truth in Tyler's assessment as well as in that of Canby: the most stunning sequences in *Purple Rain* easily are the live performance sequences, especially the film's conclusion when Prince and the Revolution perform the film's title song, and this was one of, if not the, strongest soundtrack albums of the rock era.

Let us examine, then, *Purple Rain* in the context of its music and the soundtrack album.

A native of Minneapolis, Minnesota, Prince Rogers Nelson had two parents who were musicians. When his parents divorced, Prince split his time between his parents. The relationship between Prince and his parents appears to form at least part of the basis of the storyline of *Purple Rain*. Prince's first album, *For You*, and his second, *Prince*, were released in 1978 and 1979, respectively, by Warner Bros. Although Prince later became associated with his bands the Revolution (which performed in *Purple Rain*) and the New Power Generation, on his first two albums, Prince provided virtually all the vocals and instruments, similar to what Stevie Wonder had done on his first albums after he turned 21 and entered into a new contract with Motown. The fact that Prince was an iconic electric guitarist and a technically gifted keyboardist and drummer meant that throughout his career, he was able to record numerous demo tracks, tracks that were not fully fleshed out until years later, and some which never made it to the official release. Therefore, Prince releases sometimes represented years of growth, tinkering, and development, while sometimes they were Prince-only tracks that just happened not to be released until years after they were initially recorded.

Prince certainly enjoyed chart success and was building a solid fan base at the end of the 1970s and the beginning of the 1980s. His popularity and name and image recognition, however, became more widespread with the release of the *Purple Rain* film, the soundtrack album, and the singles taken from the movie's soundtrack.

Despite the fact that Prince and the Revolution enjoyed the No. 1 pop single, album, and film during one memorable week, the album *Purple Rain* is about much more than commercial success. The songs, written by Prince alone or in collaboration with members of the Revolution aim at a wider audience than any previous Prince material, succeeding across the board. Two of the songs, the album and film's title track and "When Doves Cry," became true classics of late 20th-century pop music, and were included in various millennial lists of the most significant music of the entire rock era.

The album's opening track, "Let's Go Crazy," begins with a slow synthesized organ chorale, which supports Prince's spoken introduction. Prince portrays a preacher in his monologue. He confirms the existence of the afterlife and the bliss that it will provide. He concludes, however, by observing that in this earthly life, "you're on your own." The song itself is upbeat party material that features a stylistic blend of new wave rock and R&B. The melody of "Let's Go Crazy" is built-in short easy-to-remember phrases, as is the case with numerous pop songs of the late 20th century into the 21st century. Perhaps the most notable feature of the melody is the syncopated descending figure that accompanies the words "take us down." While this represents just a touch of musical text painting, it is not the last example on the album. In the conclusion of the track, Prince confirms his reputation as a notable lead electric guitarist with a cadenza that suggests the possible influence of 1960s icon Jimi Hendrix.

One notable feature of the lyrics of "Let's Go Crazy," which mirrors numerous other songs from throughout Prince's career, is Prince's treatment of sexuality within a religious context. As seen in songs such as this, sexual pleasure is viewed as God's gift to humankind, thus making this and other Prince songs in a similar vein almost a late 20th-century and early 21st-century musical interpretation of the Old Testament Song of Solomon integrated with Christian imagery. Similar treatments of the physical pleasure of sex can be found particularly strongly throughout this album and on *Around the World in a Day* and *1999*.

"Take Me with U," a duet with Apollonia Kotero, serves a clear function in the film, confirming the love side of what becomes a love-hate relationship between the two characters. Although the track can easily be missed, given the prominence and notoriety of "Purple Rain," "Darling Nikki," "I Would Die 4 U," and "When Doves Cry," it is one of the more effective pure love songs that Prince ever produced and is catchy, like the best pop music of its time.

Purple Rain contains three songs composed, performed, and produced by Prince, without the collaboration of the Revolution. This fact brings up one of the more noteworthy aspects of Prince's work as a musician. Although he was best known as a singer and guitarist, as mentioned earlier, Prince was also a technically and musically gifted keyboard player and drummer. Although some of the demo and finished recordings on which Prince was the sole singer and instrumentalist use drum machines, Prince left a wealth of material that showcased his expertise on percussion, keyboard, and fretted stringed instruments. The Prince-alone songs that are part of the *Purple Rain* soundtrack certainly are notable examples.

The first of the Prince-alone tracks, "The Beautiful One," is a Quiet Storm-style ballad in which Prince plays the classic role of a man whose lover has to choose between him and another man. For a Prince song, the lyrics are uncompromisingly romantic—as opposed to physical—and are supported by an engaging melody and full-sounding synthesizer arrangement and production. By contrast, "Computer Blue" combines elements of R&B and heavy metal rock. In this song, Prince addresses a woman known as Computer Blue, whom he believes needs to "learn love and lust." One of the notable features of the piece is the synthesizer figure that tops each line of the chorus. This chromatic figure bears at least some resemblance to a figure in Jonathan Richman's punk/new wave song "Pablo Picasso." Perhaps the most interesting part of "Computer Blue" is the sharp contrast between the machine-like sound of the synthesizers and Prince's virtuosic electric guitar solo. This musical contrast aligns with the contrast between the title character's machine-like precision and the pleasures of the heart and flesh, in which Prince tells her she needs to engage.

The album's next track, "Darling Nikki," gained notoriety through its association with the movement to adorn recordings that included explicit references to sex, violence, or drug use with parental warning labels. It was after finding her young daughter listening to "Darling Nikki," a song in which Prince refers to Nikki's "bumping and grinding" and masturbation, that Tipper Gore, working with other members of the Washington, D.C., political elite, founded the Parents Music Resource Center to combat such references in popular song lyrics.

"Darling Nikki" is a powerful, rhythmically heavy, slow, bluesy rock piece. Prince's melody for the verses has a sing-song quality, which he presents in a sly voice that suggests that the childlike innocence of the tune is meant to be ironic: Nikki is anything but sexually innocent. The harder-edged rock-oriented chorus, in which Prince details Nikki's highly erotic bump and grind, features more powerful vocals and distorted hard rock-style lead guitar. Although "Darling Nikki" is most famous—or infamous—for its lyrics, it is also an interesting song from a structural standpoint. Not only does Prince contrast the childlike quality of the verses with the more musically sexually energized music of the chorus he also includes a gospel-style vocal chorale as well as elements of classical minimalism near the end of the song.

Over the course of his career, Prince enjoyed a number of strong, commercially successful pop hits, including "Purple Rain" and "1999," however, arguably his most successful single was "When Doves Cry." This song topped the *Billboard* R&B charts for eight weeks and the magazine's pop charts for five weeks. In addition to making several millennial lists as one of the most important songs of the 20th century, "When Doves Cry" continues to find itself on lists of the greatest pop songs of all time. For example, in 2011 *Rolling Stone* ranked "When Doves Cry" at No. 52 in the magazine's list of "500 Greatest Songs of All Time" (The Editors of *Rolling Stone* 2011).

"When Doves Cry" makes more sense in the context of the film than it does as a stand-alone song. That being said, the song captures the sense of despair that comes out of a dysfunctional relationship. Prince also provides a musical depiction of the hollowness that his character expresses in the lyrics through the instrumental texture. Specifically, this is a rare song of the rock era that contains no bassline. The entire audio spectrum is limited to the high and middle ranges.

Prince and the Revolution's "I Would Die 4 U" is not part of the canon of contemporary Christian music; however, it is one of the most purely religious songs from this part of Prince's career. In the *Purple Rain* film, the song tends to take on multiple layers of meaning, as Prince's character is partly a messianic figure and partly simply a person who tells his lover that he is willing to sacrifice his life for her. The combination of Christian imagery and rhythmic dance music supports the overarching philosophy of life that Prince espoused in songs such as "1999," "Let's Go Crazy," and others: the Messiah will appear at the end of the world to take believers with him, but meanwhile, God's purpose for us on Earth is for us to enjoy ourselves.

Despite the immense popularity of "When Doves Cry," perhaps the most iconic song on the album and in the film is the title track. Anecdotally, this seems to be the one song from *Purple Rain* that is heard on oldies and '80s-format radio late in the second decade of the 21st century. The song also plays the most prominent role in the film. In the film, the song's music is written by The Kid's bandmates Wendy and Lisa (Wendy Melvoin and Lisa Coleman's real names are used in the film; however, Prince is known solely as "The Kid"). After refusing to use the music, The Kid finally gives in and writes lyrics to complete the song, which is performed at the band's make-or-break performance. The image of the "purple rain" can be understood as a metaphor for the appearance of God at the end of the world, and its use here reinforces that interpretation from earlier in the album.

Musically, "Purple Rain" is a mixture of the familiar and the unexpected. The chord progression of the verses and the oft-repeated chorus include the most basic of harmonies, triads (three-note chords) built on the first, fourth, fifth, and sixth notes of the major scale. This collection of harmonies would not have been outside the standard practice in Western music for hundreds of years before "Purple Rain." Thus, "Purple Rain" features a certain sense of timelessness. Certainly, the influence of early 20th-century gospel music can be heard in the vocal arrangement; this helps to lend "Purple Rain" the feeling of an anthem.

Like "Take Me with U" earlier on the album, "Purple Rain" is thoroughly engaging as a pop song, but at the same time has an unexpected and unusual phrase structure. Specifically, the end of each verse includes what might sound like an extra measure of music to some listeners. Because the overall melodic shape and the harmonic material are so typical of conventional pop music, this feeling of phrase extension tends to stand out. It sets up a focus on the start of the chorus that cannot help but draw even the most casual listener in.

The song "Purple Rain" is also a showpiece for Prince's work as a lead electric guitarist. In fact, the technical passages in his solos and the bluesy approach suggest the influences of both Jimi Hendrix and Carlos Santana. For listeners familiar with the recordings of Hendrix, the parlando vocal style that Prince uses in the verses and rhythm and the way in which he drops in pitch on the phrase "but you can't seem to make up your mind" also call to mind the work of Hendrix on slow songs such as "Little Wing" and "Hey Joe."

In the end, *Purple Rain* is a film and an album that is a pop classic, containing several significant singles; however, some of the lyrical references in songs such as "I Would Die 4 U," "Purple Rain," and "When Doves Cry" make even greater sense when placed in the context of the film. The film remains a classic of the pop music-related genre, with performance footage that adds to the impact of the music itself.

THE ROCKY HORROR PICTURE SHOW

Back in the second half of the 1970s and well into the 1980s, the movie *The Rocky Horror Picture Show* was *the* film that audiences attended perhaps primarily in the spirit of an avant-garde happening. Audience members knew the lines, sang along with the songs, danced "the Time Warp" in the aisles and in the front of the theater, used squirt guns to reenact the rain in the opening scenes, threw decks of cards in the air when the word "cards" was uttered far later in the movie, and replied to lines in unison in the same way in movie theaters across the country. In her master's thesis *Becoming the Wig: Mis/Identifications and Citationality in Queer Rock Musicals*, Samantha Michele Riley traces this phenomenon to "the film's first midnight showing at the Waverly Theatre . . . in New York City's gay neighborhood in Greenwich Village in 1976" (Riley 2008, 20). Writer Al LaValley refers to the "conscious camp" of the film (LaValley 1995, 63) and suggests that "despite its transvestite hero from Transylvania who has sex with both Brad and

Janet [two of the story's principal characters], is still largely attended by a straight teenage audience" (La Valley 64).

One might describe *The Rocky Horror Picture Show* as a cult film, but as one who participated in these happening-like events a fair number of times at the Graceland Cinema in Columbus, Ohio, back in the day, the movie was too much a part of the general slightly left-field popular culture of the time to really represent a "cult" film. Still, despite the greater-than-cult impact that *The Rocky Horror Picture Show* made in the second half of the 1970s and beyond, critics and historians still use the "cult" designation. For example, Caroline Joan S. Picart called the motion picture "the most successful cult film ever made," noting that it was still in theatrical release (Picart 2003, 62). The movie remains in limited theatrical release, now well over 40 years after it premiered.

Despite the fact that *The Rocky Horror Picture Show* is perhaps the only truly well-known and iconic version of the work, what became a popular film musical started out as a stage project, *The Rocky Horror Show*. In fact, several of the principal actors in the film, including its writer, Richard O'Brien, had starred in the original British production. Interestingly, despite some favorable reviews for the stage version, initially, the film was not widely praised. As Picart notes in her study of the film, within approximately a decade after the film's 1975 release—by which time it had achieved its "cult" status—critical reaction had shifted toward the favorable. It seems logical that perhaps part of this critical reevaluation could be tied to the almost-rabid extent to which fans had taken to *The Rocky Horror Picture Show*.

The music of the film focuses on two areas: pre–British Invasion rock and roll and 1970s glam rock. "The Time Warp," for example, exemplifies the glam style associated with David Bowie, the New York Dolls, T. Rex, and others. The movie's mad scientist, Dr. Frank N. Furter (portrayed by Tim Curry), dresses in a campy drag style that is also in line with the glam style. In contrast, "Hot Patootie—Bless My Soul," performed in the movie by American retro-rock singer Meatloaf, exemplifies the movie's musical ties to the late 1950s and early 1960s. Also, the opening introductory number "Science Fiction/Double Feature" reflects the late 1950s, one of the traditional time periods for B science fiction movies.

Although the glam style incorporated by O'Brien might not seem exaggerated compared with some of the glam work of the New York Dolls, Marc Bolan, David Bowie, or some other early-1970s practitioners of the genre, O'Brien's 1950s' style is highly stylized. For example, even though many rock and roll songs of the 1950s included screeching tenor saxophone solos, the sax solo figures in "Hot Patootie/Bless My

Soul" are decidedly over the top. Perhaps the best way to fully appreciate O'Brien's music and his script—cowritten with Jim Sharman—and Sharman's direction of *The Rocky Horror Picture Show* is to consider the movie as both a tribute to and a parody of the science fiction film genre—especially the low-budget, "B" movies of the genre—and a tribute and parody of aspects of the glam and 1950s' biker subcultures.

Part of the sense of exaggerated style that runs throughout the film can be attributed to costume designer Susan Blane. Some fans of the film back in the 1970s noted ties between Blane's costumes, the glam style of the time, as well as the punk rock fashions that had not fully emerged in popular culture at the time of the movie's release. Blane claimed that the ripped fishnet stockings and other costume design features, dyed hair, and so on that she used were part of the punk scene that was starting to develop at the time (the mid-1970s), and that the movie helped to bring that sense of fashion into public consciousness. Blane stated in an interview, "I wouldn't dream of taking the credit for inventing punk! Frankly, Malcolm McLaren should take the same attitude. It grew, and *The Rocky Horror Picture Show* was definitely a big part of that build-up." (Evans and Michaels 2002, 10). Elsewhere, Blane admitted that when American actors Susan Sarandon and Barry Bostwick were cast as Janet Weiss and Brad Majors, respectively, she used stereotypes of American fashion in designing their outfits (e.g., Brad's shortish trousers and white socks) (Siegel 2011).

One of the major themes of the movie—not to mention the glam-rock fashion and style on which it is based—is the questioning of sexuality. Clearly, Dr. Frank N. Furter, who eventually seduces both Brad and Janet, is bisexual. The seduction of Brad allows a hitherto unknown side of him to come out, and in the final "floor show" sequence, the staid and straight-laced Dr. Everett Scott (portrayed by Jonathan Adams), despite wheelchair-bound, ends up wearing fishnet stockings and garters. All of this questioning and breaking down of barriers, however, are handled in what at the time was a humorous and exaggerated campy and kitschy way. This aspect of the film seems likely to resonate less well in the social climate of the 21st century.

The attitude toward sex in general—whether heterosexual or homosexual—clearly reflects the counterculture mores of the pre-AIDS era. In fact, it is difficult to understand how *The Rocky Horror Picture Show* could have been written at any time after the early 1980s because of how sex has been treated so differently subsequent to the AIDS pandemic that so greatly affects societies around the world, coming into prominence in the mass media after the deaths of well-known entertainment figures such as Rock Hudson (1985) and Liberace (1987).

Musical highlights of the film include the introductory "Science Fiction/Double Feature" sequence. The song itself sets the stage for the film as a tribute to the "great" B-movies of the past, and in it songwriter Richard O'Brien uses a stylized 1950s ballad style with lyrics that project back to the era of *Forbidden Planet*, *The Day the Earth Stood Still*, *Plan 9 from Outer Space*, *The Attack of the 50 Foot Woman*, and so on. The reprise of the song at the end of the film is heard in the context of an even earlier reference, that of actress Fay Wray being carried up the R.K.O. tower by King Kong.

Brad Majors's biggest number "Dammit Janet," still resonates as a humorous takeoff on pop love songs. Frank N. Furter's "Sweet Transvestite" and "I'm Going Home" reflect two highly contrasting aspects of the early 1970s glam rock style. The first appearance of "The Time Warp" is greatly enhanced by the humor provided by the criminologist (portrayed by Charles Gray), who instructs the audience in the specifics of the dance moves involved. Eddie (Meatloaf) is one character that only appears alive in one major sequence; however, his "Hot Patootie/Bless My Soul" is another musical highlight. It should be noted that these songs, Janet's "Touch-a, Touch-a, Touch-a, Touch Me," and the other solo and ensemble numbers are highly context-driven. To put it another way, they relate specifically to the storyline and do not necessarily always make a great deal of sense outside the context of the storyline. That aspect of the music, combined with the exaggerated glam and old-school rock and roll styles, and the risqué nature of many of the songs make for a musical without popular record-chart hits, despite the popularity of the film itself and the accessibility of much of O'Brien's score.

Perhaps as is fitting for a movie that many still think of as a "cult" film, *The Rocky Horror Picture Show* remains a favorite and has still never been completely withdrawn from the theatrical release. Late in the second decade of the 21st century, however, it is not so much the must-participate-in-every-Saturday-night classic as much as it is a staple of the Halloween season at movie theaters across the United States. The film, however, is still a sing-along classic. This was acknowledged by Tasha Robinson in an article on the ability to sing along musicals in which she wrote that "'The Time Warp,' 'Dammit Janet,' and 'Sweet Transvestite, are winners . . . At most *Rocky Horror* showings half the audience is out of tune anyway, so even people who sing flat and can't remember lyrics half the time have a sing-along music made just for them" (Robinson 2006). In the age of streaming home video, it might be tempting to experience *The Rocky Horror Picture Show* in the comfort of one's living room. That provides only a small part of the experience;

this is one movie musical that must be experienced in a theater with all of the audience commentary, dancing, acting, use of props, and so on. Just remember to ask the question "Meatloaf again?" at the right time.

SEVEN BRIDES FOR SEVEN BROTHERS

Some movie musicals of the past were well received by audiences and critics when they first appeared but have not necessarily aged well. Such would seem to be the case with the 1954 film *Seven Brides for Seven Brothers*. Directed by Stanley Donen and starring principally Howard Keel as Adam Pontipee and Jane Powell as Milly Pontipee, *Seven Brides for Seven Brothers* featured music by Saul Chaplin and Gene de Paul and lyrics by Johnny Mercer. The plot was based on the Stephen Vincent Benét short story "The Sobbin' Women," itself based on the ancient Roman legend of the Rape of the Sabines. The film was popular when it was released, won the Academy Award for Best Scoring of a Music Picture, and was also nominated for the Academy Award for Best Picture. At the time of its release, *Variety* gave *Seven Brides for Seven Brothers* a favorable review (The Staff of *Variety* 1953), and the dance scenes—in particular, the barn raising—are still mentioned among the most memorable film dance scenes of all time. In 2006, the American Film Institute named it the 21st greatest movie musical of all time (American Film Institute 2006), and in 2004, it was added to the Library of Congress's National Film Registry. However, the plot, which included six of Adam Pontipee's brothers kidnapping six women from a small Oregon town on the other side of a mountain pass from the Pontipees' farm to marry them, has resulted in some highly negative commentary. For example, writing in the alternative press weekly *The Chicago Reader*, critic Jonathan Rosenbaum described *Seven Brides for Seven Brothers* as "profoundly sexist and hummable," adding that the story was based on the kind of "patriarchal rape fantasies that were considered 'cute' . . . at the time" (Rosenbaum 2012). Blogger for *The Paris Review* Sadie Stein wrote, "I defy anyone to watch it [the barn dance scene] and not get just a little bit cheered up. Yet we might as well admit it: *Seven Brides for Seven Brothers* is sort of . . . problematic" in reference to the nature of the storyline (Stein 2014).

Even if one is leery of the film based on the kidnap-and-forced-marriage premise, the choreography of Michael Kidd and its execution by a cast that was unusually heavy on the gymnastics and professional dance expertise remains a classic. As critic Rosenbaum noted above, the tunes—particularly "Bless Your Beautiful Hide"—are indeed hummable.

Johnny Mercer's lyrics run the gamut from clever with interesting rhymes to corny, with perhaps the corniest coming in the woodchopping scene. However, even in the scene when some of the text contains several groaners, Michael Kidd's choreography of a commonplace work activity elevates the whole to something greater than the sum of its parts.

The surface of the premise of Adam Pontipee's initial trip into town to find a bride—which he does only slightly later that day in Milly—and the Pontipee brothers' kidnapping of six other young women commoditizes women. However, it should be noted that Milly is a strong figure. She teaches Adam's brothers the proper ways to court a woman, although they soon forget that training when Adam shares with them the ancient Roman story of the Rape of the Sabine Women, which he reads from one of Milly's history books. Milly also teaches the brothers table manners, albeit with mixed success. Most importantly, however, she lays down the law when the brothers return to the farm with the six townswomen. The only evidence the audience sees that anything of a sexual nature has occurred is when Milly herself is revealed to be pregnant by her husband, Adam. Still, some 21st-century audiences will feel some discomfort as they see the women start to fall in love with the brothers.

Despite the "problematic" (Stein 2014) nature of the plot, *Seven Brides for Seven Brothers* left a legacy in the 1960s (1968–1970) with the television series *Here Come the Brides*, although the setting and time periods were slightly different (e.g., Seattle as opposed to the Oregon Territory, and the 1860s, as opposed to 1850), and the women of *Here Come the Brides* were the ones who went west in search of husbands. The women of *Here Come the Brides* were also all-in-all stronger characters, and the principal characters were three of each gender, as opposed to seven. More directly than that late-1960s television show, a stage version of *Seven Brides for Seven Brothers* was mounted in 1978, and CBS produced a short-lived television series in the early 1980s based on the movie.

As mentioned earlier, perhaps the main highlight of the movie is Michael Kidd's choreography and the dancing of the Pontipee brothers. Howard Keel (Adam) and Jane Powell (Milly) clearly are the singing stars of the film. For their singing and the impressive dancing sequences, *Seven Brides for Seven Brothers* is one of the must-see movie musicals, despite the problems posed by its plot.

SHOW BOAT

The 1927 musical *Show Boat* holds a special place in the history of the American musical. *Show Boat* was a huge almost-operatic work that stood in sharp contrast to the mostly light, sometimes thinly plotted musicals of the first quarter of the 20th century. Perhaps because of the importance of the show, perhaps because of the richness of the show's plot, and perhaps because of the quality of Jerome Kern's music and Oscar Hammerstein II's lyrics, in the quarter-century after the stage musical's premiere, *Show Boat* was adapted into the film medium three times—in 1929, 1936, and 1951, respectively.

The 1929 version of *Show Boat*, released as early as it was during the era of the so-called talkies, was not fully conceived as a movie musical. It was based on the same 1926 Edna Ferber novel, *Show Boat*, as Kern and Hammerstein's show, and was also inspired by the 1927 stage musical; however, the movie is probably best characterized as a partial talkie, not entirely committed to the brand-new medium.

The 1936 version of *Show Boat* remains the classic rendition. The American Film Institute ranked the film No. 24 on its list of the 25 greatest movie musicals of all time (American Film Institute 2006). The organization also ranked "Ol' Man River" No. 24 on its list of the 100 greatest movie songs of all time (American Film Institute 2004). The problem with this film is that in the 21st century, it is not as widely available as is the more commercially successful 1951 MGM production. The presence of Paul Robeson in the cast of the 1936 film also caused distribution challenges. When Robeson was blacklisted from Hollywood in 1950 for his communistic views, the 1936 version of *Show Boat* largely disappeared until the 1970s.

The 1951 George Sydney-directed version focuses on the African American workers and the interracial relationship between Julie and Steve less than the stage musical and less than the 1936 film. Kern and Hammerstein had replaced three songs from the original stage version with new material for the 1936 film—these were not used in the 1951 version. Adding to the removal of the 1951 version from what Kern and Hammerstein had written back in the 1920s is the fact that much of Hammerstein's book/dialogue was rewritten. It is interesting to note that both the 1929 and the 1936 films included members of the original Broadway casts. Most notable—and ultimately most damaging for the legacy of the 1936 film—was Paul Robeson's appearance as Joe, the dock worker best remembered for the song "Ol' Man River."

Although the 1936 film is difficult to find—it was not released for home video—many of the songs are available on various YouTube channels. Particularly interesting are the "Ol' Man River" sequence and the first appearance of "Can't Help Lovin' Dat Man," as sung by Julie. These sequences are fundamentally different in the 1936 and 1951 versions of *Show Boat*.

In the 1936 film, Queenie, the African American cook aboard the showboat, hears Julie singing "Can't Help Lovin' Dat Man" and recognizes it as a song that is known only by black women. Coming as it does before the audience has any evidence that Julie is of mixed race, Queenie's reaction in the 1936 film—as had been the case in the stage version of the show—portends this revelation. In contrast, the character of Queenie was significantly reduced in the 1951 film. So, instead of Queenie providing a relatively clear hint about Julie's background, the audience is left with Julie's dancing demonstration and lesson for Magnolia at the end of the song. Here, Julie teaches Magnolia some steps that are popular among black dancers but not widely known by whites.

Perhaps the starkest musical contrast between the 1936 and 1951 films is in the first "Ol' Man River" sequence (the song is reprised later in both films). In the 1936 film, Paul Robeson's Joe sings while he is sitting on the dock. Robeson's performance is cut with visual images of black men working, getting drunk, and ending up incarcerated to match the lyrical references in the song. Late in the song, Robeson is accompanied by a chorus of black laborers. The 1936 version of "Ol' Man River" is taken at a noticeably faster tempo than in the later film.

The 1936 "Ol' Man River" focuses on the harsh working conditions and the harsh life lived by black workers—it is very much a song that seems to capture the plight of blacks, and in retrospect, probably resonated especially well during the Great Depression. The tempo of the 1936 version casts "Ol' Man River" as a work song of sorts. Although this version of "Ol' Man River" sequence has been widely praised and is perhaps one of Paul Robeson's most iconic film performances, there are some ways in which William Warfield's performance in the 1951 film make a greater impact and a stronger political statement—or at least a political statement that is in keeping with a later time.

Warfield's Joe is shown in a considerably more upright position as he sings the song in 1951. The 1951 film does not include the cut-to shots of, for example, the drunk ending up in jail. The staging in 1951 presents Joe as a prouder man than the Robeson's Joe. This is a Joe who exhibits more of a tie with the post–World War II civil rights movement than the 1936 Joe. Arguably, because of Warfield's vocal style and because of the slow tempo of his performance of the song, the 1951 "Ol' Man River" is more akin to the 19th-century sorrow songs that came out of slavery. It is sadder feeling and, in some respects, speaks to the sorrow that comes out of knowing that freedom is slow to come as well as acceptance and equality. In both cases, "Ol' Man River" is the musical highlight of *Show Boat*.

One area in which the 1951 version of *Show Boat* has not aged particularly well is in Magnolia's (Kathryn Grayson) vocal style. Kathryn Grayson brings an operatic feel to the role; however, the operatic vibrato, in particular, seems out of place for the daughter of the showboat captain and his wife. She is easily the most studied female-sounding singer in the cast, despite the fact that other songs in the movie are sung by characters who are supposedly seasoned entertainers. This is perhaps most easily experienced in "Make Believe" and "You Are Love." Howard Keel's approach as Gaylord Ravenal is also more studied than what one might expect from a professional gambler; however, given his character's greater age and experience and the fact that he seems to be skilled in pretending something he is not, it is not as glaring.

One area in which the 1951 version is considerably more visually stunning than the earlier versions—particularly as the 1929 and 1936 versions were in black and white—is the full use of the Technicolor, not only in the showboat entertainers' costumes but also in their daily-wear clothes, as well as Gaylord Ravenal's outfit in the story's opening. The black children and the black laborers are not costumed as colorfully. However, the overall effect of marrying costuming and Technicolor, while visually stunning, gives the 1951 version of *Show Boat* more of a fantasy feel than the grittier setting felt in the 1936 version of the musical.

There are other differences between the stage show and the various film adaptations. Although these have little to do with the music part of the various versions of *Show Boat*, the time compression that was written into the 1951 film is worth noting. For audience members who have experienced the full theatrical experience, the truncation can seem somewhat startling.

Both the 1936 and the 1951 film versions seem to emphasize the subservient role of black characters. Although this might depict the relationship of the races in the South in the late 19th century, it also serves an important structural role in the movie, perhaps captured in the movie versions of the musical better than is possible on stage. This subservient role is confirmed in several ways, including through dialogue, how characters interact, costuming, employment, and so on.

Julie's character is interesting in the film versions. She is acknowledged as being of mixed race. Although her relationship with her husband, Steve, in the early part of the story seems strong enough, and he and Magnolia seem to fully accept her for who she is. Unfortunately, later Julie is found as a hopeless alcoholic lounge singer in Chicago. This is the setting in which the character sings the song "Bill," a song by Jerome

Kern and P. G. Wodehouse that predated *Show Boat* but was incorporated by Kern and Oscar Hammerstein into the show. Both Helen Morgan from the 1936 film and Annette Warren, who provided the singing for Ava Gardner in the 1951 film, give "Bill" a jazzy improvisatory feel. Arguably, Warren's approach in the 1951 film contrasts with her more straightforward singing in Julie's first song in the movie, "Can't Help Lovin' Dat Man," which might suggest to some viewers either that Julie is now more open about the African American side of her heritage (the performance has a more jazz-related feel than that of "Can't Help . . ."), while other viewers might interpret the relative looseness as a suggestion of Julie's state of inebriation.

In this nightclub rehearsal setting, Julie acquiesces her job as the club's vocalist to Magnolia (who does not realize that this has transpired). One could interpret this as an example of a black character acting in a subservient way for a white character; however, other viewers might interpret Julie's actions here, and when she later confronts the gambler in the 1951 film, as actions that are tied to her earlier close friendship with Magnolia.

Despite some of the racial references that have not aged well and problems with the availability of the 1936 film, *Show Boat* lives on as one of the most important Broadway musicals in history, one that was adapted into two classics of the movie musical genre.

SINGIN' IN THE RAIN

Widely acknowledged as one of the greatest films in the history of the Hollywood motion picture industry, *Singin' in the Rain* is, in essence, a movie about movies. Specifically, the premise of this film revolves around the transition from the silent films to the talkies that became all the rage after the premiere of *The Jazz Singer*. And, as is fitting for a musical comedy, all does not go smoothly for the producers, actors, and technicians during this transitional phase, which provides unintended humor and outrage from 1920s audiences and high-spirited humor for audiences of *Singin' in the Rain*.

Principally, *Singin' in the Rain* starred Gene Kelly as silent film star Don Lockwood, Debbie Reynolds as Lamont's new girlfriend Kathy Selden, Donald O'Connor as musician Cosmo Brown, and Jean Hagen as silent film star Lina Lamont. Gene Kelly and Stanley Donen directed the film.

Among the hilarious problems associated with the early sound films—of course, as depicted in *Singin' in the Rain*—include ill-placed microphones that bring out noises from costumes more than the actors' voices; actors who unwittingly turn toward and then away from microphones creating wide volume changes, out of sync soundtrack, and visuals; and eventually the exposure of overdubbing of one particular actor's voice. These technical problems alone make for a highly entertaining film.

In addition to all the technical problems contributing to the hilarity of movie, part of the humor is provided by the relationships of the characters. Lina Lamont, despite the fact that she is be barely tolerated by Don Lockwood, her acting partner, believes that his feelings for her are just like the feelings his characters have for her characters in their films. As one might expect, Lamont's jealousy of Kathy Selden also figures prominently into the storyline, as well as in the humor. Ultimately, Lamont's voice proves to be completely unsuited to the talkie medium, which results in the studio having Selden overdub her voice in place of Lamont's voice. All of this comes to a humorous head when Selden provides Lamont's vocals at a live stage appearance and is then exposed as the real vocal star of the Lockwood and Lamont films.

As detailed by Mark Juddery in an article in *History Today* (Juddery 2010), *Singin' in the Rain* was not as highly regarded in the early 1950s as it would later become. In later decades, it has been widely regarded as one of the greatest movie musical comedies ever. As Thomas S. Hischak writes in his *Musicals in Film: A Guide to the Genre*, "Even without the musical numbers, this film would have been a comic treasure, but the songs and dances are the crowning touches." He continues by praising the new songs "Moses (Supposes)" and "Make 'Em Laugh," and writes, "the rest of the score was comprised of old Brown-Freed favorites that were so marvelously staged by codirector-choreographers Kelly and Donen that the songs are usually remembered for this film rather than their initial screen appearances" (Hischak 2017, 217). Others have also recognized the entertainment significance of Donald O'Connor's song-and-dance routine in "Make 'Em Laugh" and its humorous pitfalls and near-misses. The American Film Institute, for example, ranked the movie No. 49 on its list of the 100 greatest movie songs of all time (American Film Institute 2004). The Institute also ranked Gene Kelly, Debbie Reynolds, and O'Connor's performance of "Good Morning" No. 72 on the list (American Film Institute 2004). MGM also recognized the iconic nature of both Gene Kelly's performance of the film's title song and Donald O'Connor's singing and dancing in "Make 'Em Laugh" and included both sequences in the 1974 retrospective of the studio's greatest movie musical hits *That's Entertainment*.

Singin' in the Rain has also undergone critical analysis for some of the film's subtexts. In her study, *The Musical: Race, Gender and Performance*,

Susan Smith points to the "uncomplicated wholesomeness of Debbie Reynolds' own singing voice," which lacks "the greater strength and complex tonality associated with the singing voices of stars like Judy Garland, Doris Day and Barbra Streisand." According to Smith, Reynolds's voice, particularly as she sings Don's newly written song, reinforces the conventional female role of the character. Smith writes, "That Reynolds' voice was itself dubbed, both here and during the sequences where her character is supposed to be dubbing for Lina in 'The Dancing Cavalier,' ironically reinforces this sense of her voice being more susceptible to containment and control" (Smith 2005, 74).

The continuing popularity, relevance, and significance of *Singin' in the Rain* are confirmed by the fact that the movie is still widely in circulation even late in the second decade of the 21st century. It should be noted that *Singin' in the Rain* has also taken on a second life as a staple of symphony orchestras. In summer 2018, for example, the world-renowned Cleveland Orchestra performed the orchestral soundtrack along with the voices from the original film soundtrack to a large crowd at the Orchestra's summer outdoor venue, Blossom Music Center. This digitally edited version of the film has also seen live performances by other orchestras and is on the performance schedule of orchestras going into 2020.

Although *Singin' in the Rain* might not have been the best-received example of the genre upon its initial release, the movie grew to be recognized as one of the best film musicals of all time; in 2006, the American Film Institute named *Singin' in the Rain* the No. 1 movie musical of all time (American Film Institute 2006), and the title song was named by the Institute the No. 3 greatest movie song of all time (American Film Institute 2004).

THE SOUND OF MUSIC

If one were to survey Americans familiar with *The Sound of Music* and ask who played Maria in the musical, it seems entirely logical that the overwhelming response would be: "Julie Andrews." Such is the iconic nature of this film that it tends to frame many viewers' knowledge of the show. Apologies, then, to Mary Martin who pioneered the role in the original Broadway production.

In addition to Julie Andrews, *The Sound of Music* cast included Christopher Plummer as Captain Georg von Trapp, Richard Haydn as Max Detweiler, Eleanor Parker as Baroness Elsa von Schraeder, and Peggy Wood as the Mother Abbess. The von Trapp children were played by Charmian Carr, Nicholas Hammond, Heather Menzies, Duane Chase,

Angela Cartwright, Debbie Turner, and Kym Karath. Although certainly a minor character, the casting of Marni Nixon as Sister Sophia, part of the ensemble of nuns who sing "How Do You Solve a Problem Like Maria?," is worth noting. Nixon's singing overdubs might have been a significant part of movie musicals such as *West Side Story, Gentlemen Prefer Blondes, The King and I,* and numerous others, but she was rarely cast as an on-screen character.

The 1959 stage version and the 1965 film are both more complex structurally than some audience members might appreciate, particularly in composer Richard Rodgers's use of music as part of the drama. Musicologist Raymond Knapp (2004) analyzed Rodgers and screenplay writer/director Robert Wise's use of musical motives from the secular song "Maria" interwoven into the Roman Catholic service music for the wedding of Maria and the Captain, and the more disturbing linkage of the church bells at the end of the wedding scene to the bells subsequently associated in the film with the Anschluss, the annexation of Austria by Germany. Knapp also details the mixing of the sacred and the secular in other aspects of Rodgers's music, such as the hymn-like nature of the melody and harmony of "Climb Ev'ry Mountain," a song that is at the same time closely related structurally to standard Tin Pan Alley pop-song (AABA) form. Knapp also argues persuasively that the film has less to do with actual historical events in Europe in 1938 than it does with American identity.

Interestingly, such an appreciation of these kinds of structural and rhetorical points by a musicologist of the early 21st century has little to do with the initial reaction to *The Sound of Music* by movie critics. Critics at the time—as well as movie fans and critics over the years since the film's release—complained and continue to complain about the sentimentality of *The Sound of Music*. Despite the negative press that the film received, it was the highest-grossing Hollywood motion picture of 1965 and held the title of the highest-grossing movie in history through the end of the 1960s. So, *The Sound of Music* certainly resonated with moviegoers but was not received as warmly by critics. Nevertheless, in 2006, the American Film Institute ranked *The Sound of Music* at No. 4 on its list of the 25 greatest movie musicals of all time (American Film Institute 2006).

Although the film may have represented a commentary on life in the United States more than it painted an entirely accurate historical picture of Austria on the brink of takeover by the German Nazis, and although it may have been sentimental, *The Sound of Music* certainly contained more than just a few well-remembered songs. Some of these have been recognized over the years, including by the American Film Institute, which ranked "The Sound of Music" at No. 10, "My Favorite Things" at No. 64, and "Do-Re-Mi" at No. 88 on the Institute's list of the 100 greatest movie songs of all time (American Film Institute 2004).

Robert Wise won the Academy Awards for Best Picture and Best Director, Irwin Kostal won the Academy Award for Best Music for the scoring and adaptation of the original Broadway score, James Corcoran and Fred Hynes won the Oscar for Best Sound Recording, and William H. Reynolds won the Academy Award for Best Film Editing. Although she did not win the Oscar for Best Actress in a Leading Role, Julie Andrews was one of the nominees; Andrews did, however, win the Golden Globe Award for Best Motion Picture Actress, Musical or Comedy.

The Sound of Music was not just an award-winning movie with a storyline that strayed somewhat from history, it has become one of the most beloved movie musicals of all time. The lasting impact of *The Sound of Music* can be seen in several concrete ways. Perhaps one of the clearest examples of the impact of this musical—including both its stage and film versions—is the widespread assumption that "Edelweiss" is an Austrian folksong. It was a Rodgers and Hammerstein song written for the musical. However, the song captures the character of folk music and the notion of a nationalistic song that played an important role at a time of national turmoil (at least in the musical's storyline) that many people assume that it was pre-existing source material. That this continues to be the case over half a century after the debut of *The Sound of Music* is suggested by a 2015 article in *The Atlantic* on the song's use in both *The Sound of Music* and in the 21st-century television drama *The Man in the High Castle* (Garber 2015). As Knapp (2004) argued that the entire film is more about the United States than about the Nazi takeover of Austria, Garber argues that the association of "Edelweiss" in both *The Sound of Music* and in *The Man in the High Castle* with the Nazi era has more to do with American fascination with and fear of dystopian societies than with Austria in the 1930s.

Another indication of the extent to which songs of *The Sound of Music* became etched into popular consciousness is the fact that "Do-Re-Mi" is still used as an example of how the notes of the major scale are arranged in solfege syllables. It should be noted that the persistence of "Do-Re-Mi" as an educational tool has far exceeded the persistence of many other tunes that were used in past decades to remember, for example, ascending and descending intervals in high school and college sight-singing classes.

The continuing popularity and public consciousness of songs such as "Edelweiss" and "Do-Re-Mi" might have something to do with the fact that they are relatively easy to sing and to sing along with. In fact, in 2006, film critic Tasha Robinson ranked *The Sound of Music* at no. 1 on her list of "18 Movie Musicals You Can Actually Sing Along With." Robinson explained that "sing-along-style musicals generally require catchy number with a more limited range [than *Dreamgirls*, to which she compares the musicals on her list]—most famously, like *The Sound of Music*, which is so easy to join in with that *Sound of Music* sing-alongs, with special lyrics-inclusive prints of the film, are still a regular touring event" (Robinson 2006). Similarly, over half a century after the premiere of the movie and 60 years after the premiere of the stage version of *The Sound of Music*, several karaoke sing-along recordings are widely available that include songs such as "Maria," "Do-Re-Mi," "Sixteen Going on Seventeen," "The Sound of Music," "Edelweiss," "My Favorite Things," and so on.

However, the widespread knowledge of, the popularity of, and misconceptions about songs such as these *The Sound of Music* classics cannot necessarily be tied entirely to the film. The impact on popular culture of the movie version of *The Sound of Music*, specifically, is immense and is not limited to the English-speaking world. In Salzburg and other nearby locations in Austria, for example, there is an ongoing tourism industry that revolves around locations that were used in the film and others pertinent to the storyline. The site of the wedding of Maria and the Captain, St. Michael's Church, located in Mondsee, approximately 15 miles from Salzburg, remains a popular destination for tourists well over half a century after the movie premiered, as are Nonnberg Convent, Schloss Leopoldskron, Mirabell Gradens, and other film-related locations. Even a brief internet search will reveal that several companies continue to conduct location tours late in the second decade of the 21st century, well over half a century since the film premiered, thus demonstrating its continuing popularity.

As a testimony to the movie's box office impact, a July 2019 report at CNBC indicated that if box office revenues were adjusted for inflation, *The Sound of Music* would be the third highest-grossing film of all time, bested only by *Star Wars* and *Gone with the Wind* (Whitten 2019b).

A STAR IS BORN

Of all the storylines that have been repeated and remade throughout the history of the movie musical, perhaps none is as persistent as that of *A Star Is Born*. Although fans of great musicals are likely to know the 1954 version of the movie, which starred Judy Garland and James Mason, the movie was actually a remake. In the 1937 version, the two lead characters were actors; in the 1954 musical, Mason played an alcoholic actor on a downward career spiral and Garland portrayed an aspiring singer. It was this version that set the standard, both in terms of quality and by turning the story into a musical that revolved around an undiscovered singer. The best-known later versions, the 1976 film that starred Kris Kristofferson and Barbra Streisand, and the 2018 version, that starred Bradley Cooper and Lady Gaga, provided opportunities for both leads to sing by turning the older male character into a singer whose career is on a downward spiral because of drink and drugs.

The touches of humor of the 1954 musical are carried forward into the later versions. In addition, the 1954, 1976, and 2018 versions of the story include touches that connect them to their times. For example, Judy Garland's character, Esther, works as a carhop and provides the singing voice for a marionette in a television commercial, the drive-in being a part of 1950s popular culture and television being a new in-home entertainment.

One of the interesting structural anomalies of the 1954 version of the tale is that what is arguably the best-remembered song, "The Man That Got Away," is heard early in the film. It is, in fact, the song that Maine hears Esther singing spontaneously with some of her bandmates after the club in which they're performing has closed down. The sequence is notable for how strong Esther's voice becomes—noticeably more technically impressive than it had been in the trio-backed-by-big-band performance at which James Mason's Norman Maine character first encountered Esther. In fact, Esther's huge voice dwarfs the instruments of the jazz combo that backs her up. This song became one of Judy Garland's signature songs as she increasingly turned to concertizing and television as her film career declined. "The Man That Got Away" was recognized in the 21st century by the American Film Institute as the 11th greatest movie song of all time (American Film Institute 2004).

The "Born in a Trunk" and "Someone at Last" sequences are particularly noteworthy. Although they add richness to the audience's understanding of Garland's character and provide viewers insight into her growing relationship with Norman Maine, they also provide the film's writers, producer, and director the opportunity to showcase the star. In a sense, these extended showpieces are vocal analogues to Gene Kelly's extended ballet sequences in films such as *On the Town* and *An American in Paris*.

The end of the 1954 version of *A Star Is Born* is also notable for what might tell the audience about the relationship between the public and movie and singing stars. As Susan Smith writes in the book *The Musical:*

Race, Gender and Performance, "as Esther emerges from the church following Norman's funeral, she is confronted by one of her female fans
who, insisting that she 'give us just one look,' pulls the veil away to
reveal Garland's grief-stricken face. Although itself motivated by feelings
of adoration, this act of tearing away the veil constitutes a valuation of
Esther's star identity that carries no corresponding respect for the integrity of her inner self" (Smith 2005, 93). To put it another way, although
James Mason's Norman Maine character increasingly values Esther for
who she is—and not just for how she sings—to the public Esther, the
star, becomes a commodity.

It seems that *A Star Is Born* in part defined Judy Garland. Not only
was it one of her last film musicals it also included enough seemingly
autobiographical touches in the storyline that it could be interpreted
as something of a synopsis of her early career through stardom. The
1977 film *New York, New York*, which starred Liza Minnelli, has been
interpreted as a musical that passes the mantle of the star from one generation to the next. As Jane Feuer writes, "*New York, New York* goes
so far as to replace the MGM Garland persona with her own daughter,
Liza Minnelli. The opening scene of *New York, New York* reprises Judy
Garland's initial encounter with Gene Kelly in *The Pirate*. The plot of
New York, New York reprises *A Star Is Born*. Liza Minnelli's star being
born serves to perpetuate the aura of the MGM musical, symbolized by
both her famous parents" (Feuer 1982, 120).

New York, New York, of course, was not the only mid-1970s movie
musical to bring back the basic plot theme of *A Star Is Born*. *A Star Is
Born* itself was remade by director Frank Pierson in 1976 with stars Barbra Streisand and Kris Kristofferson. The *Hollywood Reporter*'s review
of 1976 praised Kristofferson's acting; however, it found the secondary
characters to be far less than fully developed. The publication praised
the Kenny Loggins, Alan, and Marilyn Bergman song "I Believe in Love"
(Hoelscher 2018).

Other reviews of the 1976 version of *A Star Is Born* were similarly
mixed. For example, famed movie critic Roger Ebert praised Kristofferson's work—although his praise was somewhat backhanded in that
he wrote that Kristofferson "didn't exactly have to stay up nights preparing for this role" as an alcoholic, drug-abusing singer on his way
down. Ebert, however, found Streisand to be "unbelievable" as the
up-and-coming pop singer (Ebert 1976). Ebert's point could also be
extended to some of the songs in the 1976 version of *A Star Is Born*.
For example, although "Evergreen," with music and lyrics by Streisand
and Paul Williams, was a true pop hit, the song was hardly cutting edge

in the context of mid-1970s pop music. The fact that "Evergreen," more of a middle-of-the-road pop ballad than the style of music that might be more closely associated with an up-and-coming singer-songwriter of the mid-1970s, was removed from the trends of the era might give the song something of a timeless quality, but it also makes it difficult to fully accept as a vehicle for Streisand's character. Nevertheless, the American Film Institute ranked "Evergreen" No. 16 on its list of the 100 greatest movie songs of all time (American Film Institute 2004). The song also topped the Adult Contemporary charts for six weeks.

The credits of the soundtrack for the 1976 version include a large number of songwriters, although Paul Williams composed the music for several songs. Compared with the 2018 remake, this might partly account for some of the less-focused feel of the 1976 version. As mentioned earlier, though, the song "Evergreen" was a bonafide hit, with the kind of melodic and lyrical hooks that tend to stay in the listener's mind for years. To be sure, the big centerpiece, emotionally wrought tune in the 2018 remake, "Shallow," is engaging, won the Grammy Award for Song of the Year, and found its way into Lady Gaga's live shows; however, upon the release of the film it might have seemed to some audience members like it is a little short of the iconic status of "Evergreen," or even other movie hits (not necessarily all from musicals) such as "Up Where We Belong" in *An Officer and a Gentleman*, "The Rose" in *The Rose*, or Whitney Houston's cover of Dolly Parton's "I Will Always Love You" in *The Bodyguard*. This assessment changed, however, when Lady Gaga and Cooper performed the song live at the 91st Academy Awards ceremony in February 2019. The performance was widely heralded in the media as the highlight of the event, thus taking the song to a level beyond just being a very good, engaging song in a popular and critically acclaimed movie musical (see, for example, France and Gonzalez 2019). At the same Academy Awards ceremony "Shallow" won the Oscar for Achievement in Music Written for Motion Pictures, Original Song.

Within days of Gaga and Cooper's performance at the Academy Awards ceremony, it was reported that *A Star Is Born* would be released again on March 1, 2019, with an additional 12 minutes of footage cut from the first release that showed Gaga and Cooper's characters working on and performing a duet "Clover" (Moye 2019). To the jaded moviegoer the timing of the theatrical re-release of the film seemed at least somewhat suspicious and raised the question of whether the performance by the film's two stars at the Academy Awards ceremony was perhaps contrived to cash in on a re-release that was already scheduled but just not publicized.

The 2018 remake of the movie received favorable reviews. In fact, *New York Times* reviewer Manohla Dargis favorably compared the Bradley Cooper version to the "epically (empirically!) terrible" 1976 version of the story that starred Barbra Streisand and Kris Kristofferson (Dargis 2018). Similarly, the *New Yorker*'s Anthony Lane gave Cooper's version of *A Star Is Born* a favorable review, suggesting that the film only paled in comparison to the 1954 version (Lane 2018). Although the film did not fare as well as it might have done at the Golden Globe Awards, it received seven BAFTA Award nominations, including five for Bradley Cooper for Best Film, Best Actor, Best Director, Best Adapted Screenplay, and Best Original Music. It was the first time in the 70+-year history of the BAFTA Awards that a single individual had been nominated in those five categories.

Lady Gaga and Bradley Cooper won the 2019 Grammy Award for Best Pop Duo or Group Performance for "Shallow," the best-known song from the soundtrack of *A Star Is Born*. This Lady Gaga and Mark Ronson composition was performed by Lady Gaga and Cooper at the 2019 Grammy Award Ceremony. Lady Gaga used her acceptance speech to raise mental health awareness, a theme that is at the core of *A Star Is Born*.

When comparing the 2018 version to the 1954 film, the pacing might cause concern. The temporal progression seems choppier in the Bradley Cooper version. The 1954 version uses montages of sepia photographs to move the storyline forward. This smooths the sense of the progression of time. Another major difference between the films is the use of the vernacular. Although the country-rock musicians of the kind that Cooper portrays might swear as much as Cooper does, some viewers will undoubtedly find that the overuse of the profanity that begins with the letter "*F*" gets a bit tiresome. The subplot of the female lead's relationship with her father is much more fully developed in the Bradley Cooper version; the father character in the 1954 version clearly is not supportive of his daughter's focus on stardom, but in comparison, he is almost a throwaway character.

The credits at the end of the Bradley Cooper remake acknowledge that the 2018 version was based on the 1950s and 1970s versions. In fact, despite the fact that some have questioned the extent of his contributions to the 1976 version of *A Star Is Born*, the presence of Jon Peters as a coproducer of the 2018 version provides a tangible tie to the earlier Streisand and Kristofferson vehicle. In fact, some viewers of the latest remake of *A Star Is Born* might find that Bradley Cooper and Lady Gaga bear an eerie resemblance to Kristofferson and Streisand. It should be noted that although Cooper has received a great deal of attention for his acting, singing, directing, and writing for *A Star Is Born*, it is Lady Gaga who has her name most prominently included among the cowriters of the songs from the soundtrack.

In addition to the critical and commercial success of the 2018 version of *A Star Is Born*, it is interesting to note that the musical numbers—particularly those that were ostensibly written by Lady Gaga's character, Ally—tie directly into the Lady Gaga paradigm demonstrated perhaps most fully on her breakthrough album, *The Fame*, released in 2008. On that album, Lady Gaga and her producers put together a package that clearly differentiated between the Lady Gaga persona, and that of Joanne Stefani Germanotta, Lady Gaga's real name. For example, the Lady Gaga songs—such as the hit "Just Dance"—tend to be fast-paced dance pieces. The song "Lovegame" is fairly graphic in its use of sexual metaphors (e.g., "I wanna take a ride on your disco stick."). Contrast that with the poem "For a Moment," printed in the CD booklet for *The Fame* and credited to Joanne Stefani Germanotta, which is a reflection on a quiet walk through nature in the rain. Although the poem was written by Lady Gaga's aunt, whose middle name was Lady Gaga's given first name and whose first name was Lady Gaga's given middle name, the use of the Germanotta family name on the poem seems to be almost meant to be a reflection of a side of Stefani Joanne Germanotta herself that stands in sharp contrast to the Lady Gaga persona. The *Star Is Born* character Ally also exhibits an almost bipolar musical and lyrical focus. Her early songs, before she enters into a management agreement with Rez Gavron (played by Rafi Gavron), are contemplative emotional expressions that work well in coordination with the acoustic and country-rock style of her discoverer and later husband Jackson Maine (played by Bradley Cooper). Once Ally comes under the influence of Gavron, she is accompanied by dancers, changes her hair color and style, radically changes her stage costumes, and perhaps most importantly, changes her musical and lyrical style. In short, Ally transitions from a Joanne Stefani Germanotta-type persona (as reflected in Gaga's aunt's poem) to a dance music-focused *The Fame*-era Lady Gaga-style persona. What makes all of this identity interplay between the early work of Lady Gaga and the contrasting aspects of her character in *A Star Is Born* particularly effective is Lady Gaga's ability to convincingly sing in contrasting styles, something that she has demonstrated in her post-*The Fame* work under her own name (e.g., moving from electronic dance music to jazz duets with Tony Bennett).

The musical styles used in the 2018 version of *A Star Is Born* effectively connect the story to the time period, although some viewers may make connections with musical events spanning approximately a decade before the film's release. For example, the move of Ally from what is essentially an acoustic singer-songwriter style to pop dance music might be interpreted by some audiences as a reflection of the stylistic metamorphoses of 21st-century musicians such as Taylor Swift, Miley Cyrus, and others who moved away from their early-career styles into dance music in the late 2000s and into the 2010s. All of this suggests that this latest incarnation of *A Star Is Born* includes some specifics that make it accessible and relevant to the audiences of its time. It is important to note that Ally's metamorphosis from acoustic singer-songwriter (confirmed by the presence of the LP cover for Carole King's *Tapestry* on her bedroom wall) into a dance diva is presented as a selling out, a charge leveled by some fans to the stylistic shifts of the aforementioned Swift, Cyrus, and others. Perhaps most notable is that this sense that the female lead has sold out is not nearly as present in the 1954 version of *A Star Is Born*.

All three of the major musical versions of *A Star Is Born* include what seem to be autobiographical references to the female leads. Judy Garland, for example, was given theatrical prostheses (her nose), had her hairline altered by directors much as we see happening to her character in preparation for her initial screen tests. Garland's character is also given a stage name, Vicki Lester, which parallels the actress's name change from Frances Gumm to Judy Garland when she and her sisters, the Gumm Sisters, became increasingly popular as a young singing group. And the fact that Gumm/Garland grew up performing in vaudeville theaters is mirrored in Vicki Lester's performance of the extended "Born in a Trunk" sequence in the film.

The "Born in a Trunk" sequence, which was added to the film shortly before its full theatrical release, uses melodic references to old movie and musical tunes, such as "We're off to See the Wizard" and "Ol' Man River," as well as allusions to *An American in Paris* and Jacques Offenbach's "Can Can." Interestingly, there is also one brief melodic phrase that resembles the tune of "Thank Heaven for Little Girls," although that particular Alan Jay Lerner and Frederick Loewe song was first heard in *Gigi* a few years after the release of *A Star Is Born*.

It should be noted when considering the 1954 movie, the version generally found in circulation for home video in the 21st century is a 1983 restoration that includes the Harold Arlen and Ira Gershwin songs cut from the original theatrical release (e.g., "Lose That Long Face"), as well as the "Born in a Trunk" sequence, a last-minute substitute for the cut songs. As a result, the film is somewhat longer than the original theatrical release; however, it offers the viewer the entire composite of material that went into the movie as conceived and as what was experienced by audiences in 1954.

Despite the success of "Evergreen" from the 1976 version of *A Star Is Born* and the critical and commercial success of the 2018 version, the 1954 version remains the classic. The American Film Institute recognized the importance of the 1954 film when it ranked *A Star Is Born* at No. 7 on its list of the 25 greatest movie musicals of all time (American Film Institute 2006).

STORMY WEATHER

Widely heralded as one of the greatest Hollywood movie musicals with an all-African American cast, the 1943 film *Stormy Weather* brought together a number of well-known singers, instrumentals, songwriters, and dancers, including Lena Horne, Bill "Bojangles" Robinson, Cab Calloway, Fats Waller, Dooley Wilson, Katherine Dunham, the Nicholas Brothers, and others. The story roughly parallels the life of dancer Bill Robinson, who plays dancer Bill Williamson. Lena Horne plays singer Selina Rogers, a fictional character and romantic interest of Williamson. Compared with other movie musicals that contained autobiographical parallels to the principal actors, *Stormy Weather* appears more real-life than most. This aspect of the film is enhanced by the fact that the semi-autobiographical Bill Williamson and the fictional Selina Rogers—to name just the two principals—encounter and interact with famed jazz musicians Cab Calloway and Fats Waller, who both portray themselves.

Fats Waller's performances in *Stormy Weather* are particularly notable as late film documents of his work; Waller died at age 39 shortly after the film appeared. As is the case, with much of his work as a performer throughout his career, Waller, although the consummate musician, also plays the lovable clown as he mugs through his performances. Waller's main contribution was his famous composition "Ain't Misbehavin'," one of the several songs that Waller wrote during his relatively brief career that have become jazz standards.

Some critics and historians have claimed that Lena Horne's performance of "Stormy Weather" is one of her most iconic performances and one of the best interpretations of the song. In fact, The American Film Institute ranked the film's title song No. 30 on its list of the 100 greatest movie songs of all time (American Film Institute 2004). Horne's work in the film is also notable for "There's No Two Ways About Love" and her duet with Robinson on "I Can't Give You Anything But Love." Although Horne is the principal female vocalist in the movie, Mae Johnson's performance of "I Lost My Sugar in Salt Lake City" and Ada Brown's (with interjections from Fats Waller) performance of "That Ain't Right" are also highlights.

Cab Calloway's contribution as a singer and bandleader in *Stormy Weather* is also notable. This is a film that in many respects builds in musical intensity throughout and culminates in the show-within-a-show finale, in which Selina, Williamson, Calloway and his band, and the Nicholas Brothers all play prominent roles as they perform for the troops ready to ship out for World War II. Although the premise of the film's storyline is that it is about the life of dancer Bill Williamson, the Nicholas Brothers provide the most impressive dancing in *Stormy Weather*, particularly in this finale sequence.

Despite the unrivaled musical performances that fill what is actually a fairly short movie (approximately 77 minutes), some aspects of *Stormy Weather* are problematic. For example, if one considers the time period that is supposed to be represented in the film—from Williamson/Robinson's discharge from the armed forces at the end of World War I to the early 1940s—then the casting, costuming, and makeup of the characters presents problems. For example, Williamson appears to be approximately the same age in 1918 as he is in 1943, and the real-life Bill Robinson would have been approximately 65 when the film was made. For that matter, Robinson would have been around 40 at the start of World War II. From a chronological standpoint, Lena Horne's portrayal of Selina is even more head-scratching, as the real-life Horne was born only a year before the end of World War I; her character is a mature professional singer at the time of Selina's first encounter with Williamson in 1918. And, as is the case with Williamson, Selina does not appear to age appreciably in the quarter-century supposedly covered by the story.

Even if one ignores the issue with the nearly ageless appearance of the principal characters, *Stormy Weather* presents some other challenges for 21st-century viewers. Some aspects of the movie's treatment of race have not aged well. In the opening of the film, a young girl brings Bill Williamson a copy of an entertainment magazine from the mailbox. According to the title page, the issue is dedicated to the great entertainers of "the Colored Race." Although that offensive term might have been most closely associated with segregation in the Deep South, here it appears to be part of the mainstream popular media. Whether this is an accurate portrayal of mainstream entertainment publications of the time, or whether it was included to try to make a political or social point, might be debated. What is worth noting, however, is that at the time *Stormy Weather* was made race seemed to be at the forefront of media coverage of the film. The headline of a 1943 review in *The New Times*, for example, read in part "*Stormy Weather*, Negro Musical with Bill Robinson, at the Roxy" (T.M.P. 1943).

One of the most controversial aspects of the film is the inclusion of minstrel-show elements in the cakewalk sequence, particularly in the costuming. It should be noted that despite minstrelsy's association with white singers and actors performing in blackface, during Reconstruction and into the early 20th century, black performers found minstrel shows one of the few entertainment forms in which they could find employment in show business. So, the ties to minstrelsy in the production numbers that supposedly date back to the early part of the 20th century, although they can make audiences today bristle, are not too far removed from what black performers had to do to survive professionally at the time. Perhaps even more problematic to later audiences from the standpoint of references to minstrelsy is the blackface comedy routine of the Nicholas Brothers. Although the timeline of the story is not entirely clear, based on the fact that Williamson is now an established professional performer at the time of the Nicholas Brothers' routine, it would seem to be hopelessly out of date.

Despite the racial issues, the timeline issues and a plot that relies on some character stereotypes—even beyond the racial ones—*Stormy Weather* was an important movie musical on many levels. The singing, playing, and dancing is spectacular, and the film was one of the few made during this period in U.S. history that highlighted so many of the leading African American figures in the entertainment industry. Critical reaction to the film was favorable at the time of its release, and in a retrospective look at *Stormy Weather* in 2002, critic Sam Hurwitt wrote, "The rags-to-riches storyline is mere pretext for the musical numbers—but oh my stars and garters, *what* musical numbers. You don't just get the usual show tunes here; you get red-hot jazz performances by unrivaled masters Fats Waller, Ada Brown, Cab Calloway, and a number of relative unknowns" (Hurwitt 2002). In 2001, The Library of Congress recognized the historical and artistic importance of *Stormy Weather* by selecting the film for inclusion to its National Film Registry.

TOP HAT

One of the numerous movie musicals from 1930s about the entertainment industry, *Top Hat* starred Fred Astaire as Jerry Travers, a well-known American stage star brought to London by the impresario Horace Hardwick, played by Edward Everett Horton. During his stay in Europe,

Travers meets dancer Dale Tremont, played by Ginger Rogers. The meeting was instigated by Hardwick's wife, Madge, played by Helen Broderick, as well as by Travers's loud tap dancing in a hotel room. Broderick's attempts at matchmaking, however, go wrong, as Tremont mistakes the single Travers for the married Hardwick. Adding to the complications is the fact that Tremont is being actively pursued by fashion designer Alberto Beddini, played by Erik Rhodes. After Travers has fallen in love with Tremont—who continues to mistake him for Hardwick—eventually, all figure out that the intrigue was caused by mistaken identity. It is left to Hardwick's English butler Bates, played by Eric Blore, to sabotage a motorboat to give Tremont and Travers time together after all the identity issues have been resolved. At the conclusion of the story, Bates reveals that he created his own intentional mistaken identity to keep Tremont and Beddini from being married. If all of this sounds highly improbable and a bit over the top, it is important to consider *Top Hat* as one of the era's pure comedies, loaded with jokes, one-liners, dancing, and hijinks. The film, however, is also remembered as one of Astaire and Rogers's best collaborations and as perhaps one of Irving Berlin's best movie scores. Among the most memorable songs are "Top Hat, White Tie and Tails," which features an iconic Astaire tap dance solo, and "Cheek to Cheek," one of Rogers and Astaire's most iconic dance numbers.

In her analysis of Irving Berlin's changing approach as a composer and songwriter when he moved more fully from writing individual songs and for the stage to writing for films, Charlotte Greenspan (2004) traces two seemingly opposing tendencies in Berlin's writing in *Top Hat* and in other musical films from the same time period: (1) a tendency to plug in songs with catchy tunes that exhibited strength for including at various points as part of the underscoring; and (2) a tendency to write longer, sometimes more structurally complex "if he did not want a song to be played over and over again" (Greenspan 2004, 43). As Greenspan details, in *Top Hat* songs in the latter category are "The Piccolino" and "Cheek to Cheek." Both songs far exceed the standard verse-chorus structure that was commonly used throughout the Tin Pan Alley era. Not only was "Cheek to Cheek" more complicated in structure than the conventional song of the period, it was also a well-remembered classic, particularly in its performance by Fred Astaire and Ginger Rogers in the film. In fact, the American Film Institute named the Astaire-Rogers performance of "Cheek to Cheek" No. 15 on the Institute's list of the 100 greatest movie songs of all time (American Film Institute 2004).

Despite the fame of "Cheek to Cheek" and the interesting structural aspects of it and "The Piccolino," it is interesting to note that *Top Hat* is filled with underscoring. Although Greenspan (2004) focuses on Irving Berlin's use of underscoring essentially as a way of selling songs, the underscoring in *Top Hat* seems to this writer to be so pervasive that a short while into the film it is difficult to keep a mental list of all the tunes that Berlin uses. The underscoring is also used creatively to provide segues from scene to scene and locale to locale. This is most clearly evident in the transition from the "Top Hat, White Tie and Tails" sequence to the scene in Italy. The theater orchestra's performance of the song fades into an *al fresco* Italian orchestra playing the same tune, with the scoring and rhythmic style moving from Broadway to a stereotypical Italianesque sound.

It is so easy to focus on the dance numbers that some of the more subtle features of *Top Hat* can be missed. For example, early in the film, Travers sings "No Strings (I'm Fancy Free)" in response to Hardwick's suggestion that it is about time that Travers settles down and gets married. Travers then breaks into a long tap dance solo, the one that wakes up Tremont, who is sleeping in her room on the floor below. The song, dance routine, and the introduction of Rogers as Tremont tend to capture the viewer's attention. What is important to note from a structural standpoint—but easy to miss—is that "No Strings (I'm Fancy Free)" emerges directly out of the spoken dialogue. Later in the movie, dialogue segues into "Cheek to Cheek" in a similar manner. By contrast, songs such as "Isn't This a Lovely Day?" are both more conventional in form and begin after a pause in the dialogue. As a result of the fact that songs and dance numbers begin in several different ways, *Top Hat*—pardon the pun—keeps the viewer on their toes. In this respect, it seems to be more sophisticated in structure than some movie musicals, despite the almost constant humor and the near-stereotypical nature of the plot. In reference to the plot, Ginger Rogers quoted Astaire as writing a three-page letter to the film's producer Pando S. Berman that in part complained that "I cannot see that there is any real story or plot to this script" (Rogers 2008, 165–166).

Although perhaps not as well-remembered as a song per se as, "Cheek to Cheek," the "Top Hat, White Tie and Tails" dance sequence is notable for the contrasts that Astaire includes between activity and stillness, as well as for the cross-rhythms that he produces between his feet and the bouncing of his cane on the stage. The grandiose production dance sequences that introduce and follow Rogers's singing of "The Piccolino" suggests the influence of Busby Berkeley, in stark contrast to the intimacy of most other dance sequences. All in all, then, "Cheek to Cheek," "Top Hat, White Tie and Tails," "Isn't This a Lovely Day," "The Piccolino," and "No Strings (I'm Fancy Free)" exhibit a wide range of dance styles, settings, choreography, and staging. *Top Hat* is rightly, then, a movie musical that is entertaining for its dancing, songs, and for the instrumental underscoring.

Although initial reviews noted the similarities between *Top Hat* and the earlier Astaire vehicle *The Gay Divorcee* (1934), *Top Hat* gained greater recognition as time passed. In its ranking of the 25 greatest film musicals of all time, the American Film Institute listed Top Hat at No. 15; *The Gay Divorcee* was not included in the list (American Film Institute 2006). In 1990, the U.S. Library of Congress' Film Preservation Board added *Top Hat* to the National Film Registry as a significant American movie (Library of Congress 2019).

WEST SIDE STORY

The impact of Leonard Bernstein as one of the most prominent American musicians of the 20th century largely revolved around his leadership of the New York Philharmonic Orchestra, his groundbreaking Young People's Concerts, his work on television, and compositions that saw limited exposure to the general public into the mid-1950s. Sure, there was *On the Town*, but in this musical several of Bernstein's compositions were replaced with songs that were more in keeping with the commercial aesthetics of the day. All that changed in 1957 with the production of *West Side Story*, a musical that updated William Shakespeare's *Romeo and Juliet* and featured Bernstein's music and the young Stephen Sondheim's lyrics. *West Side Story* included numerous songs such as "Maria," "America," "Tonight," "I Feel Pretty," "Somewhere," and others that brought Bernstein's work as a composer/songwriter more fully into the world of popular culture than anything he had accomplished previously, the well-known song "New York, New York" from *On the Town* being the possible exception.

By moving the basic premise of *Romeo and Juliet* into the 1950s' New York City world of youth gang warfare, *West Side Story* succeeded in preserving the classic tragic love story of Shakespeare's play while providing audiences with a story that is also topical. According to the credits in the 1961 film version, the movie was produced by Robert Wise and directed by Robert Wise and Jerome Robbins with choreography by Robbins. The credit lines for the film, however, are somewhat misleading as Robbins left before the film was completed and apparently had less to do with the finished *West Side Story* than the coproduction credit would suggest.

Instead of the story revolving around two feuding families, *West Side Story* revolves around the territorial conflict between two youth gangs, the Sharks, a Puerto Rican gang, and the Jets, a more ethnically diverse—albeit white—gang that includes Italian, Polish, and other ethnicities. The combination of the two gangs produce what can be understood as a microcosm of ethnically diverse urban neighborhoods in New York; however, this can also be understood in the context of other large U.S. urban centers of the time. Interestingly, the film—and many stage productions of *West Side Story*—downplay race per se; African American characters are absent from the movie. So although the movie does not address the racial tension of the late 1950s and early 1960s, it does revolve around ethnic conflicts—the kind that were tied to some of the real-life youth gang violence of the period—and can also be understood as a larger exploration of conflict caused by varying degrees of whiteness and as an exploration of conflicts between Latino/Latina cultural and non-Latino/Latina culture.

Bernstein's music and Sondheim's lyrics are central to stage and film versions of *West Side Story*. Curiously, Stephen Sondheim later downplayed the quality of his lyrics, which were written before he became a Broadway superstar. In an interview with *ABC News* just over 50 years after the writing of *West Side Story*, Sondheim downplayed this and stated, "Most of the lyrics were sort of . . . they were very self-conscious. Bernstein wanted the songs to be . . . heavy, what he called 'poetic,' and my idea of poetry and his idea of poetry are polar opposites. I don't mean that they are terrible, I just mean that they're so self-conscious" (Berman, Apton, and Thompson 2010). Despite Sondheim's later assessment, many of the songs have become classics. Insofar as these songs are perhaps more instantly recognizable as Leonard Bernstein's music than as Sondheim's contribution, let us consider some of the qualities that Bernstein brought to songs in musicals in *West Side Story*.

One of the aspects of Bernstein's music that differentiates his work in *West Side Story* from the work of other Broadway composers of the time is the unusual approach to melody. "Maria," for example, begins with the interval of a tritone, long considered to be one of the most dissonant intervals in harmony and a melodic interval described as "the devil in music" (diabolus in musica) in musical treatises of past centuries. The upper note in the tritone interval of "Maria," however, resolves up a half-step. This pattern of tension and relaxation can be interpreted as a musical manifestation of the tension between the Puerto Rican and ethnically mixed white youths that seems—at least temporarily—to be eased by Tony meeting and being enamored with Maria. Even if one does not interpret the distinctive opening of "Maria" metaphorically, Bernstein's melodic approach and focus on the tritone is unusual enough making the start of this tune instantly identifiable.

Similarly, "Somewhere" opens with an upward leap of a minor seventh, another highly usual melodic interval. In fact, the entire melodic feel of this song seems to exude spaciousness, with a wide melodic range and more than its fair share of large intervals. This spacious melodic feel suggests the place—outside the confines of the narrow, closed-in world of the Sharks' and the Jets' little corner of New York City, where Tony and Maria can safely and securely be together. This song was named by the American Film Institute as the No. 20 greatest movie song of all time (American Film Institute 2004).

Bernstein also uses melodic connections between songs for a dramatic impact. For example the opening "Maria" melodic motive (the upward tritone) is anticipated in the bridge section of "Something's Coming." In this way, "Something's Coming" not only foreshadows Tony and Maria's meeting at the dance that evening in its lyrics it also musically anticipates Tony's reaction to the chance meeting of the two characters. Although Bernstein's use of musical connections is nowhere near as complete as, say, that of German composer Richard Wagner in his 19th-century operas, or that of the post-Bernstein American film composer John Williams in *Star Wars* and other Williams classics from the late 20th century and early 21st century, there is a certain sense of a music-as-enhancer-of-the-drama connection that runs from Wagner through Bernstein into later film and Broadway composers.

The film version of *West Side Story* starred Natalie Wood as Maria, Richard Beymer as Tony, a co-founder and former member of the Jets (although Tony remains close to the members of his one-time gang), Russ Tamblyn as Riff, the leader of the Jets and Tony's best friend. One of the notable ways in which the film differs from the stage musical is by virtue of the fact that the principal actors seemed to have been cast more for their acting and dancing abilities and, in the case of Wood, in particular, for their public recognition as stars than for their singing abilities. In fact, most of the vocal solos and small ensemble pieces relied on ghost singers.

Marni Nixon provided Maria's singing vocals and Jim Bryant provided Tony's singing vocals. In her autobiography, Nixon provides detail about how the ghost singing was accomplished (Nixon and Cole 2006, 131–136) and explains why the process caused Natalie Wood's apparent lip-synching to be slightly out of synchronization with the film's soundtrack. According to Nixon, this was because she, Nixon, had to try to synchronize her soundtrack contribution to singing that Wood had already done, but that was not, and apparently was never intended to be used in the finished film (Nixon and Cole 2006, 133–134). Although the use of Nixon and Bryant allowed the complex rhythms and melodies composed by Bernstein to come off in a way that probably would have been impossible for untrained singers, and although the ghost singers tried to make their work as believable as possible, on some songs—noticeably on "Tonight"—the singing is just too perfect to sound as though it is coming from two actors not really known for their singing abilities. There is a certain element of the polished singing styles of the old Nelson Eddy and Jeanette McDonald movies of the 1930s and 1940s. This is one of the elements of *West Side Story* that detracts from the sense of verismo that might have defined the production had the film been made at a later date. Although the ghost singers provided the voices for Natalie Wood and Richard Beymer, "Tonight" was ranked at No. 59 on the American Film Institute's list of the 100 greatest movie songs of all time (American Film Institute 2004).

Compared with later more realistic movie musicals, the settings and scenery of *West Side Story* also seem too sanitized to reflect the gritty reality of the streets of working-class New York of the time period. For example, the automobiles are too clean—almost meticulous—looking and the chain-link fence around the play area at the end of the film is just too shiny and clean to be completely believable. To be sure, though, the sets and costumes are not as highly stylized and reflective of stage aesthetics as, say, those of *The Music Man*.

On the other hand, the premise of youth gang warfare and ethnic conflict, and references to drug abuse, the politics of the McCarthy era, and domestic abuse in the songs—most notably "Gee, Officer Krupke"—give the film an edginess and topical feel like perhaps no other movie musical of the period. *West Side Story*, however, is not just a musical that takes a centuries-old premise and turns it into a topical piece for 1960, it was influential on later work in the video medium. In particular, the choreographed street rumble between the ethnically diverse Jets and the Puerto Rican Sharks can be understood as the basis for the choreographed rumble in the music video for Michael Jackson's "Beat It," one of the most iconic videos of the early 1980s. Interestingly, comparison of the gang scenes in *West Side Story* and "Beat It" suggests how much more emphasis was placed on realism in the depiction of ghetto life in the entertainment industry in the early 1980s than in the early 1960s. The scene is darker and grittier in "Beat It," and the fighting in "Beat It" looks more realistic. Adding to the realism is the fact that the Jackson video, as inspired as it appears to have been by *West Side Story*, used real gang members as dancers.

The film version of *West Side Story* includes a full theatrical-style overture, suggesting a stage production of the musical; however, immediately after the overture, *West Side Story* clearly fully becomes the product of the film medium as the viewer sees helicopter shots of Manhattan. This begins with a flyover to the island and then over the skyscrapers of the island finally before coming to the more focused neighborhood in which the story unfolds. Interestingly, the largeness of Manhattan from the helicopter shots contrasts with the relative smallness of the neighborhood, suggesting that the neighborhood plays the role of a microcosm for the City, the United States, and the world.

The film version of the musical also makes the most of close-up shots of individual characters and full-screen dance sequences that make more immediate impact than what would be possible on stage. Perhaps one of the most memorable of such dance scenes is that for "America," performed by the Sharks and the young women associated with them. This piece is also reflective of the entire approach to choreography for the film: the dance sequences associated with the Puerto Rican characters appear to be more overtly technically challenging and more precisely choreographed and performed than those associated with Jets and their entourage. One can argue that this approach perpetuates ethnic stereotypes; however, it is one of the film's clearer differentiators between the two groups. And the more individualistic approach of the Jets—perhaps more notable in the dancing in their opening number, "The Jet Song"— seems to match well with the group's identity as a multi-ethnic gang that includes members of Italian, Polish, and presumably other European descents.

Not peculiar to the film version but one of the more touching scenes is at the close of the movie in which members of both the Jets and the Sharks carry Tony's body out of the fenced-in playground area and one of the blond members of the Jets puts Maria's scarf back on her. The scarf in this context clearly becomes mourning attire. Arguably, this scene is made more for the movies than for the stage. Although the scene suggests that in tragedy differences can be set aside, it is important to keep in mind that the question of identity remains at the core of *West Side Story*.

In her article "All in the Family: Brandeis University and Leonard Bernstein's 'Jewish Boston,'" Sheryl Kaskowitz studies Bernstein's connections to Brandeis in the years leading up to the final writing of *West Side Story*. Although Kaskowitz does not reference *West Side Story* in her study, it is interesting to consider Kaskowitz's focus on the theme of identity—albeit Jewish identity—in explaining the ties between the composer and the university's mission and history (Kaskowitz 2009). Perhaps even more so than in Shakespeare's *Romeo and Juliet*, one might detect in *West Side Story*—and perhaps even more in the film than in stage productions—a similar theme of the search for and the confirmation of one's identity. And, the theme of identity in *West Side Story* is intrinsically tied to ethnic identity, much as was Bernstein's experience as an outsider in some aspects of his life and as an insider in other aspects as a Jewish American. The outsider nature of the Jets, the Sharks, and the members of their entourages, is not entirely tied to ethnicity. Their home lives, economic situations, living and employment situations, and so on set them apart from other New Yorkers. In fact, the film's opening sequence using helicopter shots of Manhattan sets up this otherness by contrasting the Statue of Liberty and the skyscrapers of the city with the neighborhood in which the characters live.

The 1961 film version of *West Side Story* was a commercial and critical smash. The movie won 10 Academy Awards, including Best Picture, Best Supporting Actor (George Chakiris as Bernardo, leader of the Sharks and Maria's brother), Best Supporting Actress (Rita Moreno, as Anita, Bernardo's girlfriend and Maria's friend), and others for musical editing, cinematography, set decorations, costumes, and so on. *West Side Story* was added to the National Film Registry in 1997. In 2006, the American Film Institute named *West Side Story* No. 2 on its list of the 25 greatest movie musicals of all time (American Film Institute 2006). Several of the musical's songs are classics and have been recognized as such. The American Film Institute, for example, named "America" the 35th greatest movie song of all time (American Film Institute 2004).

THE WIZARD OF OZ

Generally acknowledged as one of the most enduringly popular motion pictures of the 20th century, the 1939 film *The Wizard of Oz* still consistently finds its way onto "greatest movies" and "greatest film musicals" lists. The film cemented superstardom for Judy Garland, and "Over the Rainbow" is regarded as one of the greatest and most popular songs in the showtune repertoire.

In additional to Garland, who portrayed Dorothy Gale, *The Wizard of Oz* starred Frank Morgan, Ray Bolger, Jack Haley, Bert Lahr, Billie Burke, Margaret Hamilton, Clara Blandick, and Charley Grapewin. While Burke portrayed Glinda, the Good Witch of the North, Blandick portrayed Auntie Em, and Grapewin portrayed Uncle Henry, the others played multiple roles, with Morgan as Professor Marvel and the Wizard of Oz (as well as a few other minor characters), Bolger as farmhand Hunk and the Scarecrow, Haley as farmhand Hickory and the Tin Man, Lahr as farmhand Zeke and the Cowardly Lion, and Hamilton as Miss Almira Gulch and the Wicked Witch of the West.

Composer Harold Arlen and lyricist Yip Harburg provided the songs for *The Wizard of Oz*. Although both Arlen and Harburg are associated with several other significant songs of the Tin Pan Alley Era, their collaborative work for this film remains their best-remembered achievement.

The most famous song in the film, "Over the Rainbow," is sung by Judy Garland's character, Dorothy Gale, as she contemplates the life and its troubles that she endures in Kansas, not the least of which is the desire of Miss Almira Gulch to take and destroy Dorothy's dog, Toto. It is interesting that such an iconic song comes so early in the movie and in such an unassuming scene. Significantly, though, it is a near-universal song about dreaming of a better day and place and sets the stage for Dorothy's dream about being transported to such a land.

The song is one of the most honored movie songs of all time. "Over the Rainbow" was ranked No. 1 on the American Film Institute's "100 Years . . . 100 Songs" list published on the occasion of the centennial of the American film industry (American Film Institute 2004). In 2014, "Over the Rainbow" won the Towering Song Award from the Songwriters Hall of Fame (Songwriters Hall of Fame n.d.). Although "Over the Rainbow" might be the best-remembered song from the movie, it is not the only one to make "best of" lists: the American Film Institute ranked "Ding Dong! The Witch Is Dead" at No. 82 on its "100 Years . . . 100 Songs" list. Incidentally, in 2006, the Institute ranked *The Wizard of Oz* at No. 3 in the organization's list of the 25 greatest movie musicals of all time (American Film Institute 2006).

Despite the lasting popularity of "Over the Rainbow," the film is not just about the lasting significance and popularity of one or two songs. Other pieces such as "Follow the Yellow Brick Road," "If I Only Had a Brain," "Ding Dong! The Witch Is Dead," "In the Merry Old Land of Oz," "The Lollipop Guild," and "We're off to See the Wizard" feature distinctive tunes and catchy lyrics. Part of the distinctiveness of some of the songs—notably those that involve the residents of Munchkin Land—is the processed sound of the singing, which includes ultrafast vibrato, a stereotype of what munchkins might sound like. Even if one overlooks the sped-up recording technique and its inherent and intentional quirkiness, the entire soundtrack is memorable, tuneful, and invites singing along. Several of the songs are particularly easy to sing—which helps to make them popular for karaoke—because the melodies are either fairly sequential in nature (e.g., "If I Only Had a Brain") or include repeated phrases (e.g., "Ding Dong! The Witch Is Dead"). Even the wide-ranging and melodically more complex tunes, however, are easily accessible.

Although our focus is on the music of *The Wizard of Oz*, it is important to note that this musical was one of the most visually spectacular films of its day. The scenes that take place in Dorothy Gale's native Kansas both before and after she visits Oz appear in a sepia tone. This seems to reflect the reality of the decade-long Dust Bowl that afflicted the middle of the United States—from Texas through the Midwest—during the 1930s, something that was very much in the consciousness of movie audiences when *The Wizard of Oz* premiered in 1939. In fact, the use of sepia probably conveys the dustiness, the sameness, of life during the Dust Bowl better than the conventional black-and-white tones would have. After Dorothy is hit by a tornado-induced flying window frame and is concussed, she dreams that her house is transported over the proverbial rainbow to the Land of Oz. When she opens the door and steps out into Oz, she and the audience are greeted by brilliant, vivid colors. Although the technology had existed for some time before the filming of *The Wizard of Oz*, and despite the fact that it had been used in some slightly earlier films, this movie musical is widely considered to be the first film that demonstrated the possibilities of color movies. One can imagine that audiences' first view of Munchkin Land caused the kind of sensation that the first sequence of Al Jolson singing and speaking in *The Jazz Singer* had caused a dozen years before. In fact, one might reasonably argue that these two movie musicals represented two of the major steps in audiences' understanding of what to expect technically in films for the rest of the 20th century and beyond.

The movie became thoroughly ensconced in popular culture, as evidenced by its continuing popularity. Although it is possible to construe some post-1939 references to the story and the characters as being tied to L. Frank Baum's original stories, it is difficult to imagine that these came entirely or even mostly from the stories, such is the fame and popularity at the film quickly achieved. So, songs such as America's 1974 hit "Tin Man," which tells the listener that "Oz never did nothing to the Tin Man that he didn't, didn't already have," and Elton John's 1973 hit (co-written with lyricist Bernie Taupin) "Goodbye Yellow Brick Road" reflect the lasting popularity of the movie and the relevance of its messages for later songwriters.

The Wizard of Oz also inspired the 1974 stage musical and 1978 movie *The Wiz*. This adaptation, which featured music and lyrics by Charlie Smalls (some additional songs by other writers were added for the film), called for an all-black cast. Smalls's musical settings reflected some of the prevailing R&B styles of the day. Although the songs themselves and the musical styles differed from those of *The Wizard of Oz*, the functions of the songs suggested the influence of the 1939 film. Although the stage version of *The Wiz* was successful, the film, which starred Diana Ross and Michael Jackson, among others, was not.

Still, the original 1939 film lives on and finds its way onto television on a fairly regular basis, and at the time of this writing is available for in-home viewing through several streaming video services.

YANKEE DOODLE DANDY

The 1942 film *Yankee Doodle Dandy* starred James Cagney as "the man who owned Broadway," George M. Cohan. The story roughly follows Cohan's life and career from infancy through May 1, 1940, when U.S. President Franklin Delano Roosevelt awarded Cohan the Congressional Medal of Honor. The screenplay omits several important parts of Cohan's life and turns the awarding of the Medal of Honor into a fanciful meeting of Cohan and Roosevelt in the President's office during which Cohan relates his life story to the president. The screenplay suggests that the meeting was the first inkling Cohan had that he might even be in contention for receiving the prestigious reward, despite the fact that Cohan's suitability for the award had been debated in the U.S. Congress over the course of the previous several years. All in all, however, *Yankee Doodle Dandy* provides suggestions of Cohan's personality (at times cocky and abrasive), his drive (intense), his devotion to his family, and the singular role that he played in the early 20th-century development of the mature Broadway musical.

Despite the acting and musical talents of his co-stars, the film was a veritable *tour de force* for James Cagney. The role, though it reprised Cagney's start in show business in which he was a song-and-dance man, was an enormous contrast to the tough-guy gangster roles that had virtually defined Cagney's movie career throughout much of the 1930s. Although 40 years old at the time, the physicality of Cagney's dancing skills is impressive throughout the film.

Yankee Doodle Dandy reprised Cohan's hits of first several decades of the 20th century, including "The Yankee Doodle Boy," "Harrigan," "Give My Regards to Broadway," "You're a Grand Old Flag," and

"Mary's a Grand Old Name." The film also included Cohan compositions that are not as well remembered in the 21st century, both those from his days as part of the Four Cohans, and those from some of his later shows. Besides being an entertaining and informative film—as well as a highlight of James Cagney's extensive filmography—*Yankee Doodle Dandy* places many of George M. Cohan's hit songs into context. The storyline includes a depiction of the speed with which Cohan could come up with a lyric (the writing of "45 Minutes from Broadway"), as well as scenes from *Little Johnnie Jones* that place "Give My Regards to Broadway" and from *George Washington Jr.* that place "You're a Grand Old Flag" in their original—but little remembered—theatrical contexts. The movie, which was released during the United States' involvement in World War II, also places Cohan's "Over There" in both its original World War I context and its reemergence during World War II.

Undoubtedly, 21st-century viewers are not likely to notice the fact that the reenactments of parts of Cohan's early 20th-century shows largely either dispense with or significantly truncate the verses of many of the verse-chorus form songs. This reflects both the fact that the chorus was the part of the song that audiences tended to remember, and the fact that during the period in which *Yankee Doodle Dandy* was produced, jazz singers were already dispensing with the verses (which largely put the chorus into the original show's context) and focusing on the traditional usually 32-measure-long chorus.

In a television biography of James Cagney (*James Cagney: Top of the World* 1992), host Michael J. Fox explained that Cagney was especially keen to star in *Yankee Doodle Dandy* because his patriotism had been questioned as a result of his political affiliations during the 1930s. What better to prove his patriotism than to star as the writer of "You're a Grand Old Flag," "Over There," and "The Yankee Doodle Boy"? The film appears to have been successful in that regard. It was also successful at the box office and continued the legacy of Cohan's hits into a new generation. James Cagney's career did not seem to suffer as did the careers of some other actors who had been accused of being Communists during the mid-20th-century Red Scare.

Yankee Doodle Dandy was also highly regarded by critics and the Hollywood film industry: the movie earned Academy Awards for James Cagney for Best Actor, Nathan Levinson for Best Sound Mixing, and Ray Heindorf and Heinz Romfeld for Best Original Musical. Recognition for *Yankee Doodle Dandy* has continued into the 21st century: the American Film Institute ranked *Yankee Doodle Dandy* at No. 18 on its list of the 25 greatest movie musicals of all time (American Film Institute

2006). The Institute also ranked Cagney's performance of "The Yankee Doodle Boy" at No. 71 on its list of the 100 greatest movie songs of all time (American Film Institute 2004).

NOTE

1. Adapted from Perone (2012), "*Purple Rain*," vol. 3, pp. 215–221.

CHAPTER 3

Impact on Popular Culture

There are numerous ways in which the songs of movie musicals, stage musicals with film versions, and the movies themselves have impacted popular culture since the first-acknowledged movie musical, *The Jazz Singer*, appeared in 1927. Some of the impacts are easy to track, while others are more amorphous and, in some cases, may be perceived only by some people and not others. What follows is not an exhaustive accounting of the impact of movie musicals and their songs on popular culture—such an accounting and study would likely require an entire volume; however, it represents examples of some of the obvious and not-so-obvious possible impacts.

The Sound of Music is perhaps a very good place to start looking at clear examples of the impact of movie musicals on popular culture. One indication of the impact of the show on popular culture is the widespread—but erroneous—notion that the song "Edelweiss" is an Austrian folksong. Another indication is the fact that "Do-Re-Mi" is still widely recognized as a song that is constructed around the solfege syllables associated with the major scale. In fact, "Do-Re-Mi" is used by choirs as a warm-up exercise and in school music education programs to reinforce or teach the use of solfege syllables within the context of the major scale.

Songs from a musical such as *The Sound of Music* practically invite singing along. So, it is no wonder that film critic Tasha Robinson wrote about *The Sound of Music*, No. 1 on her list of "18 Movie Musicals You Can Actually Sing Along With," "sing-along-style musicals generally require catchy number with a more limited range [than *Dreamgirls*, to which she compares the musicals on her list]—most famously, like *The Sound of Music*, which is so easy to join in with that *Sound of Music* sing-alongs, with special lyrics-inclusive prints of the film, are still a regular touring event" (Robinson 2006). Similarly, over half a century after the premiere of the movie and 60 years after the premiere of the stage version of *The Sound of Music*, several karaoke sing-along recordings are widely available that include songs such as "Maria," "Do-Re-Mi," "Sixteen Going on Seventeen," "The Sound of Music," "Edelweiss," "My Favorite Things," and so on. In the middle of the second decade of the 21st century, *The Man in the High Castle*, a television series that deals with a parallel universe in which a dystopian United States is under the control of Nazi Germany, used "Edelweiss" as its theme music, which continues the connection of this song—written for a musical well over a decade after the defeat of Nazi Germany in World War II—with nationalism in the face of Nazi domination.

Well-known songs from both stage and film musicals not only have become part of the general public's and professional singers' repertoires but have also become standards among jazz instrumentalists. Perhaps one of the most famous examples of this was saxophonist John Coltrane's 1961 release of a lengthy version of "My Favorite Things" on the album of the same name. Coltrane's recording quickly became iconic, and, as an indication of how well known it became, in 2018 the album that featured the track became a rare jazz album to be certified "Gold" by the Recording Industry Association of America (RIAA). To jazz fans, Coltrane took what might have been considered a banal song from a popular stage musical and improved upon it by focusing on what at the time was a novel approach to jazz improvisation. Singer-songwriter Elvis Costello touched on this—although referencing the film version of *The Sound of Music*—in the 1994 song "This Is Hell," from the album *Brutal Youth*, in which Costello describes that his idea of hell is listening to Julie Andrews's version of "My Favorite Things" over and over and over, as opposed to John Coltrane's version of the song.

It should be noted that the widespread knowledge of, the popularity of, and misconceptions about songs such as these *Sound of Music* classics cannot necessarily be tied entirely to the film. The impact on popular culture of the movie version of *The Sound of Music*, specifically, is immense and not limited to the English-speaking world. In Salzburg and other nearby locations in Austria, for example, there is an ongoing tourism industry that revolves around locations that were used in the film and other locations pertinent to the storyline. The wedding site of Maria and the Captain, St. Michael's Church, located in Mondsee, approximately 15 miles from Salzburg, remains one of the popular destinations for tourists well over half a century after the movie premiered as are Nonnberg Convent, Schloss Leopoldskron, Mirabell Gardens, and other film-related locations. Even a brief internet search will reveal that several companies continue to conduct location tours late in the second decade of the 21st century.

The impact of *The Wizard of Oz* on popular culture can also be found in numerous places since the premiere of the film in 1939. Because there are so many examples in multiple aspects of popular culture, let us consider just a couple of musical examples. The 1973 Elton John and Bernie Taupin song "Goodbye Yellow Brick Road" was both the centerpiece of the Elton John album of the same name and lyricist Taupin's use of the "yellow brick road" to Oz as a metaphor for the aimless pursuit of the social-climbing high life. Incidentally, the cover art for the *Goodbye Yellow Brick Road* album depicts Elton John walking down a yellow brick road very much like the one on which Dorothy Gale travels in *The Wizard of Oz*. One can find an even more direct reference to the story of *The Wizard of Oz* in the 1974 song "Tin Man," recorded by the group America. This song is known for the line in its chorus, "No, Oz never did give nothing to the Tin Man that he didn't, didn't already have." Songwriter Dewey Bunnell is quoted in Hyatt 1999 as saying that *The Wizard of Oz* was "my favorite movie, I guess. I always loved it as a kid" (147). "Tin Man" was a major hit for Bunnell's band, America; it reached No. 1 on *Billboard* magazine's Adult Contemporary charts and also made it into the Pop Top 10 in *Cash Box* and *Billboard*.

Individual songs from musicals became a solid piece of popular culture. The year 1964, although perhaps best remembered as the start of the British Invasion and in the world of movie musicals as the year of the Beatles' *A Hard Day's Night,* saw the premiere of two stage musicals that later were made into films in 1968: *Hello Dolly!* and *Funny Girl*. Back in 1964, Louis Armstrong scored a No. 1 Pop and Adult Contemporary hit with the theme song from *Hello Dolly!* and Barbra Streisand—who portrayed Fanny Brice in both the stage and film versions of *Funny Girl*—enjoyed a No. 1 Adult Contemporary hit with "People." Both songs were indelibly linked with the two singers thereafter, so much so that Armstrong made a cameo appearance singing "Hello Dolly!" in the movie version of that musical.

Speaking of *Funny Girl*, Barbra Streisand's line, "Hello, gorgeous," quickly became ingrained in popular culture. She spoke the words to the statuette when she received the Academy Award for Best Actress for her role as Fanny Brice in the movie. The phrase became part of the popular lexicon and has been used in numerous other movies and television shows parodying *Funny Girl*.

A number of songs from movie musicals became signature tunes for the films' stars, so firmly were the well-known songs linked to the stars who had sung them in the movies. This certainly was the case with Judy Garland, who, when she made her comeback at the start of the 1960s, included "Over the Rainbow," "The Trolley Song," and "The Man That Got Away" in her repertoire. Garland was not the only such movie star. Performed by Doris Day in the 1956 film *The Man Who Knew Too Much*, "Whatever Will Be, Will Be (Que Sera, Sera)" became one of Day's signature songs. In fact, the song was so thoroughly connected in popular culture with Day that it became the theme song for *The Doris Day Show*, a television situation comedy that aired from 1968 to 1973. This connection of movie stars to songs also includes Lena Horne's retention of "Stormy Weather," which remained in her concert repertoire for decades after she sang it in the film of the same name. One of the more curious examples of a star's appearance in a movie musical making a lasting impact on popular culture, however, are Frank Sinatra's numerous live performances and his recordings of "Luck Be a Lady." The intriguing thing about Sinatra and this song—which actually fits Sinatra remarkably well and which deserves the designation of iconic—is that in the film adaptation of *Guys and Dolls* in which Sinatra was one of the stars, it was Marlon Brando, who portrayed Sky Masterson, who actually sang the song.

And it is not just the songs from movies that are generally considered to be classically constructed movie musicals that have made an impact on popular culture and have lived on when other popular songs from their eras have faded into memory. For example, "The Rose," featured in the closing credits of the 1979 Mark Rydell film of the same name, earned a Grammy Award for the film's star, Bette Midler, and became one of Midler's signature songs. "The Rose" also topped some of the industry's singles charts the year of its release. There are numerous other examples, but perhaps the most sensational example of a song that otherwise does not constitute a musical in the classic sense that made an indelible mark on pop culture was Céline Dion's recording of "My Heart Will Go On," from the 1997 blockbuster movie *Titanic*.

The popular culture impact of movie musicals can also be seen in the fact that the songs and dance numbers have been used in competitive figure skating and ice dancing in national and international competitions. For example, most recently, Tessa Virtue and Scott Moir used selections from the 2001 film *Moulin Rouge!* at the 2018 Winter Olympics. The close connection between this music and Virtue and Moir's gold-medal-winning performance cuts both ways: the Canadian Broadcasting

Corporation (CBC) reported that sales of the *Moulin Rouge!* soundtrack "spiked" after the team's win (Rashotte 2018). Similarly, music from *A Chorus Line*, *42nd Street*, *Meet Me in St. Louis*, *The Lion King*, *Beauty and the Beast*, *West Side Story*, and numerous other films has been used in ice dancing, singles, and couples figure skating in national and international events.

From time to time, references to various movie musicals—and musicals in general—have appeared in popular culture, sometimes decades after the shows were originally released. As a fan of the early-1990s television program *Northern Exposure*, I remember the episode "Brains, Know-How, and Native Intelligence" in which the fictional character Maurice Minnifield (played by Barry Corbin), supposedly one of the original Mercury astronauts, talked about the favorite musicals of some of his fellow astronauts on a radio program he was hosting on the radio station he owned. As part of his monologue, Minnifield also mentioned about how Yul Brynner, the star of *The King and I*, "would have made an outstanding flyboy [pilot]."

Although there is more of an indication of the impact of the songs from musicals on popular consciousness than on popular culture per se, it is worth noting that for years and years, particularly in the 1970s and 1980s, many music majors who were learning to sing particular melodic intervals learned how to sing an ascending tritone—or augmented fourth—by singing the first two notes of Leonard Bernstein's "Maria," from *West Side Story*. Similarly, music majors of the time learned or remembered the sound of an ascending minor seventh by means of the first two notes of Bernstein's "Somewhere," also from *West Side Story*.

Some of the songs from movie musicals made an immediate impact on popular culture. In February 2019, for example, "Shallow," from the 2018 Bradley Cooper production of *A Star Is Born*, was arguably the biggest highlight of the 91st Academy Awards ceremony. The song has taken on life in popular culture well beyond the film itself. The live performance at the Oscars generated a considerable amount of social media attention as well, as mentioned in Lisa Respers France and Sandra Gonzalez's report for CNN (France and Gonzalez 2019).

In fall 2018, L.L. Bean ran television commercials for their flannel shirts that used a snippet of Leonard Bernstein's music for the rumble scene between the Sharks and the Jets in *West Side Story*. What perhaps was most remarkable about this particular example of Madison Avenue adoption of musical material is the fact that this music was not one of the big popular hit songs of the show and movie.

Despite the fact that L.L. Bean's television advertising campaign suggests the extent to which instrumental music from a Broadway musical and movie can become ingrained in popular culture, it is really the songs from movie musicals that perhaps made the strongest immediate impact on popular culture and that remain part of popular culture even decades and decades later. In fact, a large number of the standards of the jazz era were part of stage musicals that became movies or from musicals that were movies from the start.

Although we would not be able to test this hypothesis scientifically, it seems likely that a movie such as *An American in Paris* was as successful as it was when it was released in 1951 because of the movie's songs, written by George and Ira Gershwin before George's death in 1937. Songs such as "Embraceable You," "Nice Work If You Can Get It," "I Got Rhythm," "Love Is Here to Stay," and "'S Wonderful," all included in *An American in Paris*, were popular hits during Gershwin's lifetime, but they remained in the repertoire of pop and jazz singers well beyond the 1951 film that brought them together in one place. In fact, several of these, perhaps most notably "I Got Rhythm" and "Embraceable You," remain part of the larger American popular culture in the 21st century.

It is not just the list of titles found in *An American in Paris*—George Gershwin classics that had been part of popular culture for years before appearing in the movie and that have continued to be firmly ensconced in popular culture into the 21st century—that exhibit a longer shelf life than the average pop song. Movie musical songs such as "New York, New York," from the 1940s musical and movie *On the Town*, and "Theme from *New York, New York*," from the 1977 film *New York, New York*, became woven into American popular consciousness and still are part of pop culture and understood as symbolic of the city of their titles decades after *On the Town* and *New York, New York* were movie hits.

Perhaps the best example of a well-known popular song that was featured in a movie musical was Irving Berlin's "White Christmas," which is reputed to be one of the most frequent songs in the history of the recording industry. Bing Crosby, who starred in *Holiday Inn*, the movie that first included "White Christmas," made the first commercially successful recording of the song and subsequently rerecorded it several times; Crosby's recording is reputed to be one of the best-selling singles of all time.

It was not only the new song "White Christmas" or the reintroduction of "Easter Parade" (an earlier Irving Berlin composition) that demonstrated the impact of *Holiday Inn* on popular culture. The movie and the fictional Connecticut inn that was the locational focal point of the film lent their name to the motel chain that was founded a decade after the film premiered (Martin 2003).

Perhaps one under-recognized gauge of the impact of movies, books, or television programs is the extent to which they become the stuff of rumors and/or urban legends. Such was the case with Disney's animated musical *The Little Mermaid*. Some of the early publicity posters and early home video releases depicted a stylized coral-like golden castle in the background. At some point after the release of the VHS home video, an urban legend developed that one of the Disney artists who was disgruntled and about to be fired drew one particular castle tower to look like a penis. The rumor-assessing website Snopes.com refutes this urban legend on the grounds that the artist did not work directly for Disney, was not on the verge of being fired, and claimed that he drew a phallic-looking tower accidentally (Mikkelson 1998). The rumor has persisted, as have other urban legends surrounding movie musicals from Disney's 1980s–1990s revival. For example, another rumor has it that dust in the stars in one scene of *The Lion King* spells out the word "SEX" (Mikkelson 1996). These and other rumors about Disney films of the era were so persistent that some conservative organizations and churches protested Disney and urged boycotts of the studio's films, amusement parks, and merchandise.

As implied by costume designer Susan Blane's statements in Evans and Michaels 2002 (10) and speculated by others, *The Rocky Horror Picture Show* may have a role in defining punk rock fashions, serving as a sort of transitional piece between the glam style of the early 1970s and the punk style that emerged mid-decade. Even if some of the film's costumes did not directly influence punk fashion, they were in keeping with what was developing in U.K. and U.S. youth fashion at the time of the film's release and initial popularity.

Although, sometimes it is difficult to gauge whether it was because a song was part of a successful stage musical or because it was part of a movie musical that it becomes part of the backdrop of popular culture. In some cases, however, it is clear. For example, because the 1933 film *42nd Street* was the first post-novel version of the story—and because a popular stage version was not produced and made available for decades—the ongoing popularity of "Shuffle off to Buffalo," "42nd Street," and "You're Getting to Be a Habit with Me" can be attributed to the 1933 film. In fact, the impact of *42nd Street* on popular culture was such that just after "You're Getting to Be a Habit with Me" appeared in the film, both Guy Lombardo and His Royal Canadians with Bing Crosby on vocals and Fred Waring and His Pennsylvanians released hit single versions of the song. "You're Getting to Be a Habit with Me" appeared in other subsequent films and became part of the standard repertoire for jazz and mainstream pop singers and was recorded over the years by artists such as Frank Sinatra, Peggy Lee, Doris Day, Diana Krall, Petula Clark, and Mel Tormé, to name just a handful.

Particularly with animated movie musicals, merchandising based on films also directly impacts and, in fact, becomes part of the popular culture. As the primary producer of animated musicals for decades, the Walt Disney Corporation has been conspicuous in tying commercial products, aspects of its theme parks, and so on to animated features, be they musicals or otherwise. This multipronged impact on popular culture seemed to become especially noticeable with the Disney Renaissance of the late 1980s through the 1990s, and it continues into the second decade of the 21st century. According to reporter Binyamin Appelbaum, in November 2014, "Disney said earlier this month that it had already sold three million *Frozen* dresses in North America, which, as it happens, is roughly the number of 4-year-old girls in North America. In January [2015], 'Frozen' wedding dresses go on sale for $1,200. Next summer, Adventures by Disney is offering tours of Norwegian sites that inspired the film's animators at prices starting north of $5,000" (Appelbaum 2014). In addition to clothing and tours, Disney's marketing of the movie included the customary soundtrack album, which hit No. 1 on the charts. Subsequently, the show remained part of popular culture by means of a stage adaptation and the production of a skating spectacular version titled *Frozen on Ice*. As of spring 2019, Adventures by Disney is no longer actively marketing the Scandinavian cruises as *Frozen* tours; however, if one searches the company's website for "Frozen," a link appears to the Norwegian tours with the text, "On the 8-Day/7-Night Adventures by Disney Norway trip, visit Bergen, Flam, Geiranger and Oslo, plus villages and landscapes that inspired Disney's '*Frozen*'" (https://www.adventuresbydisney.com/search/, accessed May 16, 2019).

The tourism industry also took advantage of Disney's 2019 remake of *The Lion King*. A luxury safari company in Kenya—The Safari Collection—offered tours that would take visitors to various locations in the country, including the site that was the inspiration for Pride Rock in the original 1994 animated musical, arrange accommodations at the same lodge at which Disney animators stayed when they were working on the film, and provide personal guided tours by Robert Carr-Hartley, who worked on the original film (Delahaye 2018).

This new, computer-generated animated version of *The Lion King* has also impacted popular culture in another way that suggests that the film perhaps is aimed at an older audience that includes teens up to those who experienced the first version the first time around. In advance of the July 19, 2019, premiere of *The Lion King*, the Danish jewelry company Pandora widely advertised a collection of bracelets and other Lion King–themed jewelry, both in television advertising and on the company's website (see https://us.pandora.net/en/campaigns/disney-the-lion-king/, accessed July 9, 2019). Other cross marketing for the 2019 remake of *The Lion King* was aimed at children and included movie-themed toys from McDonald's (The Editors of McDonald's Newsroom 2019) and Build-a-Bear Workshop (https://www.buildabear.com/disney-the-lion-king-young-simba-gift-set/27597_27365.html., accessed July 22, 2019).

On a completely different note, the style of the choreography of production numbers by Busby Berkeley beginning in the early 1930s both made a high impact on popular culture and became part of the legacy of the movie musical as a genre into the 1950s and, from time to time, beyond. Berkeley's productions often included numerous scantily clad or provocatively clad women forming gigantic geometric formations on the stage. Berkeley also made use of long, often-winding staircases in his staging design. Beyond becoming almost a standard modus operandi in movie musicals, particularly musicals about musicals, of which there have been many, this production style found its way into the popular culture outside the confines of the traditional musical.

For example, the production of the Beatles' "Your Mother Should Know," from the failed made-for-television musical *Magical Mystery Tour*, incorporates several Berkeley touches. Among these is the famous sequence in which the Beatles descend a long staircase with Paul McCartney wearing a black carnation in his lapel. (The other members of the band wore red carnations; the black carnation was taken up by some Beatle fans as evidence that McCartney had perished in an automobile accident and had been replaced by a look-alike musician.) Given the influence of early 20th-century British music hall style on "Your Mother Should Know," the staging can be interpreted as at once a celebration of Berkeley's style and as a parody of it.

Years later, in 1994, the hit Disney-animated musical *The Lion King* included Berkeley-like geometric patterns in the choreography for the song "I Just Can't Wait to Be King." Still later, the Busby Berkeley style of staging also seems to have been an influence on the return of the seriously injured Richard Hammond to the British automotive television program *Top Gear*. On a January 2007 broadcast in which Hammond returned after a near-fatal accident, he entered the *Top Gear* studio through a gauntlet of women, garbed like those in the 1930s and 1940s Berkeley-choreographed and Berkeley-directed musicals.

The 1978 film version of the 1971 musical *Grease* has a particularly interesting relationship to popular culture. The film was immensely popular when it was first released, and some critics credit *Grease* with cementing John Travolta as a major Hollywood star. *The Guardian*'s Peter Bradshaw, for example, wrote on the 40th anniversary of *Grease* that the movie "broke John Travolta through to family audiences who might have been chary about his more adulty movie sensation, *Saturday Night Fever*, the year before" (Bradshaw 2018).

Grease can be understood as part of a larger milieu of movies and television programs that reflected back to the 1950s, which included the comedy *Happy Days* (1974–1984), the film *American Graffiti* (1973), and others. This fascination with the late 1950s and early 1960s in the U.S. popular culture of the 1970s and early 1980s also included Sha Na Na (also the name of the band that appeared in *Grease*) syndicated television show (1977–1981), and the 1972 segment on the ABC television program *Love, American Style* that inspired the aforementioned *Happy Days*.

Adding to *Grease*'s intricate ties to the popular culture of its time was the fact that the theme song, written for the film by Bee Gees's member and principal songwriter Barry Gibb, was a No. 1 single hit for singer Frankie Valli. Curiously, despite the fact that the movie was a fantasy piece about high-school life in the 1950s, "Grease" reflected the popular disco style that Gibb has used in the songs he wrote and cowrote for the 1977 film *Saturday Night Fever*.

Jane Feuer's study *The Hollywood Musical* (Feuer 1982) contains a recurring theme that runs throughout the book: the prominence of the show-within-a-show in the plots of many movie musicals frees the films from the constraints associated with films that are supposed to portray reality. The premise is that by portraying a world of fantasy (the show within the show) and aligning it with what is transpiring in the outer plot, the entire piece becomes a work of entertainment. As a result, the fact that characters break into song and/or dance can be accepted (and expected) by the audience. It could also be argued that the show-within-a-show paradigm presents the audience with a particular view of what the lives of entertainers and the world of theatrical and movie entertainment are all about. To the extent that this informs popular understanding of the entertainment business and the lives of real-life entertainers, it would seem that this forms another type of impact on popular culture.

Interestingly, over the course of history, one can see evidence that the portrayal of singers, dancers, and actors—and various combinations thereof—is handled in a more realistic-appearing way—in a way that more closely aligns with the way in which some of their foibles are portrayed in the tabloid press and social media. For example, even in the remakes of a story, *A Star Is Born*, one can see how the somewhat humorous, although ultimately tragic, alcoholic Norman Maine (portrayed by James Mason in 1954) becomes the less humorous and more apparently realistic alcoholic and cocaine-abusing John Norman Howard (portrayed by Kris Kristofferson in the 1976 version of *A Star Is Born*), who in turn becomes the constantly swearing and even grittier alcohol- and drug-addicted Jackson Maine (portrayed by Bradley Cooper in 2018). Although the urinating-in-his-trousers effect is a bit over the top, Jackson Maine's appearance at the Grammy's when his wife, Ally, receives an award for Best New Artist is the kind of thing that in 2018 might immediately find its way all over Twitter, Instagram, and other social media sites. In addition, the obvious suicide of Jackson Maine—reprised from the 1954 version of the story but muted in the 1976 version—aligns with the societal concern of suicide and the self-inflicted deaths of several notable celebrities in the late 2010s. I would argue, then, that this more realistic-appearing portrayal of the lives of the famous, although it might not directly impact popular culture, at least reflects the popular culture of the time.

One of the facts about movie musicals, basically going back to the first examples of the genre, is that more than a fair share of these films presented the public with a stylized view of the life of entertainers and the entertainment industry. If this seems unlikely, consider that *The Jazz Singer* dealt with a young man who chose singing the pop music of the day over the music of the synagogue; that all three major incarnations of *A Star Is Born* dealt with a singer getting her first big break and catapulting to stardom while her Svengali descended into personal crisis and death; and that *Top Hat*, *The Band Wagon*, *La La Land*, and a host of other movie musicals were set in the world of popular music, film, or the theater.

In some cases, the entertainment industry included drug and alcohol addiction, emotional damage caused by child stardom, references to homosexuality, and so on. Although it might be difficult to trace the impact of these aspects of movie musicals on popular culture, it is possible to see a connection with popular culture and to understand some of the movie musicals as being a reflection of the popular culture of their time.

Some stage musicals and their film counterparts firmly became a part of the collective popular culture of their audiences. In some cases, this might be the wider audience or a subset for which the musical took on special significance. As described by Jewish Book Council blogger Edward Shapiro, "In the past half century *Fiddler [on the Roof]* has attained a mythic status among American Jews. There are few adult American Jews who are unfamiliar with stage or cinematic portrayal of the tribulations of Tevye, Golda, and their three eldest daughters Tzeitel, Hodel, and Chava" (Shapiro 2014). Although Shapiro's assessment of the impact of *Fiddler on the Roof* on American Jews might be accurate, there is also evidence that this stage and film musical has made a wider impact on U.S. popular culture. For example, the show's final scene—the displacement of the Jewish residents of Anatevka during the song of the same name—was parodied in the final episode of the popular CBS situation comedy *Newhart* in May 1990. Although not necessarily entirely because of the parody of *Fiddler on the Roof*, the last episode of *Newhart* has been widely described as one of the most memorable and successful television finales in the history of the medium.

As mentioned in this chapter's introduction, some possible impacts of musicals—in both their stage and film versions—may be perceived by some viewers and not by others and, in fact, may simply be in the minds of their beholders. Although it might seem to be a bit of a stretch, I believe that the possible connection is strong enough that some viewers might make it, so it is worth noting that in episodes of the British television series *Midsomer Murders* in the 2010s, Detective Chief Inspector John Barnaby's dog—a terrier that fairly closely resembled the dog Bull's Eye in the film version of *Oliver!*—was named Sykes. The dog's name could have been derived from the premise that the character of John Barnaby had studied psychology at university; however, the name of the dog raises the question of whether it also may have been in part inspired by the fact that Bull's Eye's owner in *Oliver!* was named Bill Sikes.

Perhaps one of the best examples of the impact of movie musicals—as well as other popular music of the 20th century—can be found in the highly unusual and somewhat surreal 2001 film *Moulin Rouge!*. After the familiar 20th Century Fox theme, the movie opens with a quote from *The Sound of Music*. This begins a film that is built around material from movie musicals such as *The Sound of Music* ("The Sound of Music" and "The Lonely Goatherd"), *Gentlemen Prefer Blondes* ("Diamonds Are a Girl's Best Friend"), *The Best Little Whorehouse in Texas* (Dolly Parton's "I Will Always Love You," which also played a central role in the film *The Bodyguard*), and jazz, rock, R&B, hip-hop, and other songs that cover much of the century. What a film such as *Moulin Rouge!* suggests is the extent to which songs such as "The Lonely Goatherd" or

"Diamonds Are a Girl's Best Friend" were still recognizable parts of the popular culture of 2001 as were more recent songs such as Madonna's "Material Girl" and "Like a Virgin," or Nirvana's grunge classic "Smells Like Teen Spirit."

In conclusion, it might serve us well to consider where we began this chapter: with the public's linkage of Julie Andrews—as opposed to Mary Martin—with the role of Maria in *The Sound of Music* as a gauge of the impact of movie musicals on popular culture. Although the linkage of particular singers, dancers, and actors, or the popularity of particular songs, or even the inclusion of particular expressions in the pop culture lexicon might not always have been originated from the film versions of musicals, it seems certain that greater accessibility of movie versions of musicals has helped to cement these connections between the shows and popular culture to a degree that arguably would have been impossible through the stage alone.

CHAPTER 4

Legacy

Although there is bound to be some overlap between the discussions of the impact and legacy of movie musicals, this chapter will focus on the lasting nature of films and the songs they contain. These legacies can be seen through remakes, sequels, adaptations, some recent musicals with a decidedly retrospective feel, songs that remain well known decades after the premiere of the movie, the sheer persistence of some movies, and so on. This chapter also contains a brief look at lost legacies: movie musicals that, regardless of how popular they might have been at one time, have not, for one reason or another, remained available through later theatrical release, television broadcast, or for the home market through videotape, DVD, or streaming video.

One of the important aspects of the legacy of movie musicals is that several well-known and well-loved iconic movie musicals that perhaps could have never been remade came back years later. Many of these are perhaps best considered as remakes of the original with the same basic story, characterizations that are consistent with the original, and so on. Some were remade once; however, a number of them have reappeared multiple times. For example, *A Star Is Born* came back several times with musical genres representing the times. Although the film legacy of *A Star Is Born* goes back even before the famous 1954 version that starred Judy Garland and James Mason, the film is widely viewed as the starting point, particularly because all the basic musical elements came together in this film. The 1976 version, which starred Barbra Streisand and Kris Kristofferson, was considerably less successful. The basic premise of the film remained the same; however, the musical selections and style reflected the times, as did the addictions of the male lead character.

The 2018 version of *A Star Is Born* was considerably more commercially and critically successful than the 1976 version. Like its predecessor, the Bradley Cooper–Lady Gaga film updated musical styles and the troubles and addictions of the male lead character.

A Star Is Born is not the only classic movie musical that has been remade successfully. A more recent trend in perpetuating the legacy of earlier movie musicals comes in Disney's live-actor adaptations and computer-generated adaptations of the company's animated musicals. Disney enjoyed a renaissance of sorts from the late 1980s to the late 1990s by virtue of the enormous popularity of animated musicals, such as *Beauty and the Beast, Aladdin, Mulan,* as well as other nonmusical animated films. In addition to publishing stage-ready versions of *Beauty and the Beast* and *Aladdin,* as well as "Jr." versions specially adapted for youth productions, Disney also released longer, more complex versions of the films that featured live actors. The 2017 version of *Beauty and the Beast,* for example, starred Emma Watson as Belle, and the 2019 version of *Aladdin* starred Mena Massoud as the title character. In both these movies, computer-generated special effects were used to recreate some of the spectacular effects of the original animated films. Some of these adaptations have not been entirely successful, particularly *Aladdin*—with the voice acting performance of Robin Williams and the animation of the Genie, in particular, being so iconic that the 2019 remake did not have the same impact. Disney took a different track with its 2019 remake of *The Lion King*—with turning from the conventional animation (with some computerized sequences) of the original movie fully into the world of computer animation. As was the case with *Aladdin,* the remake of *The Lion King* garnered fewer favorable reviews than the original.

It should be noted that the live-actor versions of the Disney musicals are significantly longer and somewhat more complex than their animated counterparts. In fact, the 2017 production of *Beauty and the Beast* has something of the feel of a classic late-1940s or early-1950s movie musical in the staging of production numbers, the in-jokes, and so on. If one considers the timing of these films, it might seem as though the new versions were released in an attempt to capture both the youth audience of the time of the new versions' release and the original audience—the child who was about 10 years old at the time of the release of the 1991 version of *Beauty and the Beast* would have been in their midthirties at the time of the lengthier remake. It would seem that remakes such as *Beauty and the Beast* and *Aladdin* update the stories for a more mature version of the original audience while giving the children of the original audience a version of the tales to call their own.

Part of the story of the legacy of movie musicals is the extent to which they have been reissued in various physical and streaming-video formats throughout the age of home video. As I mention elsewhere, the home-video market has been strong for some movie musicals, in particular, Disney films such as *The Lion King* and *Frozen*, among the best-selling feature film videos of all time.

Another notable reference to a highly successful earlier movie musical came in the 2018 Rob Marshall film *Mary Poppins Returns*. The fact that the film continued and rekindled the legacy of the original film and its stage version was confirmed by Lin-Manuel Miranda, who played Jack, the lamplighter in the 2018 film, who said, "There are two moments in *Mary Poppins Returns* when the grown-ups watching really lose it: Dick Van Dyke's arrival and when Angela Lansbury starts singing . . . Those are playing on a lifetime of heartstrings" (Alexander 2018, 2D). This would not necessarily have been the case were it not for the iconic nature of Van Dyke's performance in the original *Mary Poppins* movie and Lansbury's fame as a popular and award-winning stage, film, and television actress since the 1940s.

Another part of the legacy of the great movie musicals of the past is that some of the songs from the shows became well-known pieces that were reinterpreted in iconic versions. In some cases, this was true for the music itself absent the lyrics. Although numerous show tunes became jazz standards, perhaps one of the more famous jazz renditions of a tune that is closely associated with a musical is saxophonist John Coltrane's 1961 recording of "My Favorite Things," one of the well-known songs from *The Sound of Music*. Although Coltrane's famous recording was made and released before the making of the film version of *The Sound of Music*, it seems reasonable to assume that after the tremendous critical and commercial success of the film, there would always be more of a link between the Julie Andrews performance of the song and the Coltrane version than between any other singer-actor's version and Coltrane's iconic recording. As mentioned in the chapter "Impact on Popular Culture," singer-songwriter Elvis Costello made a comparison of the two versions in his 1994 song "This Is Hell."

The legacy of some films has been advanced by adaptations and updates. A creatively and sociologically interesting remake, the 1978 film *The Wiz* was a retelling of the story of *The Wizard of Oz*, but with musical and casting twists. The movie was based on an earlier stage version that featured songs by Charlie Smalls and a black cast. In the film, the Land of Oz resembles a glorified version of New York City. Diana Ross, who was born in 1944, played the 24-year-old Dorothy

Gale; Michael Jackson played the Scarecrow; Nipsey Russell played the Tin Man; Ted Ross played the Cowardly Lion; Richard Pryor played the Wiz; and Lena Horne played Glinda, the Good Witch. Despite the all-star cast, *The Wiz* was not a critical or commercial success. The 1975 stage version had fared better, earning a Tony Award for Best Musical. Despite its uneven reception, *The Wiz* was significant in bringing *The Wizard of Oz* more up to date musically and giving the story clearer relevancy for the black youth of the time. The movie's biggest hit song, Diana Ross and Michael Jackson's recording of "Ease on Down the Road" not only was *The Wiz*'s version of *The Wizard of Oz*'s "Follow the Yellow Brick Road" but also earned Jackson his first Grammy Award nomination.

While on the subject of the legacy of *The Wizard of Oz*, it should be noted that singer-songwriter-pianist Elton John and his songwriting partner, lyricist Bernie Taupin, referenced the film in their song "Goodbye Yellow Brick Road." Taupin's reference has been widely interpreted as a metaphor for the lyricist getting back to his roots, perhaps after experiencing some of the downsides of fame and fortune in the music industry of the early 1970s. Even discounting any possible autobiographical references, "Goodbye Yellow Brick Road" clearly differentiates life on a farm with the glitz and glamour of high-society city life, ultimately rejecting the latter and returning to the former, much like Dorothy in the film and in the original Frank Baum stories.

One particularly curious part of the story of the legacy of movie musicals can be found in the Mel Brooks musical *The Producers*. The original film was less of a musical than a film about a musical that the theatrical producers of the movie's title put together in an effort to enact a financial flim-flam scheme. Subsequently, Brooks mounted a fuller musical version of the story. The ironic basic premise of the storyline was that the failure of the show the two producers wrote would insure their financial success. The 1978 film featured several Brooks-penned songs, particularly noteworthy of which was "Springtime for Hitler."

The Brooks movie remained a fan favorite for years, and, in 2001, Brooks and Thomas Meehan adapted the film for a stage musical, also titled *The Producers*. The show, which starred Nathan Lane and Matthew Broderick among others in its original Broadway run, was a smash and won 12 Tony Awards. In 2005, the stage version was adapted as a film, in which Lane and Broderick reprised their roles and were joined by Uma Thurman. Unfortunately, the 2005 film did not have the commercial or critical success the stage musical or the original film did. It is, however, part of the legacy of the original film.

Another part of the legacy of movie musicals is that some aspects of films that might have seemed acceptable at one time are viewed differently in another time. For example, a 2018 online petition launched by Zimbabwean activist Shelton Mpala called on Disney to give up the corporation's trademark on the Swahili phrase "Hakuna Matata," the title of one of the best-known songs from the 1994 film *The Lion King* (Adeoye and Korium 2018). Mpala's concern was with the appropriation of a common African phrase for commercial gain. The petition drive can be understood as part of a wider reaction against cultural appropriation that generated discussions on social media and in the electronic media, particularly in 2017 and 2018.

The 2016 film *La La Land*, detailed in the chapter "Must-Hear Music," represents part of the legacy of the classic movie musicals of the 1930s–1950s. Although the storyline of the film comes from the 21st century, most of the songs and instrumental music clearly demonstrate ties to 20th-century Tin Pan Alley–style pop songs, the kind of jazz-influenced songs that populated some of the classic movie musicals of the second quarter of the 1930s–1950s, including numerous sequences in which stars Ryan Gosling and Emma Stone suddenly break into a song and/or dance, and perhaps most notably the dancing-in-the-stars sequence at Griffith Observatory.

Part of the legacy of movie musicals comes from the extent to which they are still available for viewing near the end of the second decade of the 21st century. Generally, the most iconic versions of all the movies included in the chapter "Must-Hear Music" are available in either streaming video and/or DVD or Blu-ray disc. Interestingly, the original motion picture production of *The Music Man* is difficult to come by; however, it has been available as a DVD and on VHS videotape in the past. Many public libraries still have the original film version of *The Music Man* available in physical media. Similarly, the original movie musical version of *Little Shop of Horrors* is difficult to find today, although later stage versions and the original 1960 nonmusical science-fiction version are widely available.

In addition, the vast majority of the other remakes worth watching are also available for purchase or rental. The legacy of the great movie musicals is also perpetuated by the numerous film soundtrack albums that are available in streaming audio, in digital audio for purchase, and still on CD and LP. In fact, it could be argued that given the large degree of commercial success of some movie musical soundtrack albums, they could easily generate their own independent must-hear music list.

The film that perhaps is most telling about the legacy of stage works that were made into movies is *Porgy and Bess*. Composer George Gershwin's opera of the same name received its premiere in 1935. Initially, *Porgy and Bess* did not receive an overwhelming favorable reaction. As Gerald Mast wrote in *Can't Help Singin': The American Musical on Stage and Screen*, "Because musicals so clearly inhabit this middle ground between past and present, rich and poor, high and low, they cause cultural consternation when they refuse to stay there. Take the 1935 reaction to *Porgy and Bess*" (Mast 1987, 5). Mast continues by pointing out that the critics of the day considered *Porgy and Bess* more in the context of a musical than an opera because it was socially relevant and operas were thought to be more distant from the American experience. This was despite the fact that the work had more in common with opera than much of the Broadway-style musical theater of its day. Later in the 20th century, *Porgy and Bess* was considered one of the most important American musical theater works of the century, and several of the songs—including "I Got Plenty o' Nuttin'," "Bess You Is My Woman," "It Ain't Necessarily So," and, especially, "Summertime"— are considered classics of the Tin Pan Alley era and continue to be performed live and recorded into the 21st century. Gershwin did not live to see the reaction to the opera change; he died in 1937.

The film version of *Porgy and Bess* premiered in 1959 and received a limited distribution, in part because of DuBose Heyward's controversial plot, and the movie received a wide spectrum of mixed reviews. The rights to the film reverted to the heirs of Heyward, composer George, and lyricist Ira Gershwin after 15 years. Because all three parties had to agree to keep the film in circulation for it to remain available, which they did not, the movie version of *Porgy and Bess* was pulled from circulation in the mid-1970s. As a result, the movie did not make it into the home-video market that developed in the 1970s and beyond. It should be noted that the movie had exorcised some of the nearly seamless music of Gershwin and replaced it with spoken dialogue. The Otto Preminger film, then, moved *Porgy and Bess* from the world of the folk opera, as George Gershwin described it, to the world of the more conventional movie musical, something that was apparently not fully appreciated by the Gershwin heirs but aligned with some of the critical compartmentalizing that had dogged *Porgy and Bess* since the premiere of the stage version. Today, the film versions of *Porgy and Bess* that are in circulation for purchase are from the staged performances of the full opera. As a result, the legacy of the original stage work has been preserved, at the same time the legacy of the 1959 movie has effectively been ended.

The other somewhat infamous example of a movie musical that was pulled from circulation is Disney's 1946 film *Song of the South*, which was last released for home video in 1986. As Jason Sperb writes in his book-length academic study of the film, its ramifications, and reaction to it between 1946 and the early 2010s, "Despite the film's groundbreaking technological innovation and Oscar-winning song, 'Zip-a-Dee-Doo-Dah' (for which it is still most remembered today), many post–World War II audiences in 1946 found *Song of the South* not only aesthetically underwhelming but also troubling in its regressive depiction of race relations in the American South" (Sperb 2012, 6). Sperb continues by writing that "the influential National Association for the Advancement of Colored People denounced the film as an idyllic presentation of racial relations in the post-Reconstruction South" (Sperb 2012, 7). Aside from questions about how accurately *Song of the South*—in which Uncle Remus, a former slave, happily shares stories with white children—depicts race relations during the time the Uncle Remus stories were first published (the late 19th century) or to what extent it reflects the race relations of the mid-20th century when the film was made, some viewers have described the film as racist, citing the use of racial stereotypes. Interestingly, other viewers interpret the film as a positive movie insofar as its principal African American character, Uncle Remus, is depicted as a warm, loving figure.

Regardless of how one interprets *Song of the South*, the movie clearly created controversy. Perhaps that is the reason the film has never yet been released in the digital age on DVD or as streaming video. Part of the legacy of this film, however, can be found in parodies. Perhaps one of the more memorable parodies can be seen in the 1989 film *Fletch Lives*, in which actor Chevy Chase sings "Zip-a-Dee-Doo-Dah" accompanied by the ubiquitous bluebird "on [his] shoulder" and a large cast of plantation-style-clad characters. Part of the humor of the parody can be found in the fact that Chase, a white actor, sings the song (first associated with Uncle Remus in the Disney original), and another part of the humor comes from the fact that Chase's character is dressed as a stereotypical rich plantation owner. So the *Fletch Lives* parody of *Song of the South* takes on both the racial and economic-class stereotypes of the original.

Although I discuss the impact of *Holiday Inn* on popular culture in another chapter, it is important to note that the legacy and impact of the film was felt not only through the naming of the Holiday Inn motel chain a decade after the 1942 film premiered, or through "White Christmas" becoming one of the biggest record and radio hits of all time, but can also be seen in the 1948 movie musical *Easter Parade*, which reprised

196 Listen to Movie Musicals!

"Easter Parade," a song featured in *Holiday Inn* but originally part of an Irving Berlin stage musical back in the early 1930s. The legacy of *Holiday Inn* can also be felt clearly in the 1954 film *White Christmas*, which was built around the *Holiday Inn* song of the same name.

Although the fictional Holiday Inn of the film was supposed to be in Connecticut, it is difficult to imagine that the inn itself and the premise— of someone leaving a successful career to move to an obscure country inn in the Northeast to try to turn it into a commercial success—did not, at least in some part, influence the 1982–1990 television comedy *Newhart*, and possibly even the 1987 film *Baby Boom*, in which Diane Keaton's character moves to a run-down house in rural Vermont, only to establish a successful baby food business that she runs out of her home. Although *Newhart* and *Baby Boom* might seem tangential to the consideration of *Holiday Inn*, it is possible that audiences familiar with the basic premise of *Holiday Inn* might sense a connection to the 1942 film in the later productions and sense that they continue the legacy of *Holiday Inn*.

For some actors, performances in popular movie musicals continued to, in part—and sometimes in large part—define their careers. For example, on March 8, 2019, NBC's *Today Show* reported on Olivia Newton-John's career and ongoing battles with cancer and, as a teaser for a March 11, 2019, follow-up segment, a suggestion that Newton-John would share some stories from the filming of *Grease*. Newton-John had starred in the film version of *Grease* just over 40 years before. This not only suggests the impact of *Grease* on popular culture in the late 1970s but also the lasting legacy of the film. In the context of Olivia Newton-John's career, this is particularly evident: as a recording artist, Newton-John enjoyed five U.S. Top Ten singles and several high-charting albums before she starred in *Grease* and another two Top Ten singles in the early 1980s; however, she is still widely known as Sandy Olsson, the Australian girl who moved to the United States and attended Rydell High School.

On the occasion of the 40th anniversary of *Grease*, *Entertainment Tonight*'s Paige Gawley quoted John Travolta as saying, "This is a film that's so timeless that keeps on giving to each new generation . . . When people watch this, they just get happy. They want to become the characters they're watching. They want to sing along with it, they want to dance, they want to be part of this film" (Gawley 2018).

The persistence of *Grease* on home video has also been impressive and has maintained the legacy of this musical. The releases on VHS and DVD have not only been popular but also received favorable comment from critics for over a wide time span. For example, Jane Ganahl's review of the home-video version of the film on the occasion of the 20th anniversary of the original theatrical release stated, "*Grease* has aged pretty well in the vault. Sure, it's the same trite teenage fantasy it was 20 years ago when it was first released, but somehow now the energy seems infectiously giddier, the songs zingier, the camp higher" (Ganahl 1998). Similarly, Almar Haflidason's BBC review of the 2002 DVD edition, which contained the 16-minute-long special retrospective film *The Grease Yearbook*, opened by stating, "The infectiously enjoyable comedy musical *Grease* made superstars out of John Travolta and Olivia Newton-John. As you'll find out from the new DVD release, the sheer energy of the film was very much born of a cast and crew that had a riot of fun making the movie" (Haflidason 2002). On the occasion of the 40th-anniversary re-release of *Grease*, the *Guardian*'s Peter Bradshaw summed up the legacy of the film by writing, "It's still a sugar-rush of a film" (Bradshaw 2018).

Another important part of the legacy of movie musicals is that some of the pieces associated with the movies' stars became signature songs for the performers, sometimes for decades after the premieres of the films. For example, "Over the Rainbow" was a signature song from Judy Garland, as was "White Christmas" for Bing Crosby. Perhaps one of the more unusual pairings of a star and a signature song came in the form of "Luck Be a Lady," from *Guys and Dolls*, and Frank Sinatra. As mentioned in the previous chapter, although Sinatra was one of the stars of the 1955 film, Marlon Brando, as Sky Masterson, actually sang the song in the movie. Despite that, "Luck Be a Lady" became a staple of Sinatra's concert repertoire throughout the rest of his career.

The way in which recent musicals (stage and/or film) have continued the legacy of earlier musical theater works that originally fell outside the realm of American musical theater is a distinctive aspect of the legacy of movie musicals. Within the world of late 20th-century and early 21st-century productions, perhaps the two most notable examples of this are *Rent* and *Aida*.

Rent first appeared in its stage version in official Off-Broadway release in 1996; the film version of the Jonathan Larson rock musical was released in 2005. The musical was based on the basic premise of Giacomo Puccini's famous opera *La Bohème*, the story of artistically minded but impoverished Bohemians. Larson updated the story by placing it in New York City and incorporating same-sex relationships, AIDS, drug abuse, and other contemporary social issues—not to mention current musical genres—into the show. The stage production was a greater success than the film.

Giuseppe Verdi's opera *Aida* was also remade in a rock-oriented musical. Lyricist Tim Rice, best known for his work with composer Andrew

Lloyd Webber, collaborated on a musical show version of *Aida* with the hugely successful singer-composer-pianist Elton John. After the success of the stage musical, there was speculation that Disney might turn *Aida* into a movie musical, although one has not appeared to date. Should it appear in the future, the film would not only be part of the story of the legacy of the Elton John–Tim Rice musical but also of the Verdi opera.

Despite these forays into operatic subject matters and the rest, for some movie musical aficionados, the classic films of the 1930s, 1940s, and 1950s from Metro-Goldwyn-Mayer (MGM) practically define the genre of the movie musical. Perhaps the most notable mark of the legacy of these musicals came in the mid-1970s in the form of the film *That's Entertainment!*. This 1974 work, which marked the 50th anniversary of MGM, is a documentary that intersperses commentary from MGM stars with scenes from the great MGM movie musicals from the 1920s through the 1950s. In fact, Gene Kelly, Bing Crosby, Fred Astaire, Liza Minnelli, Donald O'Connor, Peter Lawford, Elizabeth Taylor, James Stewart, Mickey Rooney, and Debbie Reynolds, all major stars in classic MGM films, introduce segments, recount their experiences with the studio's films, and, sadly, look over the formerly grand studio's decaying lot.

Most importantly, *That's Entertainment!* was a highly successful compendium of some of the best and most iconic scenes, songs, and dances from MGM musicals from 1929 into the 1950s. The film opens with an overture that contains melodic references to many of the songs and dance tunes that are highlighted later in the film. In this regard, the *That's Entertainment!* overture is constructed in a similar manner to an overture to a standard Broadway musical. The difference here is that *That's Entertainment!* is a musical documentary about one studio's musicals.

One of the more interesting early segments is a montage of various appearances of the song "Singin' in the Rain," from Ukulele Ike in *The Hollywood Revue of 1929* to renditions in later MGM films by Judy Garland and Jimmy Durante, culminating with Gene Kelly's famous performance in *Singin' in the Rain*, the movie musical that reflects back to the time period of the first movie musicals. The interesting part of this being that Kelly's performance in the movie of the same name makes it easy to forget that "Singin' in the Rain" was a much older song that had appeared in numerous films before 1952.

That's Entertainment! does not solely celebrate MGM's greatest successes; the movie also includes clips of contract performers who were put into musicals when they probably should have been cast in other types of films. For example, Joan Crawford's greatest dramatic gifts were not as a dancer; however, she was cast in musicals that included solo dance routines. Similarly, Elizabeth Taylor introduces her own film debut in an MGM musical by saying that her singing was not a threat to any of the other MGM singing actresses of her generation; the clip that appears demonstrates that Taylor's self-assessment was spot on. Mickey Rooney introduces a segment on the many films in which he starred with Judy Garland, including the popular Andy Hardy movies. The segment clearly demonstrates how similar certain types of dialogues were in the Garland-Rooney films. Another thing that the segment shows, however, is how much more elaborate the staging and the use of extras and dance ensembles became as the Garland-Rooney franchise became increasingly commercially successful.

The film, however, is mostly about the studio's greatest successes, much like a greatest-hits album. It should be noted that a high proportion of the segments feature dance routines, solos, duets, and ensembles. Included are Fred Astaire and Eleanor Powell's famous tap-dancing routine from *Broadway Melody of 1940*, Donald O'Connor's hilarious song and dance "Make 'Em Laugh" from *Singin' in the Rain*, Gene Kelly's performance of "Singin' in the Rain" from the same film, Kelly's dance routine with Jerry, the cartoon mouse of *Tom and Jerry* fame in *Anchors Aweigh*, and several others. Busby Berkeley's famous spectacular sets, direction, and choreography are highlighted, as are the elaborate synchronized swimming displays associated with and starring Esther Williams.

One of the most visually stunning sequences is the snippet from *Show Boat*. The way in which the *Show Boat* sequence was put together for *That's Entertainment!* highlights the stark contrast between the drabness of William Warfield's character, Joe, and the over-the-top brightly colored costumes of the white patrons of the paddlewheel showboat. Another visually impressive piece is the finale of *That's Entertainment!*, Gene Kelly's ballet sequence from *An American in Paris*.

Part of the story of the legacy of movie musicals can be seen in the title of this movie. The song "That's Entertainment," which was included in the 1953 film *The Band Wagon*, effectively sums up the connection of the classic movie musicals while presenting the public with a version of the entertainment industry. The importance of the song is confirmed by the American Film Institute, which named "That's Entertainment" as the 45th greatest movie song of all time (American Film Institute 2004).

Part of the legacy of movie musical classics can be found in completely unexpected places. As a perhaps-odd aside, the way in which the closing production credits are presented—panning from one to another over a background of graffiti—in *West Side Story* seems to anticipate by about half a century the presentation style of Prezi. Although one might not be able to find a direct cause-and-effect relationship between the two, connections such as this do raise the question of whether even on a subconscious level memorable things one experiences in a movie might reemerge even years later in what appears to be an unrelated realm.

To conclude, it must also be acknowledged that another part of the story of the legacy of movie musicals can be found in the fact that—while some are re-released or remade—one remains in at least limited theatrical release decades after its 1975 premiere: *The Rocky Horror Picture Show*. Because it is still officially in theatrical release even after all these years, *The Rocky Horror Picture Show* demonstrates the sheer persistence of the most iconic movie musicals.

Bibliography

Adeoye, Aanu, and Adeng Korium. 2018. "Petition Calls on Disney to Drop 'Hakuna Matata' Trademark." *CNN*, December 19. Accessed December 19, 2018. https://cnn.com/2018/12/19/africa/africans-petition-disney-over-hakuna-matata-trademark-intl/index.html.

Alexander, Bryan. 2018. "Dick Van Dyke in *Poppins*: 'He Hoofed Away on That Desk.'" *USA Today*, December 27: 2D. A report on the appearances of 90+-year-old stars Dick Van Dyke and Angela Lansbury in the 2018 release *Mary Poppins Returns*.

Alford, Robert. 2014. "Paint Your *Band Wagon*: Style, Space and Sexuality." *Screen 55*, no. 2: 49–71. A study of *The Band Wagon* in the context of what the author labels "queer" sensibilities seen more overtly in other Vincente Minnelli movie musicals.

Altman, Rick. 1989. *The American Film Musical*. Bloomington: Indiana University Press.

American Film Institute. 2004. "100 Years . . . 100 Songs." American Film Institute. Accessed September 26, 2018. afi.com/100Years/songs.aspx. A ranking of the 100 most significant movie songs from the first century of American films.

American Film Institute. 2006. "AFI's Greatest Movie Musicals." American Film Institute. Accessed February 19, 2019. afi.com/100Years/musicals.aspx. A ranking of the 25 greatest movie musicals of all time.

Andrew, Geoff. 2001. "Baz Lurhmann (I)." *The Guardian* online, September 7. Accessed July 13, 2019. https://www.theguardian.com/film/2001/sep/07/1. This interview with filmmaker Lurhmann focuses on *Moulin Rouge!*

Appelbaum, Binyamin. 2014. "How Disney Turned *Frozen* into a Cash Cow." *The New York Times Magazine*, November 18. Accessed May 8, 2019. https://www.nytimes.com/2014/11/23/magazine/how-disney-turned-frozen-into-a-cash-cow.html.

Atanasoski, Neda. 2014. "Cold War Carmen in U.S. Racial Modernity." *Cinema Journal 54*, no. 1 (Fall): 88–111. A study of Otto Preminger's movie musical *Carmen Jones*.

Barnes, Brooks. 2016. "New Musical Planned for Will Ferrell and Kristen Wiig." *New York Times* online, December 16. Accessed January 10, 2019. https://www.nytimes.com/2016/12/16/movies/new-movie-musical -planned-for-will-ferrell-and-kristen-wiig.html.

Barnes, Brooks. 2017. "Hot on the Trail of *La La Land*, Here Come More Movie Musicals." *New York Times* online, January 15. Accessed January 10, 2019. https://www.nytimes.com/2017/01/15/movies/live-action -musicals-la-la-land.html.

Barrios, Richard. 1995. *A Song in the Dark: The Birth of Musical Films*. New York: Oxford University Press.

Barrios, Richard. 2014. *Dangerous Rhythm: Why Movie Musicals Matter*. New York: Oxford University Press.

BBC. 2019. "Bill Shirley." BBC online. Accessed March 15, 2019. https://www .bbc.co.uk/music/artists/f16ca061-ead4-4334-a087-6fc2612de70b.

The Beatles. 2000. *The Beatles Anthology*. San Francisco, CA: Chronicle Books. This book includes extensive commentary from members of the Beatles about the making of the musical film *A Hard Day's Night*.

Belletto, Steven. 2008. "*Cabaret* and Antifascist Aesthetics." *Criticism* 50, no. 4: 609–630. A thorough study of the political messages in *Cabaret*.

Bergreen, Laurence. 1996. *As Thousands Cheer: The Life of Irving Berlin*. Cambridge, MA: DaCapo Press.

Berliner, Todd, and Philip Furia. 2002. "The Sounds of Silence: Songs in Hollywood Films Since the 1960s." *Style* 36, no. 1 (Spring): 19–35.

Berman, Eliza. 2016. "11 of the Most Memorable Original Movie Musicals." *Time.com*, April 15. Accessed November 9, 2018. www.time.com/429 3701/11-best-original-movie-musicals/.

Berman, John, Deborah Apton, and Victoria Thompson. 2010. "Stephen Sondheim: My *West Side Story* Lyrics Are 'Embarrassing.'" *ABC News*, December 28. Accessed December 17, 2018. https://abcnews.go.com /Entertainment/stephen-sondheim-west-side-story-lyrics-embarrassing /story?id=12345243.

Bernstein, Leonard. 1959. *The Joy of Music*. New York: Simon and Schuster. Among the topics covered are Bernstein's views on the distinctions between musicals and operas and operettas.

Block, Geoffrey. 1997. *Enchanted Evenings: The Broadway Musical from* Show Boat *to Sondheim*. New York: Oxford University Press.

Bloom, Ken. 2010. *Hollywood Musical: The 101 Greatest Song-and-Dance Movies of All Time*. New York: Black Dog & Leventhal.

Bradbury, Janine. 2018. "'Passing for White': How a Taboo Film Genre Is Being Revived to Expose Racial Privilege." *The Guardian*, August 20. Accessed May 8, 2019. https://www.theguardian.com/film/2018/aug/20/passing -film-rebecca-hall-black-white-us-rac. This article includes references to the 1951 film version of *Show Boat*.

Bradley, Bill. 2015. "Finally, the Truth About Disney's 'Hidden Sexual Messages' Revealed." Huffington Post, January 14. Accessed May 30, 2019. https://huffpost.com/entry/disney-sexual-messages_n_6452666.

Bradshaw, Peter. 2001. "*Moulin Rouge*." *The Guardian*, September 7. Accessed July 13, 2019. https://www.theguardian.com/film/2001/sep/07/nicolekidman.

Bradshaw, Peter. 2018. "*Grease* Review—Travolta and Newton-John's Summer Lovin' Still a Blast." *The Guardian*, April 18. Accessed April 3, 2019. https://www.theguardian.com/film/2018/apr/18/grease-review-john-travolta-olivia-newton-john.

Brantley, Ben. 2018. "Review: Hit Songs to Sin by in a Smashing *Moulin Rouge!*" *The New York Times* online, August 5. Accessed July 2, 2019. https://www.nytimes.com/2018/08/05/theater/moulin-rouge-the-musical-review.html.

Brett, Philip, and Elizabeth Wood. 2006. "Lesbian and Gay Music." In *Queering the Pitch: The New Gay and Lesbian Musicology*, edited by Philip Brett, Elizabeth Wood, and Gary C. Thomas, 2nd ed., 351–390. New York: Routledge.

Brett, Philip, Elizabeth Wood, and Gary C. Thomas, eds. 2006. *Queering the Pitch: The New Gay and Lesbian Musicology*, 2nd ed. New York: Routledge.

Brown, Kat. 2014. "*Frozen* Is 2014's Biggest-Selling DVD." *The Telegraph*, December 4. Accessed June 18, 2019. https://www.telegraph.co.uk/culture/disney/11272915/frozen-biggest-selling-dvd.html.

Bundel, Ani. 2019. "Disney's New *Aladdin*, Starring Will Smith, Is a Mostly Pale Imitation of the Original." *NBC News*, May 25. Accessed May 25, 2019. https://www.nbcnews.com/think/opinion/disney-s-new-aladdin-starring-will-smith-mostly-pale-imitation-ncna1010236.

Burlingame, Jon. 2017. "Will Movie Musicals See a *La La* Boost?" *Variety* 335, no. 2 (February 9): 8–14. A feature article that places *La La Land* in the context of the blockbuster 21st-century movie musicals that proceeded it, as well as its relationship to the animated musicals of the Disney studio.

Carew, Anthony. 2018. "Same Old Song: Nostalgia and Fantasy in *La La Land*." *Screen Education* 90: 8–15. A feature study of the film.

Christman, Paul. 2017. "Just His Style: The Songs Hugh Martin Created for MGM's *Meet Me in St. Louis*." *Studies in Musical Theatre* 11, no. 3 (December): 269–279.

Cohan, Steven. 2005. *Incongruous Entertainment: Camp, Cultural Value and the MGM Musical*. Durham, NC: Duke University Press.

Cohan, Steven, ed. 2002. *Hollywood Musicals, The Film Reader*. London: Routledge. This book contains critical essays on the subject of movie musicals.

Corliss, Richard. 2011. "All-TIME 100 Movies." *TIME*.com, October 3. Accessed January 2, 2019. http://entertainment.time.com/2005/02/12/all

-time-100-movies. An updated list of *TIME* magazine's 100 greatest films of all time.

Cousins, Mark. 2018. "Song and Dance Men." *Sight & Sound* 28, no. 5 (May): 11. A brief article about the lukewarm reception that *The Greatest Showman* received from male reviewers.

Coyle, Jake. 2018. "*A Star Is Born* Mania Sweeps over Toronto Film Festival." The Associated Press, September 10. A report on early favorable reception to Bradley Cooper's remake of *A Star Is Born*.

Daly, Steve. 2008. "25 Greatest Movie Musicals of All Time!" *Entertainment Weekly*, December 18. Accessed December 17, 2018. https://ew.com /gallery/25-greatest-movie-musicals-all-time-0/.

Dargis, Manohla. 2018. "Review: *A Star Is Born* Brings Gorgeous Heartbreak." *New York Times*, October 3. Accessed November 9, 2018. www.nytimes .com/2018/10/03/movies/a-star-is-born-review-lady-gaga-bradley-cooper .html?referrer=google_kp. A favorable review of the 2018 remake of *A Star Is Born*.

Decker, Todd R. 2011. *Music Makes Me: Fred Astaire and Jazz*. Berkeley: University of California Press.

Delahaye, Julie. 2018. "*Lion King* Fans Can Visit the Real-Life Pride Rock on Disney Film-Themed Holiday." *The Mirror*, December 7. Accessed June 24, 2019. https://www.mirror.co.uk/travel/africa/lion-king-fans-can-visit -13694800.

Dickerson, Kay, ed. 2003. *Movie Music, The Film Reader*. London: Routledge.

Dietz, Dan. 2014a. *The Complete Book of 1950s Broadway Musicals*. Landham, MD: Rowman & Littlefield. Like Dietz's other books in the series, this volume contains valuable information on stage musicals. Although not focused on movies per se, the book provides a broad view of the decade's musicals.

Dietz, Dan. 2014b. *The Complete Book of 1960s Broadway Musicals*. Landham, MD: Rowman & Littlefield. Like Dietz's other books in the series, this volume contains valuable information on stage musicals. Although not focused on movies per se, the book provides a broad view of the decade's musicals.

Dietz, Dan. 2015a. *The Complete Book of 1940s Broadway Musicals*. Landham, MD: Rowman & Littlefield. Like Dietz's other books in the series, this volume contains valuable information on stage musicals. Although not focused on movies per se, the book provides a broad view of the decade's musicals.

Dietz, Dan. 2015b. *The Complete Book of 1970s Broadway Musicals*. Landham, MD: Rowman & Littlefield. Like Dietz's other books in the series, this volume contains valuable information on stage musicals. Although not focused on movies per se, the book provides a broad view of the decade's musicals.

Dietz, Dan. 2016a. *The Complete Book of 1980s Broadway Musicals*. Landham, MD: Rowman & Littlefield. Like Dietz's other books in the series, this volume contains valuable information on stage musicals. Although not focused on movies per se, the book provides a broad view of the decade's musicals.

Dietz, Dan. 2016b. *The Complete Book of 1990s Broadway Musicals.* Landham, MD: Rowman & Littlefield. Like Dietz's other books in the series, this volume contains valuable information on stage musicals. Although not focused on movies per se, the book provides a broad view of the decade's musicals.

Dietz, Dan. 2017. *The Complete Book of 2000s Broadway Musicals.* Lanham, MD: Rowman & Littlefield. Like Dietz's other books in the series, this volume contains valuable information on stage musicals. Although not focused on movies per se, the book provides a broad view of the decade's musicals.

Dietz, Dan. 2018. *The Complete Book of 1930s Broadway Musicals.* Landham, MD: Rowman & Littlefield. Like Dietz's other books in the series, this volume contains valuable information on stage musicals. Although not focused on movies per se, the book provides a broad view of the decade's musicals.

Disney Miller, Diane. 2014. "Special Introduction." *The Jungle Book.* DVD. Walt Disney Studios Home Entertainment 786936833232.

Dunleavy, Steve. 1977. *Elvis: What Happened?* New York: Ballentine Books. Three former Presley bodyguards provided author Dunleavy unflattering exposé-type material on Presley shortly before the singer-actor's death.

Ebert, Roger. 1971. "*Fiddler on the Roof.*" Rogerebert.com, January 1. Accessed January 3, 2019. www.rogerebert.com/reviews/fiddler-on-the-roof-1971.

Ebert, Roger. 1976. "*A Star Is Born.*" Rogerebert.com, December 24. Accessed January 14, 2019. https://www.rogerebert.com/reviews/a-star-is-born-1976.

Ebert, Roger. 1980. "*Fame.*" Rogerebert.com, May 16. Accessed November 15, 2018. www.rogerebert.com/reviews/fame-1980. A favorable review.

Ebert, Roger. 1994. "*The Lion King.*" Rogerebert.com, June 24. Accessed November 15, 2018. www.rogerebert.com/reviews/the-lion-king-1994. A favorable review.

Ebert, Roger. 1997. "*Evita.*" Rogerebert.com, January 3. Accessed October 8, 2018. www.rogerebert.com/reviews/evita-1997.

Ebert, Roger. 2009. "*Fame.*" Rogerebert.com, September 23. Accessed November 15, 2018. www.rogerebert.com/reviews/fame-2009. A generally unfavorable review of the 2009 remake.

The Editors of *The Hollywood Reporter*. 2014. "*Frozen* Sells 3.2 Million Blu-ray, DVD Units in First Day." *The Hollywood Reporter* online, March 19. Accessed June 18, 2019. https://www.hollywoodreporter.com/news/frozen-sells-32-million-blu-689770.

The Editors of *JazzTimes*. 2018. "John Coltrane's *Giant Steps* and *My Favorite Things* Earn Gold Status." *JazzTimes*, December 13. Accessed May 16, 2019. https://jazztimes.com/features/profiles/john-coltranes-giant-steps-and-my-favorite-things-earn-gold-status/.

The Editors of McDonald's Newsroom. 2019. "McDonald's Happy Meal Makes Mealtime Deliciously Balanced, Easy and Magical for Families This Summer." McDonalds.com, July 16. Accessed July 22, 2019. https://news.mcdonalds.com/news-releases/news-release-details/disney-lion-king-happy-meal.

The Editors of *The Numbers*. 2019. "All-Time Best-Selling Blu-ray Titles in the United States." *The Numbers*. Accessed June 18, 2019. https://www.the-numbers.com/alltime-bluray-sales-chart.

The Editors of *Rolling Stone*. 2011. "500 Greatest Songs of All Time." *Rolling Stone*, April 7. Accessed September 4, 2019. www.rollingstone.com/music/lists/the-500-greatest-songs-of-all-time-20110407.

The Editors of *Rotten Tomatoes.com*. 2019. "*Fiddler on the Roof*." Rotten Tomatoes. Accessed March 22, 2019. https://www.rottentomatoes.com/m/fiddler_on_the_roof.

The Editors of *Time*. 1996. "Movie Musicals: They're Aliiiive!" *Time* 148, no. 12: 66. A brief report on *Evita, Everyone Says I Love You, Grace of My Heart, That Thing You Do!*, and *The Preacher's Wife*.

The Editors of *USA Today*. 2017. "Against *La La Land*? Try These 5 Alternative Movie Musicals." *USA Today*, February 3: 05B. A report on *The Lure, Begin Again, Romance and Cigarettes, Moulin Rouge!*, and *Dancer in the Dark*.

Evans, David, and Scott Michaels. 2002. *Rocky Horror: From Concept to Cult*. London: Sanctuary Publishing. An exploration of *The Rocky Horror Picture Show* and its stage antecedent.

Fehr, Richard, and Frederick G. Vogel. 1993. *Lullabies of Hollywood: Movie Music and the Movie Musical, 1915–1992*. Jefferson, NC: McFarland & Co.

Feuer, Jane. 1982. *The Hollywood Musical*. Bloomington: Indiana University Press.

Fischer, Lucy. 2010. "City of Women, Busby Berkeley, Architecture, and Urban Space." *Cinema Journal* 49, no. 4 (Summer): 111–130. A study of the esthetics of Busby Berkeley's choreography in the first half of the 20th century.

Fordin, Hugh. 1993. *Sunset Boulevard: From Movie to Musical*. New York: Henry Holt. Some fans of movie musicals might be interested in this book, which details the evolution of a film to a stage musical. Over the years, there has been speculation that *Sunset Boulevard* might come full circle and that Andrew Lloyd Webber might adapt the musical for film.

France, Lisa Respers, and Sandra Gonzalez. 2019. "Lady Gaga and Bradley Cooper's Oscar Performance Took People off the Deep End." CNN, February 25. Accessed February 25, 2019. www.cnn.com/2019/02/24/entertainment/lady-gaga-bradley-cooper-oscars/index.html. A report on the strongly favorable audience reaction to Lady Gaga and Cooper's live performance of the song "Shallow" from *A Star Is Born* at the 91st Academy Awards ceremony.

Ganahl, Jane. 1998. "At 20, *Grease* Is Still Slick." *San Francisco Chronicle* online, March 27. Accessed April 3, 2019. https://www.sfgate.com/news /article/At-20-Grease-is-still-slick-3097831.php. A brief highly favorable review of the home-video version of *Grease* on the 20th anniversary of the original theatrical release.

Garber, Megan. 2015. "'Edelweiss': An American Song for Global Dystopia." *The Atlantic* online, November 23. Accessed June 21, 2019. https://www .theatlantic.com/entertainment/archive/2015/11/edelwciss-an american -song-for-an-american-dystopia/417285/.

Garber, Michael G. 2016. "Tragicomedy, Melodrama, and Genre in Early Sound Films: The Case of Two 'Sad Clowns' Musicals." *CINEJ Cinema Journal 5*, no. 2: 53–86. A study of *Puttin' on the Ritz* and *Free and Easy*.

Garcia, Desirée J. 2014. *The Migration of Musical Film: From Ethnic Margins to American Mainstream.* New Brunswick, NJ: Rutgers University Press.

Gawley, Paige. 2018. "John Travolta Celebrates *Grease* 40th Anniversary by Channeling Danny Zuko." *Entertainment Tonight Online*, May 18. Accessed December 13, 2018. https://www.etonline.com/john-travolta -celebrates-grease-40th-anniversary-by-channeling-danny-zuko-102512.

Giddens, Gary. 2009. *Satchmo: The Genius of Louis Armstrong.* Boston: Da Capo Press.

Giger, Andreas. 2009. "Bernstein's *The Joy of Music* as Aesthetic Credo." *Journal of the Society for American Music* 3, no. 3 (August): 311–340.

Gooding-Williams, Robert. 1995. "Disney in Africa and the Inner City: On Race and Space in *The Lion King*." *Social Identities* 1, no. 2: 373–379.

Goodman, Walter. 1987. "Home Video; Movies." *New York Times* online archives, September 6. Accessed January 20, 2019. https://www.nytimes .com/1987/09/06/movies/home-video-movies-696287.html. A brief, albeit favorable review of the film version of *Little Shop of Horrors*.

Greenspan, Charlotte. 2004. "Irving Berlin in Hollywood: The Art of Plugging a Song in Film." *American Music* 22, no. 1 (Spring): 40–49.

Greer, Germaine. 2006. "Siren Song." *The Guardian* online, December 30. Accessed March 28, 2019. https://www.theguardian.com/film/2006/dec /30/film. This article profiles the change from the strong character types found in Hollywood films from the 1930s and 1940s to the weaker, more subservient characters of post-World War II films.

Guralnick, Peter. 2000. *Careless Love: The Unmaking of Elvis Presley* (paperback edition). New York: Back Bay Books. A profile of the later life and career of Presley.

Guthmann, Edward. 2003. "Broderick's Tepid Toot in Music Man/Unassertive Lead Weakens Musical." *San Francisco Chronicle*, February 14. Accessed October 13, 2018. www.sfgate.com/entertainment/article/Broderick-s -tepid-toot-in-Music-Man-2634696.php.

Haflidason, Almar. 2002. "Movies: *Grease* DVD." *BBC*, September 24. Accessed April 3, 2019. www.bbc.co.uk/films/2002/09/23/grease_1978_dvd _review.shtml.

Harmetz, Aljean. 2013. *The Making of* "The Wizard of Oz" (updated ed.). Chicago: Chicago Review Press.

Haskins, Jim, and N. R. Mitgang. 2014. *Mr. Bojangles: The Biography of Bill Robinson* (paperback ed.). New York: Linus Multimedia. A paperback version of the original 1988 William Morrow hardcover edition.

Hay, Peter. 1991. *MGM: When the Lion Roars.* Atlanta, GA: Turner Publications.

Herzog, Amy. 2004. "Discordant Visions: The Peculiar Musical Images of the Soundies Jukebox Film." *American Music* 22, no. 1 (Spring): 27–39.

Hess, Earl. J., and Pratibha A. Dabholkar. 2009. *"Singin' in the Rain": The Making of an American Masterpiece.* Lawrence: University Press of Kansas.

Hirschhorn, Clive. 1981. *The Hollywood Musical.* New York: Crown.

Hischak, Thomas S. 1999. *The American Musical Film Song Encyclopedia.* Westport, CT: Greenwood Press.

Hischak, Thomas S. 2011. *Off-Broadway Musicals Since 1919: From* Greenwich Village Follies *to* The Toxic Avenger. Landham, MD: Scarecrow Press. Although the focus of this volume is on generally obscure musicals, it helps to provide context to the famous, commercially successful musicals of the past.

Hischak, Thomas S. 2013. "Musical Film." In *The Grove Dictionary of American Music*, 2nd ed., vol. 5, edited by Charles Hiroshi Garrett, 617–620. New York: Oxford University Press.

Hischak, Thomas S. 2017. *Musicals in Film: A Guide to the Genre.* Santa Barbara, CA: Greenwood Press.

Hoelscher, Jean. 2018. "*A Star Is Born*: THR's 1976 Review." *The Hollywood Reporter*, October 3. Accessed January 14, 2019. https://www .hollywoodreporter.com/review/a-star-is-born-review-1976-movie -1148005.

The Hollywood Reporter Staff. 2015. "*Fiddler on the Roof*: THR's 1971 Film Review." *The Hollywood Reporter* online edition, December 20. Accessed January 3, 2019. https://www.hollywoodreporter.com/news/fiddler-roof -thrs-1971-film-850257. An online reprint of the newspaper's original 1971 review of the film.

Holusha, John. 1998. "The Theater's on a Roll, Gliding Down 42nd Street; Fast-Moving Times Square Revitalization Leaves No Stone or Building Unturned." *The New York Times* online, February 28. Accessed March 5, 2019. https://www.nytimes.com/1998/02/28/nyregion/theater-s-roll -gliding-down-42d-street-fast-moving-times-square-revitalization.html.

Hopkins, Jessica. 2011. "My Favourite Film: *Little Shop of Horrors*." *The Guardian* online, November 25. Accessed January 20, 2019. https://www .theguardian.com/film/filmblog/2011/nov/25/favourite-film-little-shop -horrors.

Hubbert, Julie. 2003. "'Whatever Happened to Great Movie Music?': *Cinéma Vérité* and Hollywood Film Music of the Early 1970s." *American Music* 21, no. 2 (Summer): 180–213.

Hurwitt, Sam. 2002. "*Stormy Weather* (1943): The Rages-to-Riches Storyline Is Mere Pretext for the Musical Numbers but Oh My Stars and Garters, What Musical Numbers." *The Austin Chronicle*, December 27. Accessed May 9, 2019. https://www.austinchronicle.com/screens/2002-12-27/stormy-weather-1943/. A highly favorable review of the musical and dance performances in the film.

Hutchinson, Pamela. 2018a. "*King of Jazz*." *Sight & Sound* 28, no. 9 (September): 86–87. A study of the 1930 film *King of Jazz*.

Hutchinson, Pamela. 2018b. "*Mamma Mia! Here We Go Again*." *Sight & Sound* 28, no. 9 (September): 71–72. A favorable review of the film.

Hyatt, Wesley. 1999. *The "Billboard" Book of Number One Adult Contemporary Hits*. New York: Billboard Books.

Internet Movie Database. 2019. "*Gigi*." Accessed March 13, 2019. https://www.imdb.com/title/tt0051658/.

James Cagney: Top of the World. 1992. Bob Lindahl, director. Turner Pictures. A *Biography* made-for-television film hosted by Michael J. Fox that is available on a bonus DVD packaged with the DVD Special Edition of *Yankee Doodle Dandy*.

John, Antony. 2001. "Songs and the Audience in Early Movie Musicals." *American Music Research Center Journal* 11: 35–45.

Jubin, Olaf. 2009. "From *That's Entertainment* to *That's Entertainment*? Globalization and the Consumption of the Hollywood Musical in Germany and Austria." *Studies in Musical Theatre* 3, no. 3: 235–251.

Juddery, Mark. 2010. "Breaking the Sound Barrier." *History Today* 60, no. 3 (March): 36–43. A feature article on the film *Singin' in the Rain* and its depiction of the start of the prominence of talkies in the movie industry.

Kael, Pauline. 1971. "The Current Cinema: A Bagel with a Bite out of It." *The New Yorker* 46 (November 13): 133. A favorable review of the film release of *Fiddler on the Roof*.

Kaskowitz, Sheryl. 2009. "All in the Family: Brandeis University and Leonard Bernstein's 'Jewish Boston.'" *Journal of American Music* 3, no. 1 (February): 85–100.

Kim, Chang-Hee. 2013. "Asian Performance on the Stage of American Empire in *Flower Drum Song*." *Cultural Critique* 85 (Fall): 1–37.

King, Barry. 1987. "The Star and the Commodity: Notes Towards a Performance Theory of Stardom." *Cultural Studies* 1, no. 2: 145–161.

King, Susan. 2017. "*Aladdin* Turns 25: Creators on the Real Beginning of the Disney Renaissance." *Variety*, November 24. Accessed October 4, 2018. variety.com/2017/film/news/aladdin-25-years-robin-williams-disney-renaissance-1202620184/.

Knapp, Raymond. 2004. "History, *The Sound of Music*, and Us." *American Music* 22, no. 1 (Spring): 133–144.

Knapp, Raymond. 2009. *The American Musical and the Performance of Personal Identity*. Princeton, NJ: Princeton University Press.

Knapp, Raymond, Mitchell Morris, and Stacy Wolf, eds. 2011. *The Oxford Handbook of the American Musical*. New York: Oxford University Press.

Kniffel, Leonard. 2013. *Musicals on the Silver Screen: A Guide to the Must-See Movie Musicals*. Chicago: Huron Street Press (American Library Association). This volume contains brief descriptions of movie musicals, good and bad, popular and obscure.

Koehler, Robert. 2000. "Different Drummers." *Daily Variety* 269, no. 8 (September 13): A1, A6. A report on *Dancer in the Dark* and *Moulin Rouge* that explores the influence of *The Sound of Music* and other classic movie musicals on both films.

Korkis, Jim. 2012. *Who's Afraid of the "Song of the South?" And Other Forbidden Disney Stories*. Orlando, FL: Theme Parks Press.

Kreuger, Miles. 1975. *The Movie Musical from Vitaphone to 42nd Street, as Reported in a Great Fan Magazine*. New York: Dover Publications. An anthology of reviews and other articles and illustrations from *Photoplay* magazine.

Kreuger, Miles. 1977. *Show Boat: The Story of a Classic American Musical*. New York: Oxford University Press.

Landon, Margaret. 1944. *Anna and the King of Siam*. New York: The John Day Company.

Lane, Anthony. 2018. "Lady Gaga Tips the Scales in Bradley Cooper's *A Star Is Born*." *The New Yorker*, October 8. Accessed November 13, 2018. www.newyorker.com/magazine/2018/10/08/lady-gaga-tips-the-scales-in -bradley-coopers-a-star-is-born. A highly favorable review of the 2018 version of *A Star Is Born*.

LaValley, Al. 1995. "The Great Escape." In *Out in Culture: Gay, Lesbian, and Queer Essays on Popular Culture*, edited by Corey K. Creekmur and Alexander Doty, 60–70. Durham, NC: Duke University Press. This chapter includes analysis of *The Rocky Horror Picture Show* and its status as a queer cult film.

Lee, Ashley. 2018. "In *Mary Poppins Returns*, Lin-Manuel Miranda Arrives as a Movie-Musical Star." *Los Angeles Times* online, December 17. Accessed January 10, 2019. https://www.chicagotribune.com/entertainment /movies/ct-ent-lin-manuel-miranda-poppins-1227-story.html.

Lewis, Hannah. 2017. "*Love Me Tonight* (1932) and the Development of the Integrated Film Musical." *Musical Quarterly* 100, no. 1 (Spring): 3–32.

Library of Congress. 2019. "Complete National Film Registry Listing." Accessed March 12, 2019. https://www.loc.gov/programs/national-film-preservation -board/film-registry/complete-national-film-registry-listing/.

Lodge, Guy. 2018. "Why Bradley Cooper Is the Real Star of *A Star Is Born*." *The Guardian*, October 3. Accessed November 13, 2018. A favorable review of Cooper's version of *A Star Is Born*.

Lott-Lavigna, Ruby. 2017. "*La La Land* Review: An Ambitious Musical Soured by Racist Overtones." *Wired*, January. Accessed October 15, 2018. www .wired.co.uk/article/la-la-land-trailer-review. Like some other mixed and negative reviews of *La La Land*, this review takes the premise of the great white savior of jazz as an example of the depiction of white superiority.

Macel, Emily. 2009. "*Fame*: The Next Generation." *Dance Magazine*, September: 28–32. A report on the remake of *Fame*.

Martin, Douglas. 2003. "Kemmons Wilson, 90, Dies; Was Holiday Inn Founder." The *New York Times* online, February 14. Accessed April 10, 2019. https://www.nytimes.com/2003/02/14/business/kemmons-wilson-90-dies -was-holiday-inn-founder.html.

Martinfield, Sean. 2017. "A Conversation with Ted Neeley, Hollywood's *Jesus Christ Superstar*." Huffington Post, December 6. Accessed March 20, 2019. https://www.huffingtonpost.com/sean-martinfield/a-conversation -with-ted-n_b_3786317.html.

Martin-Rodriguez, Manuel M. 2000. "Hyenas in the Pride Lands: Latinos/as and Immigration in Disney's *The Lion King*." *Aztlan* 25, no. 1: 47.

Mason, Keith. 2011. "*West Side Story*: Fifty Years of Cinematic Magic." *School Band & Orchestra* 14, no. 9 (September): 36–42.

Mast, Gerald. 1987. *Can't Help Singin': The American Musical on Stage and Screen*. Woodstock, NY: The Overlook Press.

McCarthy, Todd. 2001. "*Moulin Rouge*." *Variety* online, May 9. Accessed July 9, 2019. https://variety.com/2001/film/awards/moulin-rouge-6-1200468458/.

McGovern, Joe. 2017. "The Musical That Changed Movies: More Than Six Decades Before *La La Land*, *An American in Paris* Shattered the Mold, Won Best Picture, and Altered the Course of Hollywood History." *Entertainment Weekly* nos. 1451/1452 (February 2–10): 82–87. A report on the importance of *An American in Paris*.

McNary, Dave. 2018. "Steven Spielberg, Oprah Winfrey Team up for *The Color Purple* Movie Musical." *Variety* online, November 2. Accessed January 10, 2019. https://variety.com/2018/film/news/steven-spielberg-oprah -winfrey-color-purple-movie-musical-1203018808/.

McPhee, Ryan. 2019. "*Moulin Rouge!* Musical Leads Boston's 2019 IRNE Awards." *Playbill*, April 9. Accessed July 17, 2019. http://www.playbill .com/article/moulin-rouge-musical-leads-bostons-2019-irne-awards.

Messenger, Cory Luke Joseph. 2011. *Calling the Tune: Hollywood and the Business of Music* (dissertation). Brisbane, QLD, Australia: Griffith University.

Mikkelson, David. 1996. "Is the Word 'Sex' Hidden in *The Lion King*?" Snopes, December 31. Accessed May 8, 2019. https://www.snopes.com/fact -check/the-lion-king/.

Mikkelson, David. 1998. "Was a Phallus Purposely Added to the Artwork for *The Little Mermaid* VHS Cover?" Snopes, November 30. Accessed May 8, 2019. https://www.snopes.com/fact-check/phallus-purposely-added -artwork-little-mermaid-vhs-cover/.

Miller, Scott. 2011. *Sex, Drugs, Rock & Roll, and Musicals*. Boston: Northeast-ern University Press. This volume places rock-era musicals such as *The Wild Party, Grease, Hair, Jesus Christ Superstar, The Rocky Horror Show, The Best Little Whorehouse in Texas*, and others into their social context.

Moffitt, Jack. 2018. "*A Star Is Born*: THR's 1954 Review." *The Hollywood Reporter*, October 3. Accessed January 14, 2019. https://www.hollywood reporter.com/review/a-star-is-born-review-1954-movie-1149092.

Mondello, Bob. 2008. "Remembering Hollywood's Hays Coe, 40 Years On." National Public Radio, August 8. Accessed May 3, 2019. https://www.npr .org/templates/story/story.php?storyId=93301189.

Mook, Richard. 2007. "White Masculinity in Barbershop Quartet Singing." *Journal of American Music* 1, no. 4 (November): 453–484.

Morris, Mitchell. 2004. "*Cabaret*, America's Weimar, and Mythologies of the Gay Subject." *American Music* 22, no. 1 (Spring): 145–157.

Morton, John. 1996. "Simba's Revolution: Revisiting History and Class in *The Lion King*." *Social Identities* 2, no. 2: 311–317.

Moye, David. 2019. "*A Star Is Born* Returning to Theaters with New Song by Lady Gaga and Bradley Cooper." Huffington Post, February 27. Accessed February 27, 2019. https://www.huffpost.com/entry/a-star-is-born-clover -bradley-cooper-lady-gaga_n_5c76ba1ce4b0031d95646603.

Neumeyer, David. 2004. "Merging Genres in the 1940s: The Musical and the Dramatic Feature Film." *American Music* 22, no. 1 (Spring): 122–132.

Nixon, Marni, and Stephen Cole. 2006. *I Could Have Sung All Night: My Story*. New York: Billboard Books. Ghost-singer Nixon discusses her work on *West Side Story, The King and I, My Fair Lady*, and other films, in addi-tion to her credited work in the concert world, in film and on television.

Oliver, John. 2018. "10 Great British Musicals." The British Film Institute, Jan-uary 22. Accessed April 23, 2019. https://www.bfi.org.uk/news-opinion /news-bfi/lists/10-great-british-musicals.

Penner, Nina. 2017. "Rethinking the Diegetic/Nondiegetic Distinction in the Film Musical." *Music & the Moving Image* 10, no. 3 (Fall): 3–20. A study of the changing relationship between characters, storyline, and the use of music in movie musicals.

Perone, James E. 2012. *The Album: A Guide to Pop Music's Most Provocative, Influential, and Important Creations*. Santa Barbara, CA: Praeger Publishers.

Perone, James E. 2016. *Smash Hits: The 100 Songs That Defined America*. Santa Barbara, CA: Greenwood Press.

Perone, James E. 2018. *Listen to Pop! Exploring a Musical Genre*. Santa Bar-bara, CA: Praeger Publishers.

Peters, Oliver. 2017. "*La La Land*." *Sound & Video Contractor*, January: 10–12. An article about some of the filmmaking techniques used to make *La La Land* look reminiscent of classic mid-20th-century movie musicals.

Petersen, Kierran. 2014. "Disney's *Frozen* and the 'Gay Agenda'." *BBC* News, March 27. Accessed June 17, 2019. https://www.bbc.com/news/blogs -echochambers-26759342.

Peyser, Marc. 1998. "Gotta Dance." *Newsweek* 131, no. 25 (June 22): 106–107. A brief report on dance-related movie musicals.

Picart, Caroline Joan S. 2003. *Remaking the Frankenstein Myth on Film.* Albany: State University of New York Press.

Pritchard, Arthur. 2012. "Rob Marshall's *Nine*: A Film Musical Disaster or a Celebration of Failure?" *Studies in Musical Theatre* 6, no. 2: 247–253. A detailed analysis of Nine in the context of Rob Marshall's success with musicals such as *Annie* and *Chicago*.

Propst, Andy. 2019. *They Made Us Happy: Betty Comden & Adolph Green's Musicals and Movies.* New York: Oxford University Press.

Rashotte, Vivian. 2018. "Tessa Virtue and Scott Moir on 20 Years of Skating and Their Most Iconic Performances." CBC Radio, December 13. Accessed July 9, 2019. https://www.cbc.ca/radio/q/thursday-december -13-2018-tessa-virtue-and-scott-moir-joe-reginella-and-more-1.4942748 /tessa-virtue-and-scott-moir-on-20-years-of-skating-and-their-most -iconic-performances-1.4942756.

Reilly, Phoebe. 2017. "La La Landslide." *Billboard* 129, no. 5: 31–32. A report on the success of *La La Land*.

Reinstein, Mara. 2018. "The Merry Men of *Mary Poppins*." *Parade*, December 2, 14–16. A profile of and interview with Lin-Manuel Miranda and Dick Van Dyke.

Reynolds, Christopher. 2007. "*Porgy and Bess*: 'An American *Wozzeck*.'" *Journal of American Music* 1, no. 1 (February): 1–28. A study of possible connections between Gershwin's music for *Porgy and Bess* and some of the structural techniques employed by Austrian composer Alban Berg in Berg's opera *Wozzeck*.

Ribowsky, Mark. 2009. *The Supremes: A Saga of Motown Dreams, Success and Betrayal.* Boston: Da Capo Press.

Rice, Tim. 2004. "Interview." *Jesus Christ Superstar*, special ed. DVD. Universal 25786. Rice discusses the genesis and intent of the musical, casting of the 1973 film version, etc.

Riley, Samantha Michele. 2008. *Becoming the Wig: Mis/Identifications and Citationality in Queer Rock Musicals* (Masters thesis). Chapel Hill: University of North Carolina at Chapel Hill. *The Rocky Horror Picture Show* is a focal point of this thesis.

Rimier, Walter. 2015. *The Man That Got Away: The Life and Songs of Harold Arlen.* Champaign: University of Illinois Press.

Ritman, Alex. 2019. "Bradley Cooper, Alfonso Cuaron Make BAFTA Awards Nominations History." *The Hollywood Reporter*, January 9. Accessed January 9, 2019. https://www.hollywoodreporter.com/news/bradley -cooper-makes-bafta-awards-nominations-history-1174820.

Robinson, Mark A. 2014. *The World of Musicals: An Encyclopedia of Stage, Screen, and Song.* Santa Barbara, CA: Greenwood Press.

Robinson, Tasha. 2006. "Inventory: 18 Movie Musicals You Can Actually Sing Along With." *The A.V. Club*, December 22. Accessed May 8, 2019. https://film.avclub.com/inventory-18-movie-musicals-you-can-actually -sing-alon-1798210426.

Rogers, Ginger. 2008. *Ginger: My Story* (paperback ed.). New York: Harper-Collins. A paperback reprint of Rogers's 1991 autobiography.

Rooney, David. 2019. "Hugh Jackman to Lead Broadway Revival of *The Music Man.*" *The Hollywood Reporter*, March 13. Accessed March 14, 2019. https://www.hollywoodreporter.com/news/hugh-jackman-lead -broadway-revival-music-man-1194075. A report on a planned 2020 stage revival of *The Music Man.*

Rosenbaum, Jonathan. 2012. "*Seven Brides for Seven Brothers.*" *The Chicago Reader*, April 9. Accessed April 8, 2019. https://www.chicagoreader.com /chicago/seven-brides-for-seven-brothers/Film?oid=1058147.

Rubin, Martin. 1993. *Showstoppers: Busby Berkeley and the Tradition of Spectacle.* New York: Columbia University Press.

Sala, Massimiliano. 2012. *From Stage to Screen: Musical Films in Europe and United States (1927–1961).* Turnhout, Belgium: Brepols.

Schonberg, Steve. 2015. "Marni Nixon: The Voice of Beloved Movie Musicals Reflects on *The Sound of Music.*" Huffington Post, May 31. Accessed January 4, 2019. https://www.huffingtonpost.com/steve-schonberg/marni -nixon-the-voice-of-_b_6976634.html.

Scott, A. O. 2008. "Does Your Mother Know You Sing Abba Tunes?" *The New York Times* online, July 18. Accessed March 14, 2019. https://www .nytimes.com/2008/07/18/movies/18mamm.html.

Scott, A. O. 2016. "Review: Ryan Gosling and Emma Stone Aswirl in Tra *La La Land.*" *The New York Times* online, December 8. Accessed November 15, 2018. www.nytimes.com/2016/12/08/movies/la-la-land-review-ryan -gosling-emma-stone.html.

Scott, A. O. 2019. "*Rocketman* Review: The Fantastical Tale of Elton John, Survivor, Rock God, Camp Icon." *The New York Times* online, May 28. Accessed June 3, 2019. https://www.newyorktimes.com/2019/05/28 /rocketman-review.html.

Sennett, Ted. 1981. *Hollywood Musicals.* New York: H.N. Abrams.

Shang, Kaiya, Helen Fewster, Jill Hamilton, and Allison Singer, eds. 2015. *Musicals: The Definitive Illustrated Story.* New York: DK Publishing. A coffee table-style book that presents an overview of stage and film musicals.

Shapiro, Edward. 2014. "*Fiddler* at Fifty." *The Jewish Book Council*, December 9. Accessed January 3, 2019. https://www.jewishbookcouncil.org

/BlogRetrieve.aspx?PostID=1371723&A=SearchResult&SearchID=31985535&ObjectID=1371723&ObjectType=55. An overview of the reception that both the 1964 stage version and the 1971 film version of *Fiddler on the Roof* received from the Jewish community.

Shea, Christopher D. 2017. "Pharrell Williams's Life to Become a Movie Musical, *Atlantis*." *New York Times* online, March 28. Accessed January 10, 2019. https://www.nytimes.com/2017/03/28/movies/pharrell-williams -atlantis-movie.html. A brief report that hip-hop musician Williams will be involved with the movie musical about his childhood.

Siefert, Marsha. 1995. "Image/Music/Voice: Song Dubbing in Hollywood Musicals." *Journal of Communication* 45, no. 2 (Spring): 44–64.

Siegel, Marcia B. 2009. "Busby Berkeley and the Projected Stage." *The Hudson Review* 62, no. 1 (Spring): 106–112. A celebration of the sometimes critically dismissed work of choreographer-director Busby Berkeley on the occasion of a 2009 Berkeley festival.

Siegel, Robert. 2011. "Making *The Rocky Horror Picture Show*." Blu-ray.com, October 25. Accessed March 25, 2019. https://www.blu-ray.com/news /?id=7605.

Smith, Susan. 2005. *The Musical: Race, Gender and Performance*. London: Wallflower Press.

The Songwriters Hall of Fame. n.d. "Towering Song: 'Over the Rainbow.'" Accessed May 17, 2019. https://www.songhall.org/awards/winner/over _the_rainbow.

Sperb, Jason. 2012. *Disney's Most Notorious Film: Race, Convergence, and the Hidden Histories of "Song of the South."* Austin: University of Texas Press.

The Staff of *The Hollywood Reporter*. 2015. "*Grease*: THR's 1978 Review." *The Hollywood Reporter*, June 16. Accessed April 3, 2019. https://www .hollywoodreporter.com/news/grease-thrs-1978-review-802851. An online republication of the trade paper's 1978 review.

The Staff of *Variety*. 1951. "*An American in Paris*." *Variety* online, August 29. Accessed April 8, 2019. https://variety.com/1951/film/reviews/an -american-in-paris-1200417083.

The Staff of *Variety*. 1953. "*Seven Brides for Seven Brothers*." *Variety* online, December 31. Accessed April 8, 2019. https://variety.com/1953/film /reviews/seven-brides-for-seven-brothers-1200417635.

Stasukevich, Iain. 2013. "A Vibrant Holiday Musical." *American Cinematographer* 94, no. 12 (December): 28–34. A technical analysis of *Black Nativity*, a musical based on the play of the same name by Langston Hughes.

Stein, Sadie. 2014. "Beautiful Hide." *The Paris Review*, January 9. Accessed April 13, 2019. https://www.theparisreview.org/blog/2014/01/09/beautiful -hide/.

Stuckey, G. Andrew. 2014. "The World out There: Spectacle and Exposure in *Perhaps Love*." *Journal of Chinese Cinemas* 8, no. 1: 17–36. A study of Peter Ho-sun Chan's pan-Asian movie musical *Perhaps Love*.

Swain, Steve. 2004. "So Music 'More': The Music of *Dick Tracy* (1990)." *American Music* 22, no. 1 (Spring): 50–63.

Tallarico, Brian. 2018. "*A Star Is Born.*" Rogerebert.com, October 5. Accessed November 15, 2018. www.rogerebert.com/reviews/a-star-is-born-2018. A favorable review of the Bradley Cooper film.

Tang, Estelle. 2019. "Lady Gaga Devoted Her Moving Grammys Acceptance Speech to Mental Health Awareness." *Elle*, February 11. Accessed February 11, 2019. https://www.elle.com/culture/music/a26279839/lady-gaga-grammys-acceptance-speech-mental-health-awareness/.

Teachout, Terry. 2016. "Tap, Look, and Listen." *Commentary* 141, no. 2 (February): 56–59. An article about the revival of *Dames at Sea* and the rise and fall of tap dancing.

Tinkcom, Matthew. 2002. *Working Like a Homosexual: Camp, Capital, Cinema*. Durham, NC: Duke University Press.

T.M.P. 1943. "*Stormy Weather*, Negro Musical with Bill Robinson, at the Roxy—*Hers to Hold* Opens at Criterion." *New York Times*, July 1943. Accessed May 9, 2019. https://www.nytimes.com/1943/07/22/archives/stormy-weather-negro-musical-with-bill-robinson-at-the-roxy-hers-to.html. A highly favorable review of *Stormy Weather*.

Travers, Peter. 1995. "*Pocahontas.*" *Rolling Stone*, June 23. Accessed October 1, 2018. www.rollingstone.com/movies/movie-reviews/pocahontas-98358/.

Travers, Peter. 1997. "*Evita.*" *Rolling Stone*, January 10. Accessed October 8, 2018. www.rollingstone.com/movies/movie-reviews/evita-107264/.

Travers, Peter. 2008. "*Mamma Mia!*" *Rolling Stone*, July 17. Accessed March 14, 2019. https://www.rollingstone.com/movies/movie-reviews/mamma-mia-118945/.

Travers, Peter. 2016. "*La La Land* Review: Magical Modern-Day Musical Will Sweep You off Your Feet." *Rolling Stone*, December 6. Accessed October 15, 2018. www.rollingstone.com/movies/movie-reviews/la-la-land-review-magical-modern-day-musical-will-sweep-you-off-your-feet-106357/. A highly favorable review.

Tyler, Don. 2010. *The Great Movie Musicals: A Viewer's Guide to 168 Films That Really Sing*. Jefferson, NC: McFarland. Contains a synopsis and brief critical analysis of a large number of film musicals.

Wasson, Sam. 2013. *Fosse*. New York: Houghton. A biography of producer, director and choreographer Bob Fosse.

Weinstock, Jeffrey Andrew, ed. 2008. *Reading* Rocky Horror: The Rocky Horror Picture Show *and Popular Culture*. New York: Palgrave Macmillan.

Welkos, Robert W. 1993. "Will *Lion King* Be Disney's Next *Beast*?" *Los Angeles Times* online, November 29. Accessed June 25, 2019. https://www.latimes.com/archives/la-xpm-1993-11-29-ca-62180-story.html.

Whitten, Sarah. 2019a. "Disney's *The Lion King* Is 'Critic Proof,' on Pace for $175 Million US Debut Despite Mixed Reviews." CNBC.com, July 16. Accessed July 16, 2019. https://www.cnbc.com/2019/07/16/disneys-the-lion-king-on-pace-for-175-million-us-opening.html.

Whitten, Sarah. 2019b. "Hollywood Doesn't Adjust the Box Office for Inflation, But If It Did, These Would Be the Top 10 Highest-Grossing Films of
All Time in the U.S." CNBC.com. Accessed July 22, 2019. https://www
.cnbc.com/2019/07/22/top-10-films-at-the-box-office-when-adjusted-for
-inflation.html.

Wongcha-um, Panu. 2019. "The Real *King and I*—The Story of New Thai King's
Famous Ancestor." Reuters, May 3. Accessed May 20, 2019. https://www
.reuters.com/article/us-thailand-king-coronation mongkut/the-real-king
-and-i-the-story-of-new-thai-kings-famous-ancestor-idUSKCN1S90UR.

Wood, Mikael. 2018. "Nobody Loves Movie Musicals Like the HFPA, Awarding Golden Globe to 'This Is Me' from *The Greatest Showman*." *Los
Angeles Times* online, January 7. Accessed January 10, 2019. https://
www.latimes.com/entertainment/la-et-golden-globes-2018-live-updates
-nobody-loves-movie-musicals-like-the-1515379503-htmlstory.html.

Zak, Albin. 2001. *The Poetics of Rock: Cutting Tracks, Making Records*. Berkeley: University of California Press. This book deals in part with the
importance of the recording as a representation of the definitive version
of a song.

Zappa, Frank with Peter Occhiogrosso. 1989. *The Real Frank Zappa Book*. New
York: Poseidon Press. Includes Zappa's observations about the importance of the recording mix in the listener's understanding of the meaning
of a song.

Index

About the Author

JAMES E. PERONE, a native of Columbus, Ohio, earned degrees in music education, clarinet performance, and music theory from Capital University and the State University of New York at Buffalo. Jim is currently professor emeritus of music at the University of Mount Union in Alliance, Ohio. In addition to performing and teaching, he has been active as an author since the early 1990s. After researching and writing several music theory-related reference volumes and biobibliographies of American composers ranging from Howard Hanson and Louis Moreau Gottschalk to Paul Simon and Carole King, he focused his research and critical analysis more squarely on popular music. Jim's previous publications include *Paul Simon: A Bio-Bibliography* (Greenwood 2000), *Songs of the Vietnam Conflict* (Greenwood 2001), *Music of the Counterculture Era* (Greenwood 2004), *The Words and Music of Carole King* (Praeger 2006), *Mods, Rockers, and the Music of the British Invasion* (Praeger 2008), *The Words and Music of Elvis Costello* (Praeger 2015), *Smash Hits: The 100 Songs That Defined America* (Praeger 2015), *The Words and Music of James Taylor* (Praeger 2017), *Listen to New Wave Rock! Exploring a Musical Genre* (Greenwood 2018), and *Listen to the Blues! Exploring a Musical Genre* (Greenwood 2019). Jim serves as the editor of Greenwood's Exploring Musical Genres series.